OCR HISTORY B

A2

Different Interpretations of British Imperialism, c.1850–c.1950

Andrew Holland and Alexander Holland | Series editor: Martin D W Jones

www.heinemann.co.uk

✓ Free online support
✓ Useful weblinks
✓ 24 hour online ordering

0845 630 33 33

Heinemann

Part of Pearson

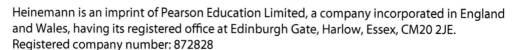

Heinemann is an imprint of Pearson Education Limited, a company incorporated in England and Wales, having its registered office at Edinburgh Gate, Harlow, Essex, CM20 2JE. Registered company number: 872828

www.heinemann.co.uk

Heinemann is a registered trademark of Pearson Education Limited

Text © Pearson Education Ltd 2010

First published 2010

16

10 9 8 7

British Library Cataloguing in Publication Data

A catalogue record for this book is available from the British Library

ISBN 978-0-435-31248-0

Edited by Caroline Sinclair
Typeset by Saxon Graphics Ltd, Derby
Illustrated by Saxon Graphics Ltd, Derby
Picture research by Zooid Pictures Limited
Cover photo/illustration © Getty Images/Popperfoto
Printed and bound in the UK by CPI Group (UK) Ltd, Croydon, CR0 4YY

Acknowledgements

The author and publisher would like to thank the following individuals and organisations for permission to reproduce photographs:

p. 18: Cartoon Stock; p. 38: Cartoon Stock; p. 49: Topham Picturepoint/PA Photos; p. 55: Getty Images/Felice Beato/Hulton Archive; p. 56: Corbis/Bettmann; p. 61: Mary Evans Picture Library; p. 77: TopFoto; p. 79: Topham Picturepoint/PA Photos; p. 82: Mary Evans Picture Library; p. 99: Getty Images/Time Life Pictures/Mansell; p. 102: Bridgeman Art Library; p. 105: (top) Alamy/The Print Collector; p. 105 (bottom) Corbis/Rykoff Collection; p. 107: Rare Book Collection, Monash University Library; p. 108: (top) Topham Picturepoint/PA Photos; p. 108: (bottom) Getty Images/Hulton Archive; p. 110: Lebrecht Music & Arts/RKO Radio Pictures/Photofest; p. 113: Corbis/Hulton Archive; p. 121: Corbis/Marcos Brindicci/Reuters; p. 124: TopFoto; p. 125: Topfoto/AP; p. 126: Getty Images/Central Press/Hulton Archive; p. 135: Getty Images/Popperfoto

Every effort has been made to contact copyright holders of material reproduced in this book. Any omissions will be rectified in subsequent printings if notice is given to the publishers.

Websites

There are links to relevant websites in this book. In order to ensure that the links are up to date, that the links work, and that the sites are not inadvertently linked to sites that could be considered offensive, we have made the links available on the Heinemann website at www.pearsonhotlinks.co.uk. When you access the site, the express code is 2480P.

Dedication: For Laura

Contents

Notes for students

This book, *Different Interpretations of British Imperialism, c.1850–c.1950,* is designed to support OCR's History B specification. It has been designed for students studying Study Topic 3 of the A2 Historical Controversies Unit F985.

How to use this book

Each unit in OCR History B is designed to be introduced through a consideration of the historical concepts. The modes of historical thinking should preface the start of every new topic and might also make valuable conclusions too. Teaching programmes might adopt a dynamic pattern of alternating between theory and topic content, the one buttressing, developing and reinforcing the other. This book will allow you to adopt either approach.

This title covers approximately one hundred years of the relevant period and encourages students to develop an understanding of the issues concerned with the nature, origins and consequences of historical controversy. Candidates are encouraged to be concerned with an appreciation and explanation of the competing views of historians, rather than categorising approaches as either right or wrong.

Students will be encouraged to:

- Understand how historians work and how the very nature of the discipline makes disagreements and different interpretations inevitable
- Appreciate how and why different methodological approaches have led to different interpretations of the events that are focused on
- Understand how these different approaches and interpretations contribute to our understanding of the events
- Think critically about the approaches, interpretations and methods adopted by historians.

You should think carefully about how useful and appropriate each approach and interpretation is when studying each part of Empire history. This is different from making value judgements (good/bad, right/wrong) about approaches and interpretations and this is certainly not a requirement of the OCR examination.

Methods of assessment

The Advanced GCE is made up of two mandatory units at AS and two further units at A2. There are three units at A2, of which candidates do two. Either:

- Unit F985 *Historical Controversies – British History* and Unit F987 *Historical Significance*

Or

- Unit F986 *Historical Controversies – Non-British History* and Unit F987 *Historical Significance.*

The Historical Controversies unit is assessed through an externally set, externally marked task. Candidates answer two questions on their chosen period. The first question requires analysis of an extract or extracts from the work of one historian and asks what you can learn from the extract about the interpretation, approach or method of that historian. The second question asks how a particular approach has contributed to our understanding of the topic. Each question is worth a maximum of 30 marks and candidates have three hours to complete the task during a two-week period nominated by OCR, under supervised conditions. Unit F987, the personal study is internally assessed and externally moderated.

Notes for teachers

How to use this book

This book has been written to support you through Unit F985, Study Topic 3 of the OCR B GCE History course, *Different Interpretations of British Imperialism, c.1850–c.1950*. It will also help you during your revision. The Exam Café sections at the end of this book will be particularly helpful as you prepare for your exam.

The book includes the following features:

■ **Sources and passages**
A wide variety of sources throughout the book will allow you to practise your historical skills.

> Source Ⓐ Joseph Chamberlain, 1897
>
> *In carrying out this work of civilisation we are fulfilling mission, and we are finding scope for the exercise of tho have made of us a great and governing race.*
>
> Quoted in E. Boehmer (ed.) (1998) *Empire Writing: An Anthology of Colonial*

■ **For discussion**
These have been designed to help you understand the specification content and develop your historical skills.

> **FOR DISCUSSION**
>
> 'Gentleman capitalists did not exist. They were invented by Cain and Hopkins'. How far do

■ **Think like an historian**
You should be thinking like an historian throughout your history course. Questions are asked about the content to encourage you to think like this; sometimes you really should just think through these ideas!

> **THINK LIKE AN HISTORIAN**
>
> The date *c.*1880 is important in the debate about informal Empire,

■ **Exam tips**
These give you advice about exam preparation to give you the best grade that you can.

> **EXAM TIP**
>
> Remember to use a dictionary if you come across a word that you are not familiar with.

■ **Quick facts and biographies**
Additional background information in the margin will give you the wider context.

> **QUICK FACT**
>
> **Government bonds** allow the public to invest money with a guarantee by the

■ **Definitions**
Definitions of new words can be found in the margin close to where the word appears in the text to help put the word in context.

> **Monocausal**
>
> Monocausal refers to a single rather than multicausal explanation of an event.

■ **Activities**
These will encourage you to consider different historical interpretations.

> What difficulties arise when using source S as evidence for local opposition to British imperialism?

■ Stretch and challenge

Questions and activities to extend your historical skills.

Stretch and challenge

What characterised a nation as a Great

■ Exam Café

In our unique Exam Café you'll find lots of ideas to help you prepare for your exams. You'll find the Exam Café at the end

of the book. You can **Relax** because there's handy revision advice from fellow students, **Get that result!** with summaries and checklists of the key ideas you need to revise and **Refresh your memory** through practising exam-style questions, accompanied by hints and tips on getting the very best grades.

Series Editor introduction

Congratulations! You are studying the most exciting and useful of the six AS/A2 History specs. OCR's History B gets to grips with what history actually is. Famously, the author of *The Go-Between* said 'The past is a foreign country; they do things differently there'. Spec B will teach you how to understand that other world: how to judge the surviving evidence; how to make sense of the past by putting that evidence together; how and why that evidence generates rival interpretations of the past; and how to measure the significance of people and their actions. Through spec B, you will see why history is alive with argument and debate, always being rethought and revised. Along the way, you will also learn to assess the motives of our ancestors and the consequences of their actions. That matters, because their decisions shaped our world; their tomorrows are our yesterdays.

Heinemann's series of books are tailored to spec B. Whichever topics you are studying, you have to learn how to think like an historian. This book will develop your thinking and understanding, and teach you the skills that you need for success. Ideas and issues are highlighted in text boxes. Case studies with sources and activities set you problems to consider. 'Think like an historian' questions encourage you to see the bigger picture. Exam tips work on your question skills. All will help you when you are starting to study a topic as well as keeping you on course during the term – and don't forget them when revising for mocks and then the real thing. Don't overlook the Exam Café, which is not just for revision – its focused advice and help are always on hand. Tips, revision checklists and advice show you how to write better essays. Get the result! offers example answers with advice about how to improve your answers.

The past is a land of controversy. 'Advances in historical knowledge arise as much from the play of debate between rival interpretations as from the efforts of individual historians' (John Tosh (2000) *The Pursuit of History*, 3rd edition, p. 200). We get used to thinking of events in a certain way. A good historian shakes the kaleidoscope and re-considers the pieces. Sometimes the old picture is confirmed, but sometimes the review shows us that things weren't as straightforward as we thought. Sometimes, the consequence is a realisation that an event was more complex than had hitherto been presumed. Often, the consequence is a shift of emphasis.

The excitement and challenge of OCR's specification B is rethinking history. History is a dynamic discipline, always being rethought and revised by the quest to fix and define. Historians offer their view – an interpretation. That is what you need to focus on. Is it narrowly focused? How well does it fit with what you know? What does it leave out? Perhaps the best way to strengthen or call into question the value of any interpretation is to cross-reference the evidence used and compare the outcome. As you do this, remember what you are evaluating: the view, the argument, the history – not the facts and not the historian.

* * * * * *

'There is no escaping the fact that the original task of the historian is to answer the child's question: "What happened next?"' (A. J. P. Taylor (1976) 'Fiction in History', in *Essays in English History* p. 9). But how do we decide? As Taylor went on to observe, 'History is a version of events. Between the events and the historian there is a constant interplay. The historian tries to impose some kind of rational pattern: how they happened and even why they happened. No historian starts with a blank mind as a jury is supposed to do' (*ibid.*). Between the historian and his or her facts there is a dialogue between the present and the past.

History is plural. There is no one single version of the past. That there is no single past is demonstrated clearly by post-colonial local histories. Representations of a united past were shattered at independence, if not before. Post-colonial local histories are quite different from previous narratives of the imperial adventure. The roles of heroes and villains are often reversed. 'Mutinies' are 'struggles for freedom'. 'Benefits' of rule are called into question. The historian of a subject like imperialism also faces what Bernard Wasserstein calls 'the difficult task of demystifying that twilight zone between living memory and written history'.

Interpretations are not themselves the past. They make claims about the past – history is constructed by historians from the evidence they use and the questions they ask. Interpretations are not evidence, so avoid trying to decide how reliable they are. Rather, ask how an historian has interpreted the evidence in response to the questions they asked. That will lead you to understand *how* differences in interpretation have been generated. In turn, that will let you make a reasoned evaluation of just *how* convincing an interpretation is. If you follow that path, you will be able to make reasoned judgements on the relative effectiveness of differing views – on *how* the evidence (factual material) is best understood and used in historical context.

In a subject like imperialism, that is vital because its historians operate in distinct spheres divided by a great chasm (except in their near universal agreement that imperialism itself is to be criticised). The few who still study the politics and economics of imperialism (traditional imperial history) tend to be eurocentric and concerned with forms of state and methods of rule – and with causation. By contrast, the great majority are post-modernist historians. They ask quite different questions of the evidence, investigating imperial culture, gender, representations of Empire – and the conquered, the marginalised, the powerless. Their interest is in consequence the impact of colonialism.

A note on the cover

Sepoy Bhandari Ram, 10th Baluchi Regiment, on the day he was presented with the Victoria Cross that he had won fighting against the Japanese in Burma on 22 November 1944.

The British raised a series of Baluchi regiments from 1820 onwards. They served the British crown in many parts of the Empire, Abyssinia and Japan as well as on the North West Frontier. In World War I, Baluchis fought on the Western Front and across the Middle East. In World War II, they took part in campaigns in North Africa, Italy and Greece as well as Malaya and Burma. They thus illustrate the enormous reliance by the British on troops raised throughout their Empire in peace as well as in war. The same is true for raw materials and foodstuffs. Yet the discourse of Empire has largely ignored this imperial contribution. Most school textbooks ignore it completely. Think about ways in which this has distorted understanding of the nature of the British Empire and assessments of the significance of British imperialism.

Martin D. W. Jones

What is the difference between an approach, interpretation and method in history?

How can you find out what approaches, interpretations and methods are used by particular historians?

Stretch and challenge

Obtain and read a copy of Niall Ferguson's *Empire: How Britain made the Modern World*. As you read it make notes on the approach, interpretation and methods he uses. What are the strengths and limitations of his approach and methods?

Introduction

'… agreement among historians is remarkably difficult to achieve, and historical events are open to a multiplicity of interpretations'

(A. Green and K. Troup (1999), p. 6)

The nature of historical debate

Factors at the root of controversy

This book is concerned with how and why historians arrive at different conclusions about the past. This is a complex and fascinating subject, but one riddled with controversy. Historians have arrived at different interpretations due to:

- the incomplete and contradictory nature of the evidence they have used
- the questions they have asked
- the historical theories they have applied to this subject
- the historical context in which their studies were written.

The nature of the evidence

The problem all historians confront, even when they are dealing with relatively recent historical events, is that the evidence they rely on is likely to be incomplete and contradictory. Everything surviving from the past that indicates something of human activity is potential evidence for the historian. The range of evidence is vast for all periods of history, and for all periods it survives in fragmentary form. Some forms of evidence are more or less lasting than others. Some types of evidence were intentionally saved for posterity; others were thrown away as rubbish. As a consequence, every historian's conclusions are influenced by their selection of evidence and their interpretation of that evidence. Furthermore, each generation of historians has access to a different range of evidence as some is lost and more is discovered.

Because of the fragmentary nature of evidence, historians need to be alert to the fact that they will never know everything about all that happened in the past. This is what makes the subject so interesting: it may be concerned mostly with the lives of dead people but, as an academic discipline, it is full of life. Academic history is often described as 'organic' – it is continually developing, often in surprising ways. The academic historian, like the designer of a modern car, builds a new history that is based on a critical reflection of the old and the availability of new techniques and new materials.

Questions and theories

Historians approach the sources with their own agendas. All good historians interrogate their sources, but the questions they ask are not always the same. These questions are shaped, in part, by what the historian is looking for. Each historian's approach to the evidence is also determined, to a degree, by who they are – their ethnicity, sex, creed and so on.

Historical context

The age in which an historian lives is also as likely as anything else to fashion their outlook and the questions they ask. The emergence of social history, for example, is very much associated with the emergence of the politics of socialism. In recent decades, many historians have adopted inter-disciplinary approaches and sometimes academics in other fields – sociologists, psychologists, anthropologists, etc. – have applied their subject-specific expertise to the construction of new histories.

The British Empire: an overview

'In carrying out this work of civilisation we are fulfilling what I believe to be our national mission, and we are finding scope for the exercise of those faculties and qualities which have made of us a great and governing race.'

(Joseph Chamberlain, 1897)

'West Africa to-day is just a quarry of paving stones for Hell, and those stones were cemented in places with men's blood mixed with wasted gold!'

(Mary Kingsley, c.1900)

The First British Empire

The origins of the British Empire can be traced to the activities of individual explorers and trading companies. Under English royal patronage, the Venetian John Cabot (Giovanni Caboto) discovered Newfoundland in 1497. Subsequent English attempts to colonise parts of the 'New World' in the late sixteenth century ended in failure. It was not until 1607 that the Virginia Company established at Jamestown the first permanent English colony in North America. In 1624, the company was dissolved and the colony was placed under royal jurisdiction. Thereafter, England's colonial presence in North America began to extend along the coastline of Virginia and New England.

Meanwhile, England started to challenge Spanish supremacy in the Caribbean. During the Anglo-Spanish War (1585–1604), English privateers had been given royal authority to disrupt Spanish commerce in the Americas. Following the cessation of hostilities, England increasingly began to colonise parts of the West Indies. It was not long before the cultivation of sugar became dominant in the regional economy. The subsequent demand for labour stimulated the West African slave trade.

Back home, the political union between England and Scotland in 1707 contributed to the formation of a strengthened British **state** which was able to pursue its imperial ambitions. In the eighteenth century, Britain's greatest colonial rival in North America was France; Spain, Portugal and the Netherlands were declining colonial powers. British ascendancy in the 'New World' appeared to have been secured following the Treaty of Paris in 1763 through which Britain acquired the French colonial possessions in North America. However, in 1776, thirteen of Britain's North American colonies rebelled over economic restrictions and attempted political interference from London; American independence was recognised by Britain in 1783.

This early stage of the British Empire (c.1600–1783) is commonly termed the 'Old' or 'First' Empire by historians. It was characterised by:

- orientation towards the Atlantic: imperial **policy** revolved around commercial activity between Britain and the colonies in North America and the West Indies.
- British settlement: colonies were populated by British settlers who were expected to contribute to the prosperity of the metropolitan state. It was intended that they would produce raw materials for Britain and provide a market for British goods. Colonisation was also seen as beneficial because it provided an outlet for Britain's surplus population, particularly those deemed undesirable. Since London was too

---

State

According to the *Oxford Concise Dictionary of Politics* a state is 'a distinct set of political institutions whose specific concern is with the organisation of domination, in the name of the common interest, within a delimited territory'.

Policy

Policy refers to the guiding principles and courses of action adopted by the authorities to achieve particular objectives.

far away to exert effective control, colonists developed a great deal of political autonomy.

- commercial regulation: the British government imposed commercial regulations designed to benefit the **metropole**. The intention was to protect and stimulate British manufacturing, reduce British reliance on foreign goods, and create public revenue through customs.

The Second British Empire: a 'swing to the East'

The Second Empire was characterised by a 'swing to the East'. Settlement colonies were founded in Australia, and more emphasis was placed on trade with India. However, the rise of Eastern commerce was not at the expense of the Atlantic trade, which remained buoyant even after 1783. Moreover, important changes had occurred before the loss of the North American colonies, particularly in relation to Britain's role in the Indian subcontinent. In 1600, the East India Company (EIC) had been granted a royal charter by Queen Elizabeth for the purpose of trading with the Indian Mughal Empire. By the early eighteenth century, Mughal rule was beginning to become very unstable, and the EIC was increasingly being drawn into local politics. The Company faced the added threat of French competition; Anglo-French hostilities in Europe in the 1740s and 1750s spilled over into India, and initially France appeared to have gained the upper hand. However, in the 1750s, the EIC took part in a number of military campaigns against hostile, local rulers who were supported by the French. Under the leadership of Robert Clive, the EIC army was remarkably successful, and French influence in India was destroyed. British supremacy was guaranteed following the Treaty of Allahabad in 1765, in which the Mughal Emperor agreed to cede the civil administration of Bengal and Bihar to the EIC. The Company would in turn attempt to restore political order and the conditions necessary for commerce to flourish. Thus, the British began to rule over a large, indigenous population. Some historians believe this represents an important shift in the nature of British imperialism; the creation of colonies populated by British migrants ceased to be seen as the most important aspect of Britain's imperial policy; instead, greater emphasis was placed on the commercial exploitation of existing societies.

Another significant event was the abolition of slavery in territory under British rule. In 1807, slave trading by British citizens in Africa was made illegal, and in 1811, the movement of slaves on the high seas was made an offence under maritime law. However, it was not until 1834 that the Abolition of Slavery Act made provisions for the eventual release of all enslaved persons living under British jurisdiction. Much debate surrounds the motives of those involved in ending slavery. The traditional orthodoxy suggested that the British government reacted to a groundswell of public opinion, which had been influenced by the propaganda of humanitarian and religious pressure groups. **Revisionists** in the 1960s countered this thesis by arguing that sugar production was a declining industry and had ceased to be of vital economic importance to Britain; hence, revisionists claimed that the real cause of abolition was the absence of powerful economic interests intent on the preservation of slave labour.

The British Empire, c.1840–c.75

From the 1840s onwards, Britain's white settler colonies began to develop 'responsible (self-)government'. This meant that each colonial government had to rule according to the wishes of an elected legislative assembly. British politicians believed that if a settler colony adopted self-government, then it should also be self-reliant. Thus, Britain was increasingly unwilling to offer military support to settler-colonists whose own policies caused conflict with indigenous populations or neighbouring states.

Metropole

The name given to the centre of the British Empire, i.e. the United Kingdom. The term has also been extended to refer to London as the metropole of the British Empire, in that British politicians and businessmen determined the economic, diplomatic and military character of the rest of the Empire.

Revisionists

Revisionist is a term given to historians whose work challenges traditional, orthodox interpretations.

Back in the metropole, Britain was beginning to embrace **free trade**. This marked a major turnaround in economic policy, and had a significant bearing on imperial affairs. Some contemporaries believed that the maintenance of Empire was now no longer necessary, nor advantageous. However, most policy-makers thought that Britain needed to protect trade using force, and this required an imperial presence.

This policy was illustrated by Britain's conflicts with China. In the early nineteenth century, Britain believed that China had the potential to become a significant market for British goods. However, China's rulers, the Qing (Manchu) dynasty, pursued an isolationist policy and did not welcome foreign commerce. In particular, they disapproved of the trade in **opium**, which was an important source of profit for the EIC. Conflict caused by the trade in opium caused two 'Opium Wars' (1839–42, 1856–60), in which China was forced to concede trading rights to Britain.

Elsewhere, Britain's involvement in India had grown considerably. Following the India Act of 1774, the British government possessed the legal powers to guide the EIC in the administration of British India. A governor-general was appointed as the overall authority for political, legal and diplomatic matters in the subcontinent, and in 1784 an Indian Board of Control was set up to supervise Indian affairs from the metropole. During the early nineteenth century, British territory in the Indian subcontinent expanded rapidly. Political instability in areas outside British control threatened trade and prompted British intervention and the annexation of new land.

A major insurrection occurred in British India in 1857–8. It was triggered by the 'mutiny' of a number of Indian soldiers in the EIC army who refused to use rifle cartridges which they believed contained cow fat (sacred to Hindus) and pig fat (unclean to Muslims). The rebellion spread to Delhi, Oudh, Cawnpore and Lucknow, and lasted for over a year. After the rebellion had been defeated, Britain introduced a number of reforms. EIC rule was replaced by Crown rule, in which the governor-general in India acted as a viceroy. The 'Mutiny' also prompted the British authorities to introduce military reforms designed to limit the power of the Indian army.

The late Victorian Empire, c.1875–1914

From c.1875 to c.1900, the **formal Empire** expanded rapidly, particularly in Africa. This was caused by international rivalry amongst the European powers, and Britain's desire to protect its economic and strategic interests. In the late 1870s, Britain and France became involved in the affairs of Egypt, which was on the verge of financial collapse. Britain decided to intervene more directly in 1882. Thereafter, Egypt became a 'veiled protectorate', in which Britain exercised power through a local ruler. In the 1880s, the rest of Africa began to be divided up amongst the European powers including Britain, France, Germany, Italy and Belgium. By 1900, over nine-tenths of Africa was under colonial rule. In southern Africa, conflict between Britain and the *Afrikaners* (colonists of Dutch origin) caused two Boer Wars (1881, 1899–1902), the second of which was won by Britain using dubious methods such as the incarceration of civilians in internment camps.

Meanwhile, in India, a nationalist movement was beginning to develop. In 1885, the Indian National Congress was established as a vehicle to campaign for Home Rule and the reform of the Indian government. Nationalists wanted the Indian Civil Service and government to become more accessible to, and representative of, Indians. The authorities made some reforms in the early 1880s, such as the introduction of elections and self-government for the local districts and municipal boards, but these were considered insufficient. Further administrative reforms were initiated by George Curzon who was appointed Viceroy of India in 1899. Many of these met with opposition, in particular the partition of Bengal; indeed, local pressure forced the reunification of

Free trade

This involved governments taking away restrictions on trade so that markets would become self regulating. Restrictions included tariffs, duties, bounties and the control of shipping.

Opium

A narcotic drug derived from the sap of the seed pods of the opium poppy.

Britain's formal Empire

The formal Empire refers to the territories that Britain officially administered and governed.

Bengal in 1911. However, Britain realised that more widespread concessions had to be made. In 1909, the Indian Councils Act was passed; this is sometimes referred to as the Morley-Minto reforms. Henceforth, Indians could be appointed to serve in the state and provincial level governments.

In Eastern Asia, growing European influence intensified nationalist sentiments among the Chinese, who were angry at foreign political, economic and cultural domination. Anti-foreign feeling finally spilled over into the Boxer rebellion (1900), the aim of which was to free China from foreign influence. Britain, France, Germany, Russia, America, Italy, Austria and Japan united to crush the rebels. In 1901, the Boxer protocol was signed in which the Chinese government agreed to pay indemnities and execute a number of Chinese officials linked to the rebellion. European trading concessions in China were subsequently partitioned; Britain retained the most lucrative region, the Yangtse valley.

The First World War, 1914–8

In 1914, tensions in Europe sparked the First World War (1914–8). During the conflict Britain prioritised the struggle in Europe over that in the colonies. If Britain had been defeated on the Western Front, then both the war, and Britain's Empire, would have been lost. However, it was still necessary to attack enemy possessions that were situated outside Europe. Germany's colonies were able to provide the German navy with the logistical support with which to disrupt British maritime commerce and communications. It was thus essential for Britain to nullify this threat. By early 1916, enemy possessions in West and South-West Africa had been wrested from German control. In East Africa, the Germans put up sterner resistance, and a German force remained active in the region until 1918. Further north, the Ottoman Empire had allied itself with Germany at the outset of hostilities. Britain responded by declaring Egypt a British Protectorate (Egypt had previously remained part of the Ottoman Empire, despite Britain's occupation and *de facto* government). Attempts by British and French forces to capture the Ottoman capital of Constantinople ended in failure after the defeat at Gallipoli in 1915. Following this, the British were mainly content to defend Egypt and the Suez Canal. They did, however, encourage the Arabs to revolt against Ottoman rule (1916–8). In 1917, British forces went on the offensive and successfully attacked Ottoman possessions in Palestine. On the other side of the world, in the Pacific, German possessions had been quickly overrun in 1914 and occupied by Australia, New Zealand and (Britain's ally) Japan.

Britain had declared war on behalf of the whole Empire, but it did not possess the authority to force the Dominions to contribute troops. Britain's initial fears that the war would be met by indifference proved unfounded, and the Dominions (as well as the other territories within Britain's Empire) contributed men and goods from the outset. However, there was some colonial unrest, much of which was directed against plans to introduce conscription.

In Britain, policy-makers were initially wary of colonial involvement, since this threatened the mother country's dominant position within the Empire. There was a belief that it was the duty, and indeed, the right, of Britain to shoulder the greater part of the military burden. A turning point occurred when David Lloyd George replaced Herbert Henry Asquith as prime minister in 1916. Henceforth, the rest of the Empire was encouraged to become more involved in the war effort. Imperial War Conferences were convened, an Imperial War Cabinet was set up in 1917, and notable imperialists such as Milner and Curzon returned to government.

Between the wars, 1918–39

After the First World War, the League of Nations allowed Britain to acquire a great deal of territory that had formerly belonged to either Germany or the Ottoman Empire. These regions were to be administered as 'mandated' territories, which meant that Britain was to rule as a guardian until each country reached political maturity, at which point they would be granted independence. In the strategically-important Middle East, Britain gained control over Palestine, Transjordan, and Iraq. However, the most immediate threat to British interests in the region lay in Egypt, where a nationalist uprising had to be suppressed in 1919. Britain responded by allowing Egypt nominal independence in 1922, but retained control over Egyptian foreign policy. In 1936, an Anglo-Egyptian Treaty was signed which stipulated that Britain was to withdraw all its troops from Egypt, except those that were situated near to the Suez Canal. In the rest of the Middle East, Britain similarly favoured the use of treaties as a means of exercising power. However, in Palestine, Britain faced serious problems, where conflict between Palestinian Arabs and Jewish settlers became increasingly violent.

Closer to home, in Ireland, the Irish Republic Army, a paramilitary group, began a guerrilla war (1919–21). Soon afterwards, Britain responded by passing the Government of Ireland Act in 1920. This created the separate political entities of Northern Ireland and Southern Ireland, and made provision for each to attain Home Rule. In 1921, an Irish treaty was signed which recognised the formation of an Irish Free State in Southern Ireland. It was agreed that the new self-governing state would be a Dominion of the Crown. However, in 1949, it became a full Republic and left the Commonwealth.

In India, there were also growing calls for greater autonomy. The Montagu Declaration in 1917 promised self government for India in the future. However, the British were still wary of Indian 'conspiracies'. In 1919, the Rowlatt Act extended emergency measures against civil disobedience that had been implemented during the First World War. This sparked much opposition, which in turn provoked repression from the authorities. The most infamous incident occurred in Amritsar, in the Punjab, where the Indian army opened fire on a crowd of civilians, killing over three hundred people. A Government of India Act was also passed in 1919. This introduced limited political reforms which reformed central and provincial government, and gave greater power to elected Indian politicians. A further declaration in 1929 reaffirmed Britain's commitment to granting India Dominion status, and in 1935, another Government of India Act effectively granted India's provinces self-government. Meanwhile the civil administration and the Indian army were slowly becoming 'Indianised'.

The Second World War (1939–45)

The Second World War was a global conflict fought across Europe, Africa and Asia. Britain's declaration of war was quickly followed by similar declarations from the Dominions. The only Dominion to remain neutral was the Irish Free State (Eire); albeit 43,000 Irish citizens volunteered to join British forces. The material support from the Dominions and Britain's other colonial possessions was crucial to Britain's eventual success. In the Indian subcontinent, the authoritarian way in which Britain conducted the war on India's behalf sparked a movement of civil disobedience in 1942, called the Quit India appeal. Nevertheless, by 1945, India had given much material support to the war effort, and around 2.25 million Indians had served in the armed forces.

It is unclear whether the Second World War altered the course of history for Britain's Empire, or simply accelerated existing trends. The Dominions continued to develop greater autonomy and began to pursue international policies that were not reliant on Britain. Australians had been told by Britain in 1940 that British naval forces were incapable of coming to their aid against a hostile Japan; Australia realised that any

future defence strategy would have to involve the United States of America, which was a Pacific Sea neighbour, rather than Britain. Elsewhere, cracks in the Empire began to appear. At the end of 1941, Japan had attacked British possessions in South-East Asia. Britain's subsequent inability to defend the region shook off the Empire's image of invincibility. Moreover, Britain was forced to train indigenous groups to fight against Japan, some of whom would later fight against British imperialism, such as the Malay communists. In India, the demands of war had been destabilising and pushed the country towards independence. Meanwhile, Africans who had fought abroad returned home with a greater awareness of the discrimination that they found in their own countries. Indeed, former troops were often at the forefront of nationalist movements, such as the ex-soldiers who held a rally in Accra, the capital of the Gold Coast, in 1948.

The beginnings of decolonisation (1945–50)

At the end of the Second World War, British policy makers realised that independence was inevitable for some colonies. However, they wanted the dissolution of Empire to appear as if it was their own choice, rather than a process forced upon them. Policy also had to take into account the financial position of Britain. Only a massive American loan of $3.5 billion dollars saved the British government from bankruptcy. It was thus crucial that very little was spent on military adventures. In India, Britain kept its promise, made in 1942, to grant the country full self-government. The greatest problem revolved around how the Muslim population was to be politically represented in the new Indian state. Initially it was proposed to create a weak federal state, since this would allow Hindu or Muslim dominated provinces to retain considerable freedom. The alternative was to partition British India along religious lines. It was the latter option that was eventually chosen by the British. The successor states, Hindu India and Muslim (East and West) Pakistan, were to remain as Dominions within the Commonwealth. British forces withdrew in August 1947. In the Middle East, the question of Palestine was handed over to the United Nations; British forces evacuated the region in spring 1948. Meanwhile, in the same year, Burma and Ceylon acquired independence from Britain, while in Malaya, communist insurgents began a guerrilla campaign against British rule.

Timeline, c.1850–c.1950

1856	→	Second Chinese Opium War (1856–60)
1857	→	Indian Mutiny/First War of Independence (1857–8)
1860	→	Taranaki Wars in New Zealand (1860–70)
1867	→	Canada becomes a Dominion
1869	→	Suez Canal opened
1874	→	The Gold Coast becomes a colony
1875	→	Britain buys Suez Canal shares
1876	→	Victoria becomes Empress of India
1877	→	Annexation of Transvaal
1878	→	Second Afghan War (1878–80)
1879	→	Zulu War; Anglo–French control over Egypt
1880	→	First Boer War (1880–1)

1881	→	Sudan conflict (1881–9)
1882	→	Occupation of Egypt begins
1884–5	→	Berlin Conference
1885	→	Indian National Congress formed
1886	→	Royal Niger Company Charter awarded; Colonial and Indian Exhibition
1895	→	Jameson Raid
1898	→	Fashoda Crisis
1899	→	Second Boer War (1899–1902)
1906	→	Muslim league established in India
1910	→	Union of South Africa formed
1914	→	First World War (1914–8)
1916	→	Easter rising in Dublin
1917	→	Balfour declaration promises Palestine to the Jews
1919	→	Amritsar massacre in India; Arab rebellion in Egypt
1926	→	Imperial conference defines Dominion status
1931	→	Statute of Westminster
1932	→	Ottawa agreement promotes imperial trade
1933	→	Bodyline Cricket tour of Australia
1935	→	Government of India Act allowing limited local government
1937	→	Arab–Jewish conflict in Palestine
1939	→	Second World War (1939–45)
1942	→	Fall of Singapore, Malaya and Burma
1947	→	Indian Independence; partition of India and Pakistan
1948	→	Ceylon and Burma become independent; communist insurgency in Malaya; Israel created
1949	→	Ireland leaves the Commonwealth

Areas of historical controversy

Formal and informal Empire

Traditionally, the Mid-Victorian Empire was seen as an era of apathy. This could be contrasted with the period of New Imperialism which was characterised by the rapid expansion of Empire. However, historians such as Gallagher and Robinson began to challenge this thesis in the 1950s; they argued that British imperial policy remained more or less constant throughout the nineteenth century and it was only the

international climate that changed; thus, the expansion of Empire was caused by changing events in Europe rather than Britain becoming more imperialistic.

The causes and motives for Empire

A great deal of debate has surrounded the causes and motives for Empire. Some historians and commentators such as Hobson, Lenin, and more recently Cain and Hopkins, have chosen to focus on economic causes and the relationship between capitalism and imperialism. Other historians have chosen to focus on how Britain's political and strategic interests affected the development of Empire.

Violence and the maintenance of Empire

A number of historians argue that Empire could only have been maintained through violence and coercive measures. Other historians emphasise that Britain lacked the resources to rule great swathes of territory without the consent of local peoples.

Ideological control and Orientalism

More recently, much scholarly energy has been directed at the way in which Britain exercised ideological control over indigenous and non-white peoples. The most important arguments were put forward by Edward Said who identified a discourse of **Orientalism** in Western culture, in which Europeans constructed and promoted a distorted and negative view of non-Europeans.

Popular support for Empire in Britain

The extent to which people in Britain supported Empire, or were merely apathetic, has caused considerable debate. In particular, historians argue over whether the period of New Imperialism was really characterised by intense, popular **jingoism**.

Decolonisation

Historians have debated the reasons why the British Empire broke up and the extent to which Britain 'jumped' of its own free will, or was 'pushed' by nationalist movements and the international climate of the twentieth century.

Historiographical trends and influences

The centre and the periphery

Before the 1960s, most historians of the British Empire adopted a top-down approach, focusing on official sources and decisions taken in the metropole. However, from the 1960s onwards, scholars from the periphery began to research the histories of their own countries from a different perspective. This resulted in a profusion of area studies in which the pre-colonial history of a region was given much more prominence. In consequence, imperial history began to lose popularity and status. This trend was heightened by the declining interest in Empire shown by people in Britain. More recently, imperial history has revived, and syntheses of the various area studies have given a clearer picture of how the Empire functioned. From the end of the Second World War until the present, imperial scholarship has also been influenced by wider academic trends and influences.

Modernisation

In the 1950s and 1960s, there was an emphasis on development and the need for 'traditional societies' to become more like 'modern societies'. This was partly inspired by the desire to demonstrate the supremacy of the 'Free World' and was given impetus by the post-war economic boom. However, in the late 1960s and early 1970s, these assumptions were challenged. In particular, the moral and economic impact of the

---

Orientalism

A term used originally by Edward Said to describe antagonistic and disapproving views of the East by the West, shaped by the attitudes of imperialism in the eighteenth and nineteenth centuries.

Jingoism

Excessive patriotism.

Vietnam War caused many people to re-evaluate the supposed superiority of Western modernity. Increasingly, the negative aspects of modern culture, such as ugly towns and urban poverty, came to be emphasised. By the early 1970s, the ex-colonial world ceased to be seen simply as the antithesis of the modern West. Indeed, many of the former colonies were shown to have rich pre-colonial histories that were as different from each other as they were from Europe.

Dependency theory: the 'development of underdevelopment'

In opposition to ideas of modernisation, a new theory of 'dependence' began to gain popularity. This held that **colonialism** was responsible for imposing a relationship of dependence on indigenous societies, thereby preserving and increasing economic inequality.

Marxism

Gradually, from the mid-1970s, dependency theory was taken over by more general **Marxist** theories of Empire. In particular, greater emphasis was placed on analysing the modes of production of colonial societies. Marxists believed that history was characterised by the progression of different modes of production, and that one day the industrial working class would become dominant. However, historical study began to demonstrate that pre-industrial and colonial societies possessed very different modes of production, and did not fit into any neat scheme of historical development. More damage was done to Marxist scholarship when the Communist bloc began to collapse in 1989.

The *Annales* School

The *Annales* School provided another significant influence on historical study. Two French historians, Lucien Febvre and Marc Bloch, had founded the journal *Annales d'histoire économique et sociale* in 1929. A good deal of prominence was placed on identifying long-term historical structures, and attempting to uncover the *mentalités* of particular epochs. In the 1960s, the work of the historian Fernand Braudel began to popularise the ideas of the *Annales* School. Braudel's approach influenced other historians, including those who were studying the British Empire.

Britain, the Empire, and the teaching of history

In Britain, the declining significance of Empire sparked less interest in imperial history. This was compounded by a growing sense of guilt about Britain's role as an imperial power. Moreover, particularly since the 1980s, history lessons in school have increasingly become obsessed with foreign 'baddies' such as Hitler and the Nazis, or Stalin and the Soviets.

Post-modernism

In the last couple of decades, 'post-modern' scholarship has come to dominate (although the meaning of the term 'post-modern' is disputed). Generally, 'post-modernists' tend to reject the idea of absolute, objective knowledge, and instead focus on how 'truth' has been used to construct lopsided accounts of historical events.

Post-colonialism

A body of work known as **post-colonial** theory developed in the aftermath of independence. Academics, mainly from the periphery, attempted to reveal how imperial history had inaccurately represented colonial peoples in order to perpetuate and justify colonial rule. Post-colonial theory has certainly contributed to a greater

---

Colonialism

The 'systems of rule by one group over another, where the first claims the right (a 'right' again usually established by conquest) to exercise exclusive sovereignty over the second and to shape its destiny' (Stephen Howe (2002) *Empire*, pp. 30–1).

QUICK FACT

Marxism is an ideology based on the writings of Karl Marx (1818–83). Marxists are generally critical of imperialism as they view it as exploitative, unjust and a major cause of world conflict. They also see imperialism as a particular stage in their predictive model of historical change, which suggests that the exploited, via revolutions, will eventually replace the exploiters as the rulers of society.

Post-colonialism

Either the era after colonialism, or the body of academic work concerned with giving colonial and ex-colonial subjects an historical voice.

understanding of imperialism. However, there is still considerable debate about post-colonial methods and assumptions.

Jargon and obscure theory

Critics have pointed out that some of the work written by leading post-colonial theorists is simply unreadable. In a review of Gayatri Chakravorty Spivak's *A Critique of Post-Colonial Reason: Towards a History of the Vanishing Present*, the Marxist literary critic Terry Eagleton suggests that:

> 'You do not need to hail from a shanty town to find a Spivakian metaphorical muddle like "many of us are trying to carve out positive negotiations with the epistemic graphing of imperialism" pretentiously opaque [...] Post colonial theory makes heavy weather of a respect for the Other, but its most immediate Other, the reader, is apparently dispensed from this sensitivity [...] It might just be, of course, that the point of a wretched sentence like 'the inchoate infant aboriginal para-subject cannot be theorised as functionally completely frozen in a world where teleology is schematised into geography' is to subvert the bogus transparency of Western Reason.'
>
> (T. Eagleton (May 1999) *The London Review of Books*, vol. 21, No. 10)

Race and the Other

The post-colonial theorist Robert Young has described what it means to be an 'Other' in the following terms:

> 'Have you ever been the only person of your own colour or ethnicity in a large group or gathering? It has been said that there are two kinds of white people: those who have never found themselves in a situation where the majority of people around them are not white, and those who have been the only white person in the room. At that moment, for the first time perhaps, they discover what it is really like for the other people in their society, and, metaphorically, for the rest of the world outside the West: to be from a minority, to live as the person who is always in the margins, to be the person who never qualifies as the norm, the person who is not authorised to speak. This is as true for peoples as for persons. Do you feel that your own people and country are somehow always positioned outside the mainstream? Have you ever felt that the moment you said the word "I", that "I" was someone else, not you? That in some obscure way, you were not the subject of your own sentence? Do you ever feel that whenever you speak, you have in some sense been spoken for? Or that when you hear others speaking, that you are only ever going to be the object of their speech? Do you sense that those speaking would never think of trying to find out how things seem to you, from where you are? That you live in a world of others, a world that exists for others?'
>
> (R. Young (2003) *Postcolonialism*, p. 1)

Much of Young's plea is very persuasive, but some of his assumptions about being an 'Other' ought to be approached with caution. Post-colonial theory tends to assume that all aspects of identity are subservient to the concept of race, and in particular the broad categories of East/West and black/white. The possibility that somebody might feel excluded, or seek to exclude others, for a reason other than being Eastern or Western, black or white, is rarely considered. It seems reasonable to think that most people possess very complex identities based on locality, ethnicity, gender, sexuality, age, appearance, ability, religion, values, ideas, and personal experiences. A person living in a far-off land might very well consider him-or-herself as an 'Other' in relation to the West. Equally, more powerful identities might be formed in opposition to neighbouring ethnic groups, a situation which has been illustrated by violent conflicts such as the Rwandan Civil War and genocide of the early 1990s.

Furthermore, since post-colonial theory assumes that East/West and black/white are the most important classifications, any other basis for the inequality of power is relegated to the margins. It is certainly true that the European powers dominated and exerted power over indigenous peoples through formal and informal Empire. However, post-colonial theorists sometimes ignore the possibility that comparable inequalities of power can and indeed did exist within non-white society. This has the effect of concealing power-relations within and between societies, and devaluing identities that emerged as a response to non-European oppression.

Critics, particularly Marxists, have also pointed out that the emphasis on racial identity serves to diminish the importance of class as a factor. For example, Terry Eagleton has criticised many post-colonialists for failing to address the fundamental issues surrounding the inequalities of wealth in capitalist society.

> 'There are discreditable as well as creditable reasons for the speedy surfacing of post-colonialism […] Its birth, for example, followed in the wake of the defeat, at least for the present, of both class-struggle in Western societies and revolutionary nationalism in the previously colonialised world...post-colonialism is a way of being politically radical without necessarily being anti-capitalist, and so is a peculiarly hospitable form of leftism for a "post-political" world.'

> (T. Eagleton (May 1999) *The London Review of Books*, Vol. 21, No. 10)

The influence of scholarship from the United States of America

How historians approach the past is heavily influenced by the problems facing their own societies. Thus, Eagleton notes that 'a good deal of post-colonialism has been a kind of "exported" version of the US's own grievous ethnic problems, and thus yet another example of God's Own Country, one of the most insular on Earth, defining the rest of the world in terms of itself'.

This helps to explain why the concept of the 'Other' is so heavily linked with the idea of being part of an ethnic minority. It reflects to a greater extent the position of non-white people living in the West today, rather than the position of colonised peoples in the time of Empire. The indigenous people of a colony might have resented and felt humiliated by British rule without ever considering themselves as an excluded *minority*. Ironically, it is more likely to have been British Empire-builders who felt like 'outsiders', albeit with the ability to exercise a good deal of power over local peoples.

2 Formal and informal Empire

Passage

The end of the nineteenth century is commonly seen as the great age of imperialism… We think that theorising of this sort needs to be totally overhauled.

R. Robinson and J. Gallagher with A. Denny (1965) *Africa and the Victorians: The Official Mind of Imperialism*, p. xi

---

Key Questions:

- Why has the middle of the nineteenth century traditionally been seen as a period of anti-imperialism?
- Why has the end of the nineteenth century traditionally been seen as the 'great age of imperialism'?
- How significant is Gallagher and Robinson's thesis of informal Empire?

The mid-Victorian Empire: an age of indifference

Key Question:

Why has the middle of the nineteenth century traditionally been seen as a period of anti-imperialism?

TRADITIONAL APPROACH AND INTERPRETATION

Approaches:

- an emphasis on areas of the globe which Britain formally controlled
- a comparison of the mid-Victorian Empire with the New Imperialism of the late nineteenth century

Methods:

- an analysis of the extent to which the formal Empire expanded
- an analysis of official metropolitan documents

Interpretation:

- the mid-Victorian Empire was an era of indifference

The traditional interpretation: indifference and anti-imperialism

Before the 1950s, the mid-Victorian Empire (c.1850–c.1875) was usually seen as an age of 'indifference'. The period was identified as 'anti-imperialist' because it was characterised by very little territorial expansion of the formal Empire, and by Britain's willingness to allow the development of self-government in the white settlement colonies. Historians tended to link this to Britain's adoption of free trade in the middle of the nineteenth century; the ideology of free trade appeared to contradict notions of Empire, since imperial expansion usually involved the acquisition of foreign territory in order to regulate trade and commerce.

The development of responsible government

In the 1840s, Britain's remaining North American colonies were allowed to develop 'responsible (self-)government'. The origins of this lay with the 1839 Durham Report. From 1837 to 1838, the French population in the British colony of Lower Canada had rebelled; they were angry that they lacked political representation in the colonial government. Britain defeated the rebels, and in 1839 Lord Durham was sent to North America to discover the causes of political discontent, and recommend necessary changes. He advocated uniting (English-speaking) Upper Canada with (French-speaking) Lower Canada, and allowing the North American colonies to adopt 'responsible government'. This meant that the government of each colony in the region was to be held responsible to, and rule according to the wishes of, its elected legislative assembly. In essence, this gave the elected representatives of a colony the ability to determine domestic policy, such as how taxation was to be spent. New Brunswick was the first colony to receive responsible government in 1848, and the other North American colonies soon followed.

Before long, the remaining white settlement colonies were clamouring for similar concessions. Those that wished to acquire responsible government had to demonstrate that they were financially self-sufficient and possessed the ability to govern competently. The Australasian colonies secured responsible government from the 1850s onwards. At around the same time, the Cape colony in Southern Africa gained representative institutions, but only achieved full self-government in the early 1870s. The position of the West Indies was complicated by the uneasy coexistence between a white planter minority and emancipated blacks. Attempts at introducing forms of self-government here were a failure.

Earl Grey and imperial defence

The middle of the nineteenth century marked an important shift in Britain's strategy of imperial defence. In 1846, the Colonial Secretary, Earl Grey, had published a review about Britain's overseas military strength. He recommended that Britain ought to concentrate its armed forces at home. If a particular threat to a colony emerged, Britain had the technological capabilities to respond rapidly and effectively. Moreover, it was believed that the settler colonies, having now received self-government, should provide for their own self-defence and internal security. The British government accepted these proposals and between the late 1840s and late 1870s withdrew many troops from the colonies. In Canada, the strength of the British garrison fell from 16,000 in 1841 to 2800 in 1856. Meanwhile, in 1860, a conflict erupted in New Zealand between settlers and the indigenous population. Britain was initially obliged to support the colonists, and by 1864 had provided around 18,000 troops. However, there was a big debate over whether the war was being fought in the interests of the Empire as a whole or in the interests of the colonists; many in Britain believed that if settler colonies such as New Zealand chose to be aggressive, then they ought to bear the consequences. New Zealand was thus coerced into adopting 'self-reliance', and a local defence force was raised. Britain began to withdraw troops, and, even when hostilities between settlers and locals were renewed in 1868–9, refused to send reinforcements; the last regiment left in 1870.

The adoption of free trade

The repeal of the Corn Laws in 1846 marked a radical change in British economic policy. Thereafter, the British government adopted a policy of free trade. Protectionist legislation was scrapped, and measures were taken to limit government interference in commerce, culminating in the free trade budgets of the 1850s and 1860. Advocates of free trade believed that British manufacturing would be stimulated; free trade would make it easier for other countries to earn sterling through the export of raw materials, and these countries could then buy British manufactures. Hence, the developing international division of labour would strengthen Britain's **comparative advantage** in the world economy. It was also argued that free trade brought moral benefits, as it would foster an ethos of work and enterprise.

Contemporaries realised that free trade between nations did not depend on the acquisition of colonies. Therefore, there were many free-traders, such as **Richard Cobden**, who believed that colonies were an unnecessary burden. It was argued that the costs of colonial involvement to the British taxpayer outweighed the benefits.

> ### BIOGRAPHY
>
> #### Richard Cobden (1804–65)
>
> Richard Cobden was born in Sussex, the son of an impoverished farmer. He became a successful businessman in the textile trade before beginning a campaign against the Corn Laws in the late 1830s. These were tariffs imposed on the import of foreign corn, and were designed to protect Britain's farmers; in 1845/6, they were abolished by the Prime Minister Robert Peel. Cobden subsequently continued to promote free trade principles and the need for Britain to pursue a pacific foreign policy.

However, most people believed that the British government still had a role in ensuring that obstacles to free trade were removed. **Palmerston** noted that 'it is the business of the Government to open and to secure the roads for the merchant' (quoted in A. Porter (ed.) (1999) *The Oxford History of the British Empire: The Nineteenth Century*, p. 105). As Foreign Secretary and then Prime Minister, Palmerston consistently intervened in defence of free trade principles. Britain coerced foreign nations into agreeing free trade treaties and then used force, or the threat of force, to ensure that they were adhered to. This aggressive foreign policy has been termed 'gunboat diplomacy'.

> ### BIOGRAPHY
>
> #### Viscount Palmerston (1784–1865)
>
> Henry John Temple (Viscount Palmerston) was the son of an Irish peer. In 1807, he entered politics as the Tory MP for Newport (Isle of Wight). He subsequently served for many years in government as the Secretary for War. However, around 1830, his support for Catholic emancipation and political reform obliged him to change allegiance to the Whigs. He served as Foreign Secretary in a number of Whig governments (1830–4, 1835–41, and 1846–51), and was also appointed Home Secretary (1852). In 1855, he became Prime Minister, and served two terms (1855–8, and 1859–65).

QUICK FACT

Comparative advantage. A country can sometimes use its resources more efficiently to produce one type of good rather than another. If the advantage of specialising in the production of good *x* is greater in country *a* than in country *b*, then country *a* has a comparative advantage over country *b* in relation to the production of *x*. In other words, country *a* benefits more from producing good *x*, than country *b* would. It therefore makes sense for countries to specialise in the production of goods for which they have a comparative advantage, and participate in international trade in order to import the goods that it is disadvantageous for themselves to produce. In the nineteenth century, Britain had a comparative advantage over other countries in the production of manufactured goods. Free trade encouraged countries to specialise in the production of other goods, which in turn reinforced Britain's manufacturing advantage.

New Imperialism, c.1875–1914

> **Key Question:**
>
> Why has the end of the nineteenth century traditionally been seen as the 'great age of imperialism'?

TRADITIONAL APPROACH AND INTERPRETATION

Approaches:

- an emphasis on areas of the globe which Britain formally controlled
- a comparison of late-nineteenth century imperial enthusiasm with mid-nineteenth century imperial apathy

Methods:

- an analysis of the extent to which the formal Empire expanded
- an analysis of official metropolitan documents

Interpretation:

- the late nineteenth century was the 'great age of imperialism'

The approach that focuses on New Imperialism and the thesis of discontinuity

The traditional approach identified significant **discontinuity** between mid-Victorian imperial apathy and the development of strong imperial sentiments in the latter part of the nineteenth century, a period which was characterised by the expansion of the formal Empire. This revival of imperialism ('New Imperialism') was prompted by concerns that free trade was no longer working and that security could only be found by expanding imperial markets.

The New Imperialism interpretation

From c.1875 a number of European states rapidly acquired a great many formal colonies. This period of expansion is often called 'New Imperialism' and was the result of several economic and political factors. Nations such as Germany and Italy had recently undergone political unification, and this strengthened the ability of each to engage in external enterprises. Politicians in these states also hoped that imperial ventures would promote nationalist sentiments and prevent internal unrest. Moreover, countries such as France, Germany and the United States of America had begun to industrialise and were eager to contest Britain's dominant position in the world economy. Crucially, however, a period of economic depression between 1873 and 1896 encouraged European states to adopt **protectionist** policies. This also provided an important motivation for the acquisition of colonies. It was believed that colonial expansion would provide markets for domestic goods and sources of raw materials. In Britain, these developments were viewed as alarming. Foreign colonial expansion endangered British commercial and strategic interests, such as the route to India.

Imperial defence and strategic interests

This threatening international climate persuaded British policymakers to develop an all-encompassing defensive strategy for the entire British Empire. A particular point of concern was the damage that might be inflicted on British commercial shipping in wartime; this would have a catastrophic impact, since Britain imported many basic foodstuffs and resources. Hence, imperial defence was to be based on a strong naval presence. From the late 1880s, an expensive programme of naval construction attempted to create a 'two-power standard' of superiority, in which British naval strength was to match that of any two other countries combined.

QUICK FACT

The thesis of discontinuity was a useful means of identifying key ways in which the Empire of c.1850 differed from that of c.1900. It also sparked an important debate in which the underlying assumptions of the interpretation and the approach began to be challenged. In the 1950s, a number of historians rejected the traditional focus on formal Empire, and instead developed the concept of informal Empire.

Protectionism

Policies instituted by governments which restrict trade between nations through tariffs, quotas and other regulations in order to protect a country's own industries and economy.

However, important figures in the British army believed that Russia posed the greatest threat to the Empire, and that British India was particularly vulnerable to Russian invasion through Afghanistan. From the 1860s, Russia had dramatically expanded its territory in central Asia and was gradually moving closer to the Indian subcontinent. Britain attempted to create secure buffer states around India through diplomacy and the extension of informal control. If this proved impossible, the British engaged in 'little wars' against intransigent and hostile local rulers. The Mediterranean route to India was also threatened by Russia. The major power in the area had traditionally been the Ottoman Empire, which was too weak to pose a significant threat to Britain. However, there was a very real possibility that the Ottoman state might collapse, and if this happened Russia appeared to be keen on extending its influence in the region.

The occupation of Egypt

In the nineteenth century, Egypt was nominally part of the Ottoman Empire, but its rulers (the Khedives) enjoyed a great deal of political freedom. From the 1850s, the Egyptian government began to borrow heavily from Europe to fund development in the country's economic infrastructure. However, these attempts at rapid modernisation led to a severe financial crisis in the mid-1870s. Britain believed that Egyptian bankruptcy would lead to internal instability and this would jeopardise British financial and strategic interests. In particular, the security of the route to India through the **Suez Canal** (opened in 1869) would be threatened.

QUICK FACT

The Suez Canal was built by French engineers and opened in 1869. It linked the Red Sea port of Suez with Port Said in the Mediterranean. Britain became very interested in the project because it dramatically shortened the distance for steamships to travel between Britain and India. In 1875, the British government became the largest shareholder of the Suez Canal Company. British troops were stationed in the canal zone from 1882 until 1956 in order to ensure that the Canal was kept open.

Source **A** This cartoon from 1875, captioned 'Moses in Egypt' shows the British Prime Minister, Disraeli, with the 'key to India' – the Suez Canal.

"Mosé in Egitto!!!"

The British Prime Minister Benjamin Disraeli decided to shore up Egypt's finances by buying the Khedive's shares in the Suez Canal. Despite these actions, the Egyptian government was declared bankrupt in 1875–6. The Khedive was forced to ask for European assistance in dealing with the crisis, and in 1876 Britain and France assumed joint responsibility for Egypt's finances in a system called 'Dual Control'. Strict financial measures were subsequently introduced and this caused much resentment amongst Egyptians, including the Khedive. In response, the Europeans forced the Ottoman sultan to depose the Egyptian ruler in 1879, and he was replaced by his more pliant son.

However, many Egyptians remained unhappy that their economy was being managed by, and for the benefit of, foreigners. By 1881, these grievances had spawned a broad-based nationalist movement. The Egyptian ruler became worried that his army might start a rebellion and depose him. Consequently, an Anglo-French naval force was sent to Egypt in January 1882 in order to support the authority of the Khedive. However, this made the situation even more volatile. In Alexandria, bouts of rioting killed around 50 Europeans, and this finally persuaded Britain to launch a military invasion. Initially, the British intended to restore internal stability swiftly and then withdraw. However, it soon became clear that there was no existing Egyptian leader who would be able to ensure security without British support. Britain was thus forced to remain in Egypt for the foreseeable future.

The subsequent occupation was called a 'Veiled Protectorate', since Egyptian ministers, who were really just puppets, governed the country under the direction of British advisors. After 1882, Britain's ties to Egypt grew considerably. Egyptian cotton became very important for British mills, and Egypt became a significant market for British goods. It was also a place where British administrators could forge a career. Thus, the longer Britain remained in Egypt, the more difficult it became to leave.

The partition of Africa

Before the occupation of Egypt, the British presence in Africa had been confined to Cape Colony and Natal in the south, and the coastal enclaves of Gambia, Sierra Leone, the Gold Coast, and Lagos in the west. By the turn of the twentieth century, Britain had gained nearly 5 million square miles of additional African territory. The formal extension of British authority occurred mainly as a response to the threat posed by the colonial ambitions of other European powers. Between 1880 and 1900, the major European powers, including Britain, acquired jurisdiction over nine-tenths of Africa.

West Africa

British commercial interests in West Africa were mainly concerned with the production of palm oil. Initially there was little need for formal British intervention in the region, since indigenous elites were willing to cooperate with British traders. However, in the 1880s, France, Germany, and King Leopold of Belgium decided to claim territory in West Africa. This threatened Britain's commercial dealings in the region, particularly because the other European countries were beginning to introduce protectionism. Matters were resolved at the Berlin Conference (1884–5) in which the European powers laid down rules for future colonial conduct in Africa. In effect, West Africa was divided up between France, Germany, Britain and King Leopold. The agreement meant that Britain was able to retain dominance over the Niger Delta and the palm oil trade.

East Africa

From the 1880s, Britain vied with Germany for influence in East Africa. German expansion in the region was dangerous because it threatened the source of the Nile, and hence, Egypt. Initially, Anglo-German rivalry was conducted through competing commercial companies. The Imperial British East African Company had been granted a royal charter in 1888 to develop the economic potential of the area. The company had

gained a great deal of territory by the 1890s, but it soon became clear that it was incapable of competent governance. In 1895, therefore, the British government was obliged to transfer the administration of British East Africa to the Foreign Office.

Southern Africa

By the mid-1870s in southern Africa, Britain possessed crown colonies at the Cape and Natal, but lacked jurisdiction over the Orange Free State and the Transvaal, which were Afrikaner (Boer) communities. Many Boers had become unhappy with British rule in the early nineteenth century, and in particular Britain's decision to abolish slavery. In the 1830s, around 10,000 of them migrated from the Cape into the interior and established independent communities in Natal and beyond the Orange and Vaal rivers. Britain annexed Natal in 1843–84, but recognised the other two regions as autonomous Afrikaner states in the 1850s. Matters were complicated because the expansion of European settlement caused much conflict with the indigenous population, and these hostilities endangered the security of the British colonies. A number of British officials wanted to create a federation of southern African states. It was believed that this would cheapen the administration of the region, and provide a centralised body that could effectively manage relations between settlers and natives. Afrikaners were less keen on the idea. However, in the 1870s, the Transvaal government was in a state of political and financial crisis. Moreover, they needed British support to deal with the threat posed by neighbouring Zulus. This gave the British authorities the opportunity to annexe the Transvaal in 1877. After Britain had defeated the Zulus (1879), they decided not to restore Transvaal independence. This, in turn, infuriated the Boers and in 1881 they attacked the British at Majuba Hill and won a famous victory in what is called the First Boer War. Britain was forced to back down, and the Boers regained their political autonomy. However, there were provisos, and Britain retained the right to direct Transvaal foreign policy.

Anglo-Boer relations were also deeply affected by the discovery of diamonds and gold in southern Africa. In particular, the discovery of large gold deposits in the Transvaal in 1886 meant that the British colonies were now in the vicinity of an extremely rich and rather hostile neighbour. The British attempted to counter this threat through territorial expansion around the Transvaal. It was hoped that Britain could retain commercial dominance in the region by preventing the Afrikaners from reaching the sea, and thus gaining access to ports outside British territory. Encircling the Transvaal would also hinder any possible alliance between the Afrikaners and a rival European power such as Germany.

The Second Boer War

As another consequence of the discovery of gold in the Transvaal, 41,000 *uitlanders* (European, non-Afrikaners) came to work in the mines. Britain (and British mine owners) wanted the Transvaal to grant these workers full citizenship and voting rights. However, the Transvaal government believed that this was an attempt to undermine Afrikaner independence. Britain's case was pressed by **Cecil Rhodes**, the Prime Minister of Cape Colony (1890–6) who had made a fortune from gold and diamonds. Rhodes believed that the *uitlanders* would very soon rebel against their Transvaal rulers. He hoped to take advantage of the situation and establish British dominance over the region. In 1895, he encouraged a Briton, Dr Jameson, to launch a raid against the Transvaal in the hope of sparking an *uitlander* uprising. It was a complete failure. Rhodes was forced to resign and, since Britain was implicated in the affair, relations with the Transvaal became even more hostile.

The situation was made even worse when **Alfred Milner** was appointed High Commissioner for South Africa. He was not very sympathetic towards the Afrikaners and stirred up a great deal of righteous anger against them in the British press. Negotiations between the Transvaal Prime Minister and Milner over the *uitlander* question ended in failure. In 1899, British troops were sent to South Africa to place greater pressure on the Transvaal, but this simply provoked the Afrikaners into attacking Cape Colony. Britain won the subsequent (Second Boer) war (1899–1902). However, the victory was accomplished through the use of some unsavoury methods. Many Afrikaner civilians were rounded up and placed in internment camps. This prevented them from giving material support to the Boer soldiers, who had begun to employ guerrilla tactics rather than engage in open warfare. It is estimated that over 20,000 Afrikaners died whilst being held by the British, mainly through disease. The conditions in the camps caused an international scandal and placed major moral question marks against the British Empire.

After the war Britain paid a great deal of money in compensation to Boers who had been damaged by the conflict. Self-government, which Britain had taken away from the Boer states during the war, was restored to the Transvaal in 1906 and to the Orange Free State in 1907. In May 1910, all the southern African states established the Union of South Africa.

The Constructive imperialism interpretation

From the 1880s, a number of individuals in Britain sought to promote closer imperial relations. They believed that the construction of a more politically-cohesive Empire was essential if Britain was to remain a world power. Only the economic and military resources of the colonies would allow Britain to compete with nations such as Germany and the United States of America. The term 'constructive imperialism' was coined to describe these views by the economist W. A. S. Hewins in 1899.

Joseph Chamberlain is the man who is most commonly identified with constructive imperialism. He held the position of Colonial Secretary from 1895 until 1903. While in office, he attempted to develop the infrastructure of Britain's tropical colonies, although financial restrictions meant that the impact of this policy was marginal. He also became a great supporter of plans to introduce **reciprocal preferential imperial tariffs**. Since imperial preference would help to provide guaranteed markets for British and colonial goods, it was argued that each colony would have an economic interest in retaining the integrity of the British Empire. Critics argued that this would be detrimental to Britain, since the colonial trade was only worth a small part of Britain's total international trade. Nevertheless, there was a broad measure of support for imperial preference in the metropole and in the colonies. In 1903, Chamberlain resigned from the government and formed the Tariff Reform League, which sought to reverse Britain's long standing policy of free trade.

Constructive imperialists also attempted to foster imperial sentiments through the promotion of a pan Anglo-Saxon racial identity. For the most part, they equated Empire with Britain's white settlement colonies. They believed that the concept of race was sufficiently inclusive for national and imperial identities to coexist.

Yet constructive imperialism failed. Five colonial conferences were held between 1887 and 1911 as forums for the discussion of imperial policy, but preferential tariffs were not introduced. Many politicians and businessmen agreed that closer imperial links might be beneficial, but there was very little agreement about how this ought to be achieved. The adoption of imperial preference would have been impossible in some cases, since Britain had already concluded favoured-nation treaties with other states.

Moreover, there was still great support for the idea of free trade, and many people believed that the cohesiveness of Empire should not rely on sordid material interest. Neither could constructive imperialists count on the support of the masses.

BIOGRAPHY

Joseph Chamberlain (1836–1914)

Joseph Chamberlain was born and educated in London. He moved to Birmingham and became a prominent local politician and social reformer. From 1873 until 1875 he served as Mayor before becoming a Liberal MP in 1876. In 1880, he entered Gladstone's Cabinet as President of the Board of Trade, but resigned in 1886 in opposition to the Irish Home Rule Bill. He became Colonial Secretary in Lord Salisbury's Conservative-Unionist government in 1895. In 1903, he resigned in order to champion tariff reform. Three years later he was paralysed by a stroke and was forced to withdraw from political life.

QUICK FACT

Reciprocal preferential imperial tariffs. The idea was that countries within the Empire would place higher tariffs on goods imported from outside the Empire. Thus, imperial goods would have a larger share of the imperial market, because goods produced elsewhere would be more expensive.

If preferential tariffs were given to colonial produce, then at least some tariffs would
have to be placed on non-imperial products (otherwise there would be no preference),
which included many basic foodstuffs. The British electorate would not be happy with
the introduction of '**stomach taxes**'. Finally, by placing such significance on the white
settler colonies, constructive imperialists tended to ignore very important parts of the
Empire, such as India. British policymakers still believed that they had an obligation of
trusteeship towards the non-white populations of the Empire. Moreover, the emphasis
on an Anglo-Saxon 'race' excluded, and would potentially alienate, the Boers in South
Africa, and those of French origin in Canada.

The approach that focuses on the imperialism of free trade

Key Question:

How significant is Gallagher and Robinson's thesis of informal Empire?

GALLAGHER AND ROBINSON'S REVISIONIST APPROACH AND INTERPRETATION

Approach:
- the use of the concept of informal Empire

Methods:
- an analysis of official policy
- a comparison of mid- and late-nineteenth century official policy

Interpretation:
- the policy adopted by British governments towards the Empire in the
  nineteenth century displayed more continuity than change

The revisionist interpretation: Robinson and Gallagher

In 1953, John Gallagher and Ronald Robinson published an article in *The Economic
History Review* entitled 'The Imperialism of Free Trade'; this presented a major challenge
to the traditional orthodoxy. Gallagher and Robinson argued that in the middle of the
nineteenth century, Britain sought to open up foreign markets to British commerce
through political, and therefore imperial, pressure. Only occasionally, however, did the
furthering of British interests require formal annexation of territory; Britain 'followed the
principle of extending control informally if possible and formally if necessary' (J.
Gallagher and R. Robinson (1953) 'The Imperialism of Free Trade', *The Economic History
Review*, 6:1, p. 13). There was thus significant continuity in British policy throughout the
nineteenth century – the major difference after c.1875 was the more hostile international
climate. Thereafter Britain was often unable to achieve **paramountcy** through informal
means. Thus, Robinson and Gallagher forcefully argued a case for the equal importance
of informal and formal control of regions; the traditional view had focused more on the
latter. By introducing the idea of informal expansion they were able to support their
argument that the whole period was one of continuous imperial development.

Critical analysis

The Robinson and Gallagher thesis created great controversy. Some historians adopted
much of their thinking, but were unsure about some of the underlying assumptions
made by the two academics.

- Gallagher and Robinson believed that free trade was compatible with imperialism (hence the term 'imperial free trade'). This was attacked by Macdonagh who argued that many free traders such as Cobden were staunchly anti-imperialist.

- The 'Imperialism of Free Trade' thesis was in some ways too universal. It skipped over the differences in metropolitan attitudes towards Empire and seemed to underestimate the strength of anti-imperial feeling.

- Gallagher and Robinson suggested that informal control was gained through trade, investment, migration and cultural links. Some historians have pointed out that the nations most significantly affected by these factors were *not* part of the Empire, for example, the United States of America.

- D. C. M. Platt, an Oxford historian, argued that Gallagher and Robinson exaggerated the role of governments, and that British influence was mainly exerted by 'men on the spot'. He also claimed that although an informal Empire emerged, this was not until well after 1860.

ACTIVITY

1. Working by yourself, reflect on the titles 'An age of indifference' or the 'Imperialism of Free Trade' – two labels used to generalise about the period.
   a) Construct a table that lists the advantages and disadvantages of using labels to describe periods of time in history; you may use examples from any period of history to illustrate your answer.
   b) Using the material in this section, construct another table that shows the evidence for and against the use of these labels as appropriate generalisations about the period, c.1850–c.75.

Label	Evidence for:	Evidence against:
Age of indifference		
Imperialism of Free Trade		

   c) Finally, invent your own label for the period and write a justification for why you think it is suitable. Compare your label with those from the rest of the group. Which do you think is most applicable, and why?
2. Consider the following 'facts', stated by Robinson and Gallagher in passage 2.

> **Passage** (2)
>
> *Between 1841 and 1851, Great Britain occupied or annexed New Zealand, the Gold Coast, Labuan, Natal, the Punjab, Sinel and Hong Kong. In the next twenty years British control was asserted over Berar, Oudh, Lower Burma, and Kowloon, over Lagos and the neighbourhood of Sierra Leone, over Basutoland, Griqualand and the Transvaal; and new colonies were established in Queensland and British Columbia.*
>
> J. Gallagher and R. Robinson, 'The Imperialism of Free Trade', *The Economic History Review*, 2nd Series, Vol. 6, No. 1 (1953), pp. 9–10.

This information was provided to support the argument that the mid-Victorian period was not one of indifference towards Empire. What does this information tell you about the approaches and methods used by Robinson and Gallagher? Refer to the extract and your own knowledge.

3 Economic explanations for the growth of Empire

> **Passage 1**
>
> *It is admitted by all business men that the growth of the powers of production in their country exceeds the growth in consumption, that more goods can be produced than can be sold at a profit, and that more capital exists than can find remunerative investment. It is this that forms the taproot of Imperialism.*
>
> J. A. Hobson (1902) *Imperialism: A Study,* p. 8

Economic forces interpretations

Economic forces interpretations deal with how the production of material goods and the acquisition of wealth influenced imperialism. For instance, the British government often felt obliged to protect British citizens who were engaged in the expansion of commercial activity. This sometimes led to 'informal imperialism', and sometimes to the acquisition of formal colonies.

Key Questions:

- How has Hobson's approach and interpretation contributed to our understanding of the way in which **economic forces** affected imperialism?
- How has Lenin's approach and interpretation contributed to our understanding of the way in which economic forces affected imperialism?
- How has Cain and Hopkins' approach and interpretation contributed to our understanding of the way in which economic forces affected imperialism?

J. A. Hobson and overseas investment

Key Question:

How has Hobson's approach and interpretation contributed to our understanding of the way in which economic forces affected imperialism?

HOBSON'S APPROACH AND INTERPRETATION

Approach:
- Hobson took a moral standpoint and linked this with his belief in **New Liberalism**

Method:
- the scrutiny of financial records

Interpretation:
- imperialism was the result of the search for new and lucrative investment markets by greedy financiers. This had the unfortunate result of making poverty in the metropole worse

QUICK FACT

New Liberalism

This, in theory, involved a move away from old liberalism based on laissez-faire individualiam to a 'new' liberalism centred around the vision of society as an organic, integrated entity that needed supporting by state intervention.

Hobson's approach

John Atkinson Hobson was born in Derby in 1854. He was educated in a local grammar school and progressed to Lincoln College, Oxford, where he studied Classics and Modern Greats, graduating in 1880. He then moved into a teaching career, specialising in classics and economics. By the late 1880s, Hobson had started to focus his own work on criticising older, classical ideas about economics and developing new approaches to solving what he believed to be the crucial economic issue of the time: the unequal distribution of wealth. This concern over inequality, injustice and the plight of the poor in general, was undoubtedly influenced by his experience of living in London and the findings of the great social investigators of the time, **Booth** and **Rowntree**.

BIOGRAPHY

Charles Booth

Charles Booth was a social investigator who surveyed the extent of poverty in London from 1886 to 1902. He discovered that 30 per cent of the people of London were living 'in poverty or want'.

BIOGRAPHY

B. Seebohm Rowntree

B. Seebohm Rowntree, son of the founder of the York-based chocolate making business, also turned to social investigation partly as a wish to 'do good'. He researched poverty in York from 1899 to 1901 and revealed that the percentage of those in poverty was not too far below the figure for London. This was shocking given that York was considered to be a relatively wealthy rural-based county city.

Hobson was a prolific writer and published his views on economics in a book called *The Evolution of Modern Capitalism* (1894). The thrust of his argument was that poverty was caused by the rich continuing to accumulate income, which they kept in the form of savings, rather than pumping money back into the economy. This meant less for the poor and a slowing down of economic growth, which in turn led to unemployment. These ideas were to be applied at a later date to Hobson's theory about the causes of New Imperialism.

When living in London, Hobson also became associated with a group of progressive radicals, who were to influence what has been called 'New Liberalism'. At the core of their ideology was the belief that society was organic, i.e. like a biological mechanism. It was thought to consist of individuals who were governors (politicians), and the governed (other citizens) who were dependent on each other (just as the human body is dependent on individual cells and vice versa). Thus, the state was responsible for the well-being of its citizens and, in return, citizens had a duty to be law abiding and morally upright to ensure social stability and peaceful coexistence. This belief set also influenced Hobson's concerns about the Empire.

Hobson also worked as a journalist. In 1899, he was employed as a special correspondent by the *Manchester Guardian* to report on the Second Boer War. He was shocked by what he observed and believed that the terrible bloodshed he witnessed was totally unnecessary. For him, the war was simply the result of the actions of greedy capitalist financiers such as Rhodes and the **Rothschilds**. His experience in Africa partly laid the foundation for two important written works: *The Psychology of Jingoism* (1901) and the more influential *Imperialism: A Study* (1902). In the latter, Hobson identified what he called 'the economic tap-root of imperialism' and linked this with the policies and actions of politicians.

BIOGRAPHY

The Rothschild family

The Rothschilds were a family of extremely wealthy Jewish merchant bankers who made considerable investments in the Empire.

The First World War witnessed a split in the Liberal party. Hobson became disillusioned with liberalism and the idea of peaceful coexistence, and joined the Labour party. He spent the rest of his life writing about possible solutions to international economic problems. He died in 1940, aged 81.

Hobson's interpretation

Hobson believed that imperialism was morally wrong as it led to inequality and injustice. More often than not it was enforced using violence. The main cause was the greed of those with 'idle hands': capitalist financiers who had made fortunes out of investing, mainly in British industry. However, in the late 1870s, the industrialising process had slowed down and many enterprises were experiencing a situation of excess production. This appeared to be a result of a combination of factors: markets were saturated with goods that consumers no longer needed or could not afford, and there were cheaper goods flooding the country from competitor nations such as the US and Germany. All of this made investing in British industry less attractive. The alternative was to seek new investment opportunities overseas.

Hobson argued that the most lucrative markets had to be in territories that could be 'newly acquired'. This explained, in particular, the 'scramble for Africa' and the targeting of Egypt and the Transvaal. The prospect of finding an abundance of gold and diamonds was too much for people like Rhodes to ignore. More specifically, money was to be made by buying into the infrastructure required to mine and sell gold and diamonds. What is more, they received the support of government through subtle manipulation and propaganda. By the time of the Boer War, the exploitation of Africa was well under way. The consequences of this investment were far reaching. Newly-acquired territories became political and actual battlegrounds as nations with imperial intentions fought over the chance to become even wealthier. The metropolitan economy was also affected. Hobson thought that investment overseas resulted in less investment at home at a time when it was most needed. This in turn led to further reduced consumption, less production, unemployment and subsequent poverty. The gap between the rich and poor was widening as never before. For Hobson, the solution to this dilemma was simple: wealth had to be redistributed and the main way to do this was through progressive taxation.

At the time, Hobson's theory was very persuasive and was taken up by pro-Boer Liberals with gusto. But by the end of the Second World War it carried less weight and, until recently, was largely discredited.

Critical analysis

Hobson's approach and interpretation focused on economic forces and, partly because of this, has been associated with Marxism. Historians have viewed it as a **polemical** (i.e. controversial) approach that missed out important bits of the story. Thus, Niall Ferguson believes that 'like those modern conspiracy theories which explain every war in terms of the control of oil reserves, the Radical critique was an over-simplification' (N. Ferguson (2004) *Empire: How Britain Made the Modern World*, p. 284).

More specific criticisms of Hobson's approach and interpretation have been put forward.

- ◼ Eldridge has argued that Hobson overestimated the number of investors who had excess capital to invest in newly-acquired territories, although this view has recently been challenged by Cain and Hopkins.

- ◼ A common criticism is that Hobson focused most of his attention on newly-acquired territories and ignored the importance of the US and Latin America as investment

Polemic

Describes the practice of disputing accepted political, religious or philosophical conclusions. A polemic text on a particular subject is written to dispute or refute a theory that is generally acknowledged and established.

markets. In fact, as Fieldhouse has shown, the largest amount of new investment was made in these new settlement colonies.

- The analysis of newly-acquired territories largely ignored the importance of other factors. Gaining influence in Egypt was also about controlling the Suez Canal and trade routes to India. The occupation of the Transvaal could be viewed as a way of stopping the Boer domination of the Cape and therefore another possible impediment to Indian trade. However, such objections overlook the fact that protection of trade was still linked to profit making.

- The chronology of the Hobson thesis appears weak. He viewed the period from 1875 to 1895 as being crucial with respect to overseas investment. In fact, most statistical indicators show that overseas investment was rather sluggish during this time and did not really pick up until after 1900.

- With hindsight we know that returns from investment in Africa and parts of South-East Asia were seldom substantial. Some organisations such as the Imperial British East Africa Company never paid dividends! However, some care needs to be taken when dealing with this issue. Initially, it was the *possibility* of making profit that motivated individuals.

- Hobson probably overstated the detrimental effect that overseas investment supposedly had on the home economy. For example, when railways were constructed in southern Africa, this boosted demand for iron (and therefore coal) produced in Britain.

Despite these criticisms, Hobson's work is still of considerable value. It tells us much about how Radicals and New Liberals viewed imperialism at the turn of the twentieth century and the core of his message continues to provoke debate.

ACTIVITY

Source A is a quotation about Cecil Rhodes, one of the capitalist financiers highlighted by Hobson, and was written by Henry Labouchere, a Radical MP of the time:

> **Source**  **A** **Henry Labouchere**
>
> *Rhodes was an Empire jerry-builder, who has always been a mere vulgar promoter masquerading as a patriot, and the figurehead of a gang of astute Hebrew financiers with whom he divides the profits.*
>
> Quoted in N. Ferguson (2004) *Empire: How Britain Made the Modern World*, p. 284

What can you learn from this extract about the validity of Hobson's interpretation about the motives of imperialists? Refer to the extract and your own knowledge to explain your answer. (Remember that the source was not written by Hobson. You need to think about the extent to which it supports his views.)

Stretch and challenge

Explain how the context within which Hobson was writing influenced his views. What problems are involved in drawing conclusions about the importance of context when assessing the work of historians?

Lenin and the crisis of capitalism

> **Key Question:**
>
> How has Lenin's approach and interpretation contributed to our understanding of the way in which economic forces affected imperialism?

LENIN'S APPROACH AND INTERPRETATION

Approach:
- an argument based on Marxist-Leninist ideology

Method:
- Lenin borrowed material from other commentators such as Hobson and applied Marxist theories

Interpretation:
- Imperialism was inevitable as it was 'the highest stage of capitalism'. It was also bound to lead to further world conflict

Lenin's approach

Vladimir Ilich Ulyanov (Lenin) was born in Simbirsk, Russia in 1870. After a disrupted education he eventually graduated from the University of St Petersburg with a degree in Law. From a young age Lenin was moved to campaign against Tsarist autocratic rule which he considered to be oppressive and undemocratic. Along with other opponents of the Tsar, he studied the works of Karl Marx and was driven to help peasants and workers prepare for the overthrow of the regime. The authorities quickly identified him as a potentially dangerous activist and from 1896 until 1917 he was consistently imprisoned or forced into exile.

Lenin produced a profusion of pamphlets that outlined how revolution in Russia might be achieved but was puzzled as to why the prophecies of Marx were slow to materialise. In particular, he was concerned at the way attention was being averted from international conflicts within nations to those between nations. The arms race, conflicts in the Balkans, and the 'scramble for Africa' in the last quarter of the nineteenth century were examples of escalating international tensions. Lenin noted that this seemed to coincide with a second industrial revolution characterised by rapid technological developments such as a global telegraph system and machine guns. The most notable change, though, was the way in which world political and economic affairs seemed to be dominated by one or two global powers. Lenin formulated a theory that helped explain why these developments had occurred and why Marxists revolutions had been delayed. He published his ideas in 1917 under the title *Imperialism: the Highest Stage of Capitalism*.

Lenin's interpretation

Lenin viewed imperialism as a stage in economic development. This fitted perfectly with Marxist views about how the history of the world was to unravel. Before 1873 (the start of the 'Great Depression') industrialised countries, led by Britain, thrived on free trade. However, the crisis of the 1870s resulted in small-scale businesses either folding or being taken over by bigger concerns, resulting in **monopolies**. The result was a group of powerful institutions that could dictate price levels and trade agreements; 'free trade' was no longer free.

By the outbreak of the First World War, monopoly capitalists were making vast amounts of money which they were ploughing into what they anticipated would be the most

Monopoly

A monopoly occurs when an individual or business has the sole power in selling particular goods and services. Thus, a monopolist usually has total control over what prices to set for goods, how much to produce and the quality of finished articles.

profitable enterprises. Lenin agreed with Hobson in stating that territories in untapped parts of the world were being fought over to provide markets for the 'new' money to be invested. Lenin differed with Hobson over the impact of this on the home economies of imperialist nations. He claimed that through unifying the nation, imperialism discouraged people from protesting against adverse living and working conditions. Being part of a strong empire seemed to offer hope for the future. Lenin also emphasised the power of monopolies which was far greater than that of the individual investment capitalists that Hobson seemed to have in mind. Lenin called imperialism the highest stage of capitalism because he believed that it would inevitably lead to further world conflict (i.e. world wars) and result in poverty which workers would blame on leaders.

Critical analysis

Non-Marxists have been highly dismissive of Lenin's approach. The main concern is that he was selective in the 'facts' he used so that they would fit his ideology. Other criticisms include the following.

- Lenin borrowed much of his material from Hobson but more significantly from a fellow Marxist intellectual of the time called Rudolf Hilferding. After Hilferding began to moderate his political views, Lenin turned against him claiming he was a 'petty bourgeois disguised as a socialist' and refused to acknowledge his debt. Although this is a criticism of Lenin rather than his thesis, it illustrates how unoriginal his work was and that it is Hilferding's work that really needs scrutinising.

- Lenin's theory was predictive and not especially accurate in this sense; imperialism did not lead to revolutions with resultant governments controlled by workers in either the periphery or the metropole. However, nationalist independence movements were often influenced by Marxist-Leninist ideas.

- Lenin largely ignored other factors and concentrated solely on those of an economic nature, assuming that governments were mostly encouraged to support expansion due to the desire to acquire raw materials, new profitable markets and highly lucrative investment opportunities. In reality, Britain often looked to invest in countries without wishing to exert political control, such as in Argentina.

- Generally, investments in other industrialised areas were often more valuable than investment in the colonies. North America was, for example, always a better investment market than most of Africa.

> **FOR DISCUSSION**
>
> How far do you agree with the view that Lenin's interpretation of the causes and motives for imperialism is irrelevant because it was largely based on a Marxist predictive model?

Cain and Hopkins: the concept of gentlemanly capitalism

> **Key Question:**
>
> How has Cain and Hopkins' approach and interpretation contributed to our understanding of the way in which economic forces affected imperialism?

CAIN AND HOPKINS' APPROACH AND INTERPRETATION

Approach:
- emphasis on the role of economic history but also a multi-disciplinary approach to studying the Empire

Method:
- the selection, presentation, interpretation, analysis and evaluation of quantitative material

Interpretation:
- imperialism came about due to the emergence of 'gentlemanly capitalists'

Cain and Hopkins' approach

P. J. Cain and A. G. Hopkins are two prominent academics working in British universities who, from the 1980s until the present, have focused on explaining how British Imperialism was mainly due to economic activity in the metropole. They are both economic historians, but their work does attempt to show how '…material forces… were linked to social and political developments' (P. J. Cain and A. G. Hopkins (2002) *British Imperialism 1688–2000*, p. 2).

Their first major work, *British Imperialism: Innovation and Expansion 1688–1914* was published in 1993 and was quickly followed by a second companion volume which dealt with the period up to the mid-1940s. An expanded second edition of their writing which took into account the influence of **globalisation** came out in 2002. The latter is significant as it implies that the relatively new concept of globalisation can help historians view the origins of the British Empire in a different light. It is an example of how current thinking about world affairs can shape how we interpret the past. The British Empire could be viewed as an early example of the move towards globalisation that failed. In addition, Cain and Hopkins implied that they were influenced by the economic crises of the late 1980s and early 1990s. The end of Thatcherism seemed to signal the beginning of uncertainty about future economic performance, and in particular, concerns over **deindustrialisation**.

Cain and Hopkins' interpretation

From the end of the Second World War to the 1970s, historians generally believed economic influences to have been less important than those of a political, social and cultural nature. The work of Cain and Hopkins and, more recently, Ferguson has, however, reopened the debate. Cain and Hopkins argued that the link between the Industrial Revolution and British Imperialism was greatly exaggerated. This was due to the evolutionary rise of a new 'social' group from the time of the Glorious Revolution of 1688: gentlemanly capitalists, based mainly in the City of London. This group consisted of individuals from families associated with commerce, the professions, and/or landed interest. In turn, they seemed fused together by a set of values inculcated by the public schools and elite universities. Such values consisted of placing duty before self-advancement and gaining an education that would give them such a high level of social prestige that they would not have to 'work', but could use leisure time to think, plan and be creative. Working was associated with industrialisation and manufacturing activities linked with classes of a lesser rank. These gentlemen were 'made as well as born', although their roots were mainly in the old landed gentry of England. They emerged around the time that the landed classes found it increasingly difficult to earn income from agricultural activity. Gentlemanly capitalists began to realise that investment of substantial amounts of money in a variety of service enterprises, both at home and especially abroad, would yield enormous returns.

Thus, links were forged with the commercial and financial hub of the nation: the City of London. It was from here that the gentlemanly capitalists started to dominate the service industry, particularly banking, and influence decisions about the quantity and direction of finance capital to various parts of the Empire. Imperial projects where significant returns on investments could be gained encouraged gentlemanly capitalists, such as the 8th Duke of Devonshire, to shift their assets out of both agriculture *and* industry. After 1890, for example, Devonshire invested heavily in overseas railways and government stocks, which provided a considerable amount of his income before 1914 and the major part of it by the 1920s.

The most important elite investors came from the Rothschild family, who had accumulated assets worth £41 million by the end of the nineteenth century, most of

---

Globalisation

This is the process whereby world-wide, international concerns are placed above national or local concerns.

Deindustrialisation

This is the move away from an economy based on manufacturing (secondary level production) to one dependent on services (tertiary level production).

which was invested in **government bonds**. In turn, a large number of the bonds were investments in Egypt and South Africa.

The Rothschilds also had close links with politicians, which supports another observation made by Cain and Hopkins: gentlemanly capitalists needed the support of governments to protect their investments, both directly and indirectly. Equally, politicians appeared to value highly the services of the 'aristocratic' investors, both privately and publicly. Disraeli, Randolph Churchill and the Earl of Rosebery were all linked to the Rothschild dynasty. As Niall Ferguson has pointed out, the case of Rosebery is of particular note since he was in close communication with senior members of the Rothschild family, and, in 1878, married Lord Rothschild's cousin, Hannah. Although Rosebery held senior positions in government for relatively short periods of time (Foreign Secretary 1886, 1892–4; Prime Minister 1894–5) there is evidence to suggest that he did provide valuable inside information and assistance to his relatives that helped protect their interests.

Gladstone is another interesting example of a politician who seemed to mix with gentlemanly capitalists. He invested heavily in the Egyptian economy via the Ottoman Egyptian Tribute loan of 1871. By 1891, he had made a capital gain of 130 per cent on his initial outlay and had much to lose if financial instability occurred within the area. Unsurprisingly, as Ferguson points out, the monitoring of affairs in Egypt for the last part of the century was placed in the hands of a member of another great financier family of the time, the Barings.

Critical analysis

Cain and Hopkins' research has been very important in revitalising the debate over what caused the expansion of the Empire in the latter part of the nineteenth century. They revisited the role of the metropole and claimed that gentlemanly capitalists were the driving force behind British Imperialism, rather than a mixture of other influences. Criticism has been aimed at the findings of Cain and Hopkins, although they have been very astute and thorough in defending their thesis. The main areas of concern have been as follows.

- ■ Fieldhouse has pointed out that the Cain and Hopkins approach is **monocausal**. However, this does not mean that they are wrong, even though events are often the culmination of complex interplay between a number of factors.
- ■ Bernard Porter has concerns that the thesis underplays the importance of the periphery. He believes that it is too Anglo-centric, focusing far too much on activity originating from an elite based in the City of London.
- ■ A far more common criticism is that expressed by historians such as Daunton, who claim that industrialists *did* play a significant role in empire building and that Cain and Hopkins chose to ignore evidence that did not fit with their thesis. In fact, they do acknowledge the importance of manufacturing groups, but claim that this factor was nowhere near as influential as that of gentlemanly capitalists.
- ■ Finally, some of the material used to explain how gentlemanly capitalists influenced government policy is rather flimsy. More research still needs to be carried out on the interaction between individuals and groups, although, as Cain and Hopkins point out, their aim was to establish a general theory of causation rather than investigate the motivations of the key 'players'.

Explanations of political and social forces in the metropole

Key Questions:

- How has the 'international' approach and interpretation contributed to our understanding of the way in which political forces affected imperialism?
- How has the 'metropolitan politics' approach and interpretation contributed to our understanding of the way in which political forces affected imperialism?
- How has the concept of informal imperialism contributed to our understanding of the way in which political forces affected imperialism?

Political causes of Empire are linked to the interest of nations in the acquisition and maintenance of political power. This, in turn, often meant demonstrating authority and control over territory using diplomatic means and/or military force. The land in question may not necessarily have become part of a formal Empire but the influence exerted was seen as a way of enhancing prestige and status on the world stage. Strategic causes refer to the need to plan to protect acquisitions for their economic value. Many political and military actions were taken for strategic reasons, i.e. to protect parts of the Empire that were deemed irreplaceable due to their commercial value. This was especially true of India; much of British imperial policy up to 1914 was aimed at protecting the 'jewel in the crown'. This highlights the strong interrelationship between political, strategic and commercial factors.

Imperial rivalry among the Great Powers

INTERNATIONAL APPROACH AND INTERPRETATION

Approach:
- an emphasis on international relations in an historical context

Method:
- the analysis of official and unofficial written sources

Interpretation:
- expansionism and, in particular, the 'scramble for Africa' was a result of Great Power rivalry

Key Question:

How has the 'international' approach and interpretation contributed to our understanding of the way in which political forces affected imperialism?

A. J. P. Taylor's approach and interpretation

In *The Struggle for Mastery in Europe* (1954), A. J. P. Taylor argued that the so-called 'New Imperialism' of the latter decades of the nineteenth century was primarily about the 'scramble for Africa' (a term first used by *The Times* in 1884). Africa acted as a kind of stage on which the major Western European powers (Britain, France, Germany and Italy) could act out a power struggle. Tensions could be released, threats made and 'fights' participated in, without recourse to a full-blown war. At the same time, all of this was on 'foreign' soil, and often to the detriment of the indigenous populations. For Taylor, this was a completely unplanned and even irrational development, especially as the economic costs of partitioning Africa seemed to outweigh the benefits for all of the players concerned.

P. Kennedy's approach and interpretation

To an extent, this interpretation has been supported by more global approaches adopted by scholars such as Paul Kennedy. In *The Rise and Fall of the Great Powers* (1988), he argued that Britain's expansion of Empire was a response to the attempt by other budding world powers to emulate Britain. These other 'Great Powers' tried to match the British with respect to industrialisation, trade, naval power, overseas investment and the acquisition of colonies. In turn, Britain wanted to maintain its pre-eminent position as a world power, and therefore had no option but to compete with the others to acquire new land. The Kennedy view is useful as it emphasises the complex interplay between the powerful European nations, and the consequences of a changing balance of power. However, it is worth considering the position of each 'Great Power' in order to assess the foundations of the Taylor and Kennedy arguments.

Approaches and interpretations that emphasise European rivalry

Some historians have approached the study of the growth of Empire by emphasising the complex interplay between European rivals. Below is a summary of interpretations of the role played by each European nation with imperial interests.

France

The heavy defeat of France during the Franco-Prussian War (1869–71) left French leaders and the people embittered, especially as they had to cede the valuable province of Alsace-Lorraine to Prussia. However, this did not halt their imperial ambitions; if anything, it strengthened their will to expand further, especially if it was at the expense of the newly-unified Germany or Britain.

French imperialism gained momentum from the 1860s with territorial gains in Indo-China (Vietnam). By the 1880s, they had pushed towards southern China, Burma and Siam (now Thailand). In Africa they made great strides south of the Sahara, so that, by the end of the century, their empire in that continent was vast and impressive, even if mainly on 'light soil' (desert land).

> **Stretch and challenge**
>
> What characterised a nation as a Great Power in the nineteenth century? Was it necessary to be imperialist to become a Great Power? Was it inevitable that being imperialist at some stage would lead to the eventual downfall of a Great Power?

QUICK FACT

The Fashoda Crisis. In 1898, the British government sent troops commanded by Lord Kitchener to the Sudan to protect the upper reaches of the Nile from a possible French incursion. Kitchener met a French force under the command of Marchand at the small town of Fashoda; Marchand laid claim to Fashoda on behalf of France while Kitchener asserted that the whole of the Sudan belonged to Britain. After the Prime Minister, Lord Salisbury, refused any attempt by the French to compromise and put the Royal Navy on alert, Marchand was forced to withdraw. In March 1899, France renounced all claims to the Nile valley.

The Entente Cordiale

This was an agreement, signed between France and Britain on 8 April 1904, to remain allies and to show 'mutual goodwill'.

Kolonialverein

A pressure group made up of industrialists and businessmen, formed in 1882, which aimed to persuade Bismarck to follow an expansionist imperial policy for commercial purposes.

The occupation of Egypt (1882) by the British, while the French made territorial gains in West Africa, confirmed by the 1884–5 Berlin Conference, certainly increased tension between Britain and France. Anglo-French rivalry in central Africa continued throughout the 1890s with France attempting to gain better trade and border agreements, and the British attempting to maintain (but not expand) their territorial influence. The **Fashoda Crisis** of 1898 brought matters to a head and forced the French to realise that they lacked the power to oppose Britain in Africa. At this point, it was not likely that an *entente cordiale*, such as that of 1904, would ever be achieved.

French acquisitions in Africa were not seen as economically important and nor were they seen as a threat to trading routes. Thus, French imperialism did not seem to pose much of a threat to the British and was not really a prompt to scramble for more territory.

Russia

British governments feared Russia as an expansionist force for most of the nineteenth century. As Russia moved further eastwards into central Asia and Siberia, concern mounted about a possible Russian invasion of India. These fears caused Britain to invade and occupy Afghanistan in 1879, since the country was considered a vital buffer state between Russian territory and British India. By the mid-1880s, Russia retaliated by annexing Merv and moving towards the Persian-Afghanistan border. After a direct threat from Gladstone, Russia backed off, but politicians of all persuasions began to accept that India had to be defended beyond the Indus. Russia also looked to expand further east via the acquisition of Port Arthur in north China in 1898, which provided a base for incursions into Korea. These ambitions were ended by defeat in the Russo-Japanese War (1904–5), but until then they added to anxiety over the possible challenge to eastern trading routes.

As with France, there is little to indicate that Russian imperialism stimulated British expansionism. Disraeli did not sanction the invasion of Afghanistan. This was done independently by the Viceroy for India, the Earl of Lytton. In fact, Disraeli was shocked by such action, and retorted 'When Vice-roys and Commanders-in-Chief disobey orders, they ought to be sure of success in their mutiny. Lytton, by disobeying orders, has only secured insult and failure… To force the Khyber, and take Cabul is a perilous business' (quoted in C. C. Eldridge (1978) *Victorian Imperialism*, pp. 110–1). Russia was obviously seen as a strategic threat, but not one to directly threaten political world standing. The 1905 revolution, the weak attempt to form a constitutional monarchy that followed, and the revolutions of 1917 appeared to provide reassurance that the 'Russian bear' was not very frightening. After the First World War, Bolshevism caused consternation, but mainly among Conservatives, who feared the spread of communism throughout Europe, and who saw the Empire as a kind of antidote to the growth of socialism at home.

Germany

Before the mid-1880s, the British eyed Germany with some suspicion, mainly due to Chancellor Bismarck's foreign policy aims. However, these appeared to be focused solely on Europe. Bismarck seemed entirely uninterested in colonial expansion, claiming that 'Here lies Russia, and there lies France, and we are in the middle. That is my map of Africa'. In 1883, a dramatic change of policy occurred, as the German leader called for a meeting of the Great Powers to 'carve up' parts of West Africa. The British were taken by surprise, and Gladstone was rather dismissive of the action seeing it as an 'election gimmick'. It was more than that though, as Bismarck was under considerable pressure from the ***Kolonialverein*** to take action.

By 1886, Germany had acquired significant imperial territory. The Cameroons and Togoland were taken as a result of the Berlin West African Conference of 1884–5, and Tanganyika followed by way of a separate agreement. In the Pacific, north-eastern New Guinea and a number of islands further north and east were also annexed by Germany. This sudden turnaround in German foreign policy undoubtedly sparked an expansionist response from Britain, although this was also aided by changing domestic circumstances which made expansion more acceptable.

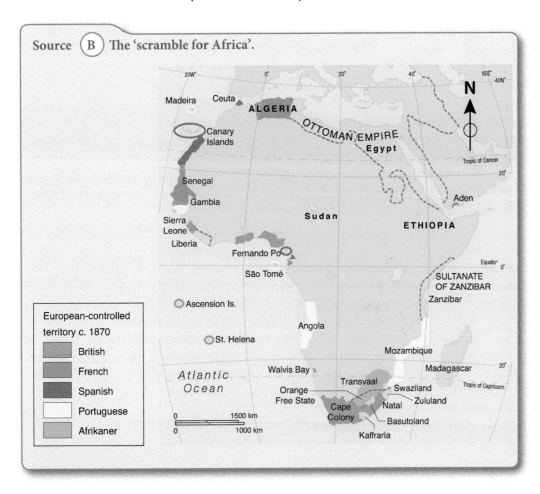

Source **B** The 'scramble for Africa'.

The reaction came mainly in the form of providing backing to 'men on the spot'. In 1886, a Royal Charter was granted to Sir George Goldie's National Africa Company (later renamed the Royal Niger Company) which resulted in a virtual monopoly of British trade around the Niger. In 1889, Cecil Rhodes was also granted a charter for his British South Africa Company, leading to the occupation of land north of Bechuanaland and the Transvaal. By 1891, the company was granted further permission to go into lands north of the Zambezi (Northern Rhodesia, now Zambia) and Rhodes also influenced the declaration of a protectorate over Nyasaland in 1891 by guaranteeing to fund it for at least four years. In East Africa, William McKinnon was granted a charter to run the Imperial British East Africa Company. This was partly so that McKinnon might eventually take Uganda, which would help to prevent the spread of German influence via the trader and explorer Carl Peters. Finally, an agreement with Germany in 1890 over East African claims resulted in German recognition of British claims to Zanzibar and Uganda in exchange for Heligoland and extension of German influence from Dar-es-Salaam to Lake Tanganyika. Salisbury also used the opportunity to gain an agreement over British control of Northern Rhodesia, Bechuanaland and eastern Nigeria. By 1891, partition of Africa was pretty much complete.

Counter-factualism

In March 1890, Bismarck was forced to resign as Chancellor of Germany by the Kaiser, Wilhelm II. He died in 1898. If he had been allowed to continue with his own foreign policy would this have changed Britain's approach to Empire? Make a list of the changes that you think may have occurred. How does this kind of approach add to our understanding of the development of the Empire?

However, this was not the end of Anglo-German tensions over Africa. In 1895, the Kaiser sent a telegram to Paul Kruger, President of the Transvaal, congratulating him on repelling a 'raid' by the British adventurer, Leander Jameson, who had been intent on stirring a rebellion to unseat Kruger. This created a certain amount of hysteria in Britain as it was seen as the first sign of a pact between Germany and the Transvaal, aimed at eventual takeover of South Africa. During the first decade of the twentieth century, Germany also flexed its muscles over French claims to Morocco, culminating in the Agadir crisis of 1911, in which the Kaiser sent the German battleship *Panther* to the Moroccan port in order to force the French into making territorial concessions. Given the close relationship that had developed between France and Britain by that time, such an action was viewed as outrageous, humiliating and threatening.

This raises a very significant point about the relationship between imperialism, military technology and Anglo-German rivalry. James Roll has pointed out that Wilhelm II, in particular, valued the acquisition of colonies in Africa as it provided a testing ground for new German technology, especially warships. Plans for an expanded and modernised German navy developed in 1897 under Admiral Tirpitz and began to be implemented from 1900. It was the start of a naval arms race, which was to have serious financial implications for participants but, more significantly, played a role in the outbreak of World War One.

German imperialism was undoubtedly a trigger for change in British imperial policy and contributed to the partition of Africa. This partly supports Taylor's view that imperial expansion was a power struggle between the two nations. However, the evidence suggests that the leaders of Germany and Britain acted under pressure from sections of society who welcomed expansionism for a variety of commercial, humanitarian, political and strategic reasons, rather than as a result of personal ideology. Finally, the naval arms race provides useful support to the Kennedy thesis. Britain had ruled the waves via the British navy, and to achieve similar status Germany had to compete at sea and copy its imperial rivals. Naval supremacy could only be tested through ownership of an empire.

Metropolitan political ideology

Key Question:

How has the 'metropolitan politics' approach and interpretation contributed to our understanding of the way in which political forces affected imperialism?

METROPOLITAN POLITICAL APPROACH AND INTERPRETATION

Approach:
■ the identification of how political ideology affected decisions taken in the metropole

Method:
■ an analysis of official political documents

Interpretation:
■ political ideology affected imperial expansion

Approaches that emphasise metropolitan politics and imperialism

The struggle between world powers gives us some idea of why nations such as Britain embraced imperialism. However, many historians have also emphasised the significance of political ideology within the metropole. Historians who approach imperialism from this angle focus on the values and beliefs held by particular politicians and parties, and how this affected the actions taken by different governments. This approach is significant since it explores the way in which individuals could alter imperialism, and the way in which Britain was not merely reacting to external, global events.

Interpretations of the role played by political parties

The Liberal Party

During the second half of the nineteenth century, the Liberal Party was dominated by the leadership of William Ewart Gladstone who was in office as prime minister on four occasions (1868–74, 1880–5, 1886 and 1892–4). The Gladstonian stance on Empire was fairly constant during this time: he believed it was his duty to govern efficiently over the Empire, but to consolidate rather than expand it. Expansionism and direct control of colonies was viewed as costly, and led to conflict. It also went against the basic tenet of liberalism, which focused on providing freedom and rights to peoples who were governed. Gladstone's aim was to allow colonies responsible self-government and encourage them to become self-reliant.

During Gladstone's first ministry there were times when he was vilified for lacking patriotism and any genuine concern for imperial affairs. In early 1870, troops were withdrawn from Canada and New Zealand at a time of internal upheaval. The Canadian Prime Minister, Galt, was given a knighthood despite being a proponent of independence, and, in June 1870, the Gambia was handed over to France. These events caused some historians to label 1869–70 as the 'climax of anti-imperialism', but the Gladstonian approach needs to be seen in context. There were genuine concerns over budgets, implementing **Edward Cardwell**'s proposed military reforms of 1869, coping with changing European relations (as a result of the Franco-Prussian War) and the need to strengthen bonds with the USA. Besides, both Gladstone and his Colonial Secretary, Granville, sincerely believed that the withdrawal of military assistance was the best way to allow self-government while maintaining 'prosperous and cordial friendships'. This did not mean a separatist approach, that is, the break up of Empire, but one whereby 'a Colony might be great and self-reliant, and still maintain an intimate connection with the mother country' (Knatchbull-Hugessen, Liberal spokesman for the Colonial Office speaking in the House of Commons, May 1871).

However, Gladstone's second and subsequent ministries revealed divisions in the Liberal camp over Empire. The majority of Liberals adopted a moderate position based on consolidation and informal control, whilst a significant Whig group pushed increasingly for expansionism, which was more aligned to the 'Forward' school of thought that pervaded the Conservative party. To make the matter even more complicated, Gladstone had to deal with the demands of Radicals and Irish Nationalists, both groups severe critics of Empire, but whose support was crucial in dealing with the Irish Question and a range of other domestic issues. Given the pressure from the Whig elements, and the sudden switch by Bismarck to imperialism, it is not totally surprising that Gladstone moved towards a more expansionist approach (to the extent that some historians believe he was responsible for the 'scramble for Africa'). But this was not apparent in the lead up to the 1880 election; Gladstone's famous Midlothian campaign attacked Disraelian imperialism as being inhumane, unjust and expensive (source C).

Gladstone's intention on taking office in March 1880 was to reverse the path taken by Disraeli, and to consider a more federalist approach to governance of Empire. With the

BIOGRAPHY

Edward Cardwell

Edward Cardwell was Minister for War during Gladstone's first ministry. He carried out a number of army reforms to improve military performance. These included reducing the length of service from 12 years to 6, reorganisation of the battalion system, the introduction of breech-loading rifles and the abolition of the purchase of commissions.

Suzerainty

This means that one country has power or control over the affairs, usually foreign, of another country.

Transvaal, Gladstone initially attempted to keep it 'federated' with Frere still in charge (see page 39 on the Conservative party), but this backfired as the Boers revolted, resulting in the death of the Governor of Natal at Majuba Hill in February 1881 (the First Boer War). In response, a convention was held at Pretoria in August 1881, which restored Boer self-government, but with British **suzerainty** over external affairs. The latter was not clearly defined and was completely ignored when renegotiations took place in 1884. The British were left without any kind of 'effective control', whilst the Boers were buoyed by their efforts to repel the imperial aggressors.

> Source **C** A cartoon of the time relating to Gladstone's Midlothian campaign.
>
> The McGladstone!
>
> " To land McGladstone lightly sprang,   With note prolong'd and varied strain,
>   And thrice aloud his bugle rang   Till bold Ben-Gholl replied again."
>   " *Lord of the Isles.*"   Canto IV.

The Eastern Question

This refers to the problem of what was to happen in south-eastern Europe as a result of the decline of the Turkish Ottoman Empire during the second half of the nineteenth century.

Retrenchment

Reduction in expenditure.

Gladstone seemed to have more success over mopping up problems in Afghanistan, but this sill required military intervention. Moderate Liberals, meanwhile, had been very critical of Conservative support for Turkey and their policy over the **Eastern Question** in general. Gladstone was successful in dropping the scheme to defend the Turkish Empire in Asia, and he placed pressure on the Sultan to keep agreements made at the Berlin summit of 1878. The occupation of Egypt in 1882, however, was seen as a clear reversal of Gladstonian thinking, particularly when it became apparent that it would not be temporary. Finally, the handling of the Mahdi uprising in the Sudan from 1881 to 1885 culminating in the death of Gordon and the fall of Khartoum, was nothing short of a disaster. Gladstone was forced to intervene due to the threat posed to Egypt, but with hindsight, chose the wrong person to administer a peaceful solution to the conflict. Thus, overall, Gladstone struggled to consistently follow a policy of **retrenchment** over Empire, due to a mixture of external events and the need to keep factions in his party happy. Moderates felt he had gone back on his principles, while Whigs believed he had not gone far enough to address the challenges of New Imperialism as witnessed by his hesitancy over the Sudan crisis.

Splits in the party were even more apparent in June 1886 when 93 Liberal Unionists, led by Lord Hartington and Joseph Chamberlain, voted against the first Irish Home Rule Bill. By 1887, they had formed an alliance with the Conservatives and Chamberlain went on to serve them as Colonial Secretary from 1895 to 1903. By the time of the Second Boer War (1899–1902), the Liberal party was in total disarray over imperial matters. The Liberal Imperialists ('Limps'), including Asquith, Grey and Rosebery, favoured the Conservative party position on the war, whereas Radical Liberals, such as Lloyd George, found the war 'senseless and unnecessary'. The moderate position was summed up by Sir Henry Campbell-Bannerman, who stated:

'I have never uttered a pro-Boer word; I have been anti-Joe [Chamberlain], but never pro-Kruger' (quoted in C. C. Eldridge (1978) *Victorian Imperialism*, p. 88). This lack of unity was always evident before 1914, although it is fair to say that post-1906 Liberal governments were distracted from imperial affairs by domestic issues and the continuing question of Irish Home Rule. After 1914 they were never in power again and therefore had no direct control over the future of the Empire.

The Conservative Party

The Conservatives were undoubtedly the party of Empire throughout the period, and against the 'freedom and voluntarism' of the Liberals. Both Disraeli and Salisbury were intent on defending Britain's imperial strategic interests and also adopted policies that used the Empire as a tool to maintain world political status.

Disraeli (Prime Minister 1868, 1874–80) set his stall out in 1872 with his Crystal Palace speech in which promised to uphold Empire. Although historians have debated his motives, some believe he was genuinely concerned about the Empire. Others, however, view his actions as opportunistic and based on the chance to further 'dish the Whigs'. What followed was a flurry of activity which can be interpreted in different ways. Extensions of control in West Africa and Malay states and the annexation of Fizi in 1874 were carried out reluctantly, and were really extensions of previous Liberal strategies. The purchase of Suez Canal shares in 1875, the annexation of the Transvaal and the occupation of Cyprus in 1878 occurred for strategic reasons. Attempts at expansion in Zululand and Afghanistan in 1879 were made by 'men on the spot', mostly against the overt wishes of Disraeli. In fact, most developments during this time were due to individuals such as Cross, Viscount Sandon, the Earl of Carnarvon, and the Earl of Derby without close co-operation with the Prime Minister. Disraeli nearly always publicly supported the actions of his ministers to sustain party unity, but he was not as aggressively expansionist as is sometimes made out.

A fairly similar line was taken by Salisbury, who was in power as Prime Minister on three occasions: 1885–6, 1886–92 and 1895–1902. Like Gladstone, he was caught up in the whirlwind of changing world affairs from the mid-1880s onwards, and was spurred to react against the new European imperialism that emerged. His tenure was most notable for Britain's participation in the naval arms race, Chamberlain's attempts to install a new form of imperial integration and the Second Boer War. The work of Chamberlain is of particular significance. His policies centred around creating a strong union between Britain and the colonies of settlement, which he believed was the solution to the economic and social challenges the nation had started to face. A reorganised Empire would boost supplies of raw materials, create even bigger and more favourable markets, and result in more job opportunities. In turn, this would aid the funding of social reform (Social Imperialism), which started to become a burning issue with the revelations of social investigators such as Booth and Rowntree, and evidence provided by recruitment offices during the Boer War about the poor medical condition of numerous volunteers. His ideas culminated in a Tariff Reform Programme, launched in 1903, which was not adopted at the time, although a variation of it appeared during the interwar years.

FOR DISCUSSION

How important were the Liberals compared with the other major political parties in determining the course of British imperialism throughout the period in question?

After the debacle of the Second Boer War, the Conservatives' policy towards Empire lacked support and credibility. By the interwar years they returned to power with renewed impetus and new ideas about the importance of Empire. The Conservative Secretary of State for the Colonies, Leo Amery, promoted Empire as an antidote to socialism. The public could be persuaded to take pride in imperial achievements, which would take their minds off the problems associated with economic slumps and prevent them from turning to extreme political ideologies and groups (i.e. socialists, communists). But, increasingly during this period, the Empire seemed to hold less political and strategic purpose, becoming more useful as a potential solution to the economic ills of the time; hence, the implementation of **Imperial Preference** by the National Government in the early 1930s. Moreover, developments in India suggested that a unified Empire would be difficult to sustain, even if desired, and that the great age of Empire was beginning to wane.

Imperial Preference

This was the planned policy of favouring nations of the Empire through special trading concessions, such as lowering the tariffs on imperial goods to a level below that of foreign goods, guaranteeing to export a certain amount of goods to colonies.

ACTIVITY

The historian C. C. Eldridge believes that, on balance, Disraeli was not a staunch imperialist. Imagine that Disraeli was called to a press conference in 1872 to present and defend his views on Empire. What questions would he be asked and how would he respond? Set this up as a role-play exercise with other members of your history group. Appoint someone to play Disraeli and others to act as key members of the Cabinet who would be in a position to support him at a press conference. The rest of the group can act as journalists. Make certain that:

■ your teacher ensures that the class is crystal clear about the learning outcomes for the exercise

■ those playing Disraeli and his Cabinet are well briefed about imperial affairs at the time and individual attitudes, beliefs and values that link to Empire. This could be linked to a research exercise that involves looking for primary and secondary material that provides evidence about what the key players believed (e.g. speeches, letters, diary entries)

■ those playing the role of journalists are also well informed about imperial developments and Conservative party ideology. They should obviously be given time to construct meaningful and probing questions

■ anachronisms are avoided, that is, assigning something to an earlier or (less strictly) to a later age than it belongs to

■ your teacher chairs the meeting and acts as a quality controller with respect to how well the Conservatives are briefed and the nature of questions asked by the journalists

■ records are kept by all of the group of the material that is used to inform the press conference

■ your teacher uses an appropriate assessment tool to check whether learning has taken place. This could take the form of an extended piece of writing that involves answering the following question.

Some historians have stressed the importance of looking at the motives of key politicians in the metropole when analysing the reasons for imperialism in the late nineteenth century. With reference to Disraeli in particular, explain the extent to which this approach adds to our understanding of why the Empire grew so rapidly during this time. What are the strengths and limitations of interpreting motives for the expansion of Empire using mostly a 'top down' (and political) focus? (N.B. 'top down' means from the perspective of those in power. This activity can easily be adapted to apply to other politicians of the time.)

Schumpeter and the sociology of imperialism

SCHUMPETER'S APPROACH AND INTERPRETATION

Approach:
- an emphasis on the importance of social scientific knowledge and understanding

Method:
- the scrutiny of records dealing with social stratification

Interpretation:
- 'hereditary elites' needed the Empire to justify their role and status in society

J. Schumpeter's approach

Joseph Schumpeter (1883–1950) was born in Triesch, Moravia, part of the old Austro-Hungarian Empire. He studied law and economics at the University of Vienna and went on to become an academic of considerable standing, finishing his career at Harvard University (1932–50) as Professor of Economics. He also held the post of Austrian Minister of Finance (1919–20) and president of the Biedermann Bank (1920–4). Most of Schumpeter's approach revolved around promoting the benefits of free trade and capitalism. This helps explain the views he held about imperialism, as he believed this was a hindrance to the functioning of the 'free market'. His views on empire building were most clearly expressed in an essay published in 1918 entitled 'The Sociology of Imperialism'. It was at a time when many intellectuals were reflecting on the Great War and attempting to offer explanations as to why the tragedy had occurred.

Schumpeter's interpretation

Schumpeter defined imperialism as 'the objectless disposition of a state to expansion by force, without assigned limits'. The British 'state' by 1918, was still dominated and controlled by an aristocratic elite, despite the fact that the franchise had been extended to the working classes and most of the population had some representation in parliament. The elite took an interest in the expansion of trade and investment opportunities and therefore embraced, to an extent, the entrepreneurialism of the middle classes. However, Schumpeter believed that the aristocracy as an institution was so firmly entrenched in British society that it would never give way to the challenge posed by business and professional people. In fact, this made them even more determined to protect their status, which they proceeded to do by pushing for the expansion of the Empire. Land acquisition, as had always been the case with the feudal aristocrats of Europe, meant prestige and widening political power. This led Schumpeter to describe imperialism as 'an **atavism** of social structure and of individual habits'.

An important strand to this theory was that empire building was inextricably linked to the use of force. This was due to it providing the opportunity for aristocrats, who were naturally inclined to be warlike, to reassert their dominant status; indeed, the scramble for Africa provided plenty of examples of mini-wars to bear this out. Moreover, opportunities to engage in violent conflicts were often taken without consideration of what the precise objectives might be. This made expansion a sinister exercise. Schumpeter pointed out, though, that the use of military force was partly aimed at reassuring the capitalists that their imperial investments would always be protected and, hence, helped the ruling elites maintain a position of dominance over their 'class' rivals. Schumpeter believed that as imperialism was always associated with war, it was a negative phenomenon. War, in turn, was an impediment to the development of a free

FOR DISCUSSION

'Schumpeter was primarily an economist and sociologist. He was not trained in the discipline of history and therefore his views can be easily discredited.'

How far would you agree with this statement?

Atavism

The process of returning to an ancestral or 'primitive' state.

market economy. The only way to eradicate imperialism was to somehow conjure up the disappearance of the aristocracy who perpetuated it.

Critical analysis

The Schumpeterian view is valuable, since it emphasises the importance of the interaction of social groups on the expansion of the Empire, especially from 1880 onwards. However, it has been criticised on the following grounds.

- Schumpeter emphasised the psychological and emotional factors that influenced groups. Hence, he talked about the 'martial dispositions' of the aristocracy, which is fine except that it is very difficult to measure whether one social group in the past has been *naturally* more warlike than others.

- The ruling elites were far less homogenous than Schumpeter suggested. As we have seen, Cain and Hopkins have highlighted the existence of gentlemen capitalists who pushed for a peaceful approach to imperial economic development.

- Equally, the 'men on the spot', such as Rhodes, often acted independently without direct control from the metropole.

- Imperial wars often had very precise *strategic* objectives and were not carried out simply to provide a **cathartic** channel. This was true of the Ashanti and Zulu Wars, and the Boer Wars. The outcome of conflicts may have been miscalculated and even disastrous on occasion, but the motives behind forcible expansionism were seldom irrational (or illogical).

- Finally, Schumpeter excluded discussion of the humanitarian motives of the 'higher classes'. Thus, missionaries, philanthropists, explorers and scientists were excluded from his analysis.

Cathartic

In this context this means the cleansing or purifying of feelings and emotions.

Metropolitan influence on the informal Empire

Key Question:

How has the concept of informal imperialism contributed to our understanding of the way in which political forces affected imperialism?

GALLAGHER AND ROBINSON'S APPROACH AND INTERPRETATION

Approach:
- an emphasis on areas of the globe where Britain exerted influence rather than direct control

Method:
- an analysis of official documents

Interpretation:
- the influence exerted by Britain counts as informal Empire

Gallagher and Robinson's approach and interpretation: Britain's informal Empire

One of the most important debates about British imperialism has revolved around the significance of Britain's dealings with states outside its formal Empire. In the 1950s, Gallagher and Robinson suggested that Britain's economic and cultural influence over some independent states amounted to 'informal Empire'. This was particularly true for Britain's relationship with China and South America. From the 1830s to the 1860s, the

British government intervened in these regions with the intention of removing barriers to British commerce and finance. Britain was often the dominant partner in the subsequent economic relationships. It has thus been argued that some states came to rely on Britain's commercial and financial contributions to such an extent that they were compelled to make decisions that were beneficial to Britain. If they did not, British goods and capital might go elsewhere. Gallagher and Robinson's approach thus involved constructing a theoretical concept (informal Empire) which they then attempted to match against the 'facts'.

The approach and interpretation that emphasises the limitations of metropolitan power

Nevertheless, some historians have pointed out that there were serious limitations to the power of British influence, and that the impact of informal Empire on the metropole and periphery was often negligible. The volume of trade and investment between Britain and its 'informal Empire' was relatively low before 1880. In China, for example, although trade with Britain was growing during this period, it was still marginal to both the British and Chinese economies. This was partly because trade was limited to a few 'treaty ports' along the coastline of China, but also because the Chinese population had little disposable income. Besides, most needs could be satisfied by local goods, sold by local traders. Chinese merchants understood local tastes and promoted 'buy Chinese' sentiments. They were also able to acquire similar tax exemptions to those obtained by the British government for British merchants operating in China.

Moreover, politicians of 'subordinate' states retained the ability to make decisions that were detrimental to British commerce if it served the interests of their own country. For example, in the mid-nineteenth century, Britain was unable to 'manage' the price of Peruvian guano (bird excrement), which was essential as a fertiliser for Britain's agriculture. Furthermore, despite Britain's obsession with free trade, Latin American governments were able to maintain some tariff controls. British influence was also affected by foreign competition since Britain did not seek to place restrictions on trade between other nations. In the mid-Victorian period, Britain's industrial and financial supremacy gave it a significant advantage over competitors. But this was not to last. By the end of the nineteenth century, many countries in Britain's 'informal Empire' were able to deal with rival European and American merchants and financiers.

Stretch and challenge

Read Passage 1 by the historian Martin Lynn. What can you learn from this extract about the historian's approach and interpretation? Refer to the extract and your own knowledge to explain your answer. You will find it useful to read the case study on Argentina (pp. 126–9) before answering this question.

Passage

The metaphors [of 'informal Empire' and 'informal control'] not only distort what should be seen as a more ambiguous, fluid, and infinitely graded continuum of influence between Britain and the wider world. They are also unhelpful in implying… that this influence simply reached one way, from Britain into the world outside.

Martin Lynn in A. Porter (ed.) (1999) *The Oxford History of the British Empire: The Nineteenth Century*, p. 120.

THINK LIKE AN HISTORIAN

The date c.1880 is important in the debate about informal Empire, since it roughly marks the beginning of New Imperialism and the scramble for Africa. Gallagher and Robinson were thus keen to demonstrate that British policymakers contributed to the development of (informal) imperial control before this date.

Robinson and Gallagher believe that British governments' policies towards a 'free trade Empire' were best summed up by the following statement; 'trade with informal control if possible; trade with rule when necessary'. What does this tell you about their interpretation of the motives of British politicians towards maintaining and expanding the Empire in the second half of the nineteenth century?

EXAM TIP

Remember to use a dictionary if you come across a word that you are not familiar with. For example, it may be useful to look up the words metaphor, ambiguity, and continuum, all of which occur in the extract from Martin Lynn.

5 The exercise of imperial power on the periphery

> **Source** (A) **A colonial governor of Kenya, at the turn of the twentieth century**
>
> *Here we are, three white men in the heart of Africa... administering and policing a district inhabited by half a million well armed savages... the position is most humorous.*
>
> Quoted in B. Porter (2004) *The Lion's Share*, p. 222

Key Questions:

- How has the study of metropolitan policy contributed to our understanding of the way in which factors on the periphery affected colonial rule?
- Why have historians attempted to uncover the way in which factors on the periphery affected colonial rule, and how significant are their findings?
- How has the debate about coercion added to our understanding of the nature of colonial rule?
- Why have some historians decided to use the concept of hegemony to study Empire, and how significant are their findings?

The exercise of imperial power involved a variety of relationships between Britain and subordinate states and peoples. These reflected and influenced the way in which Britain attempted to rule and the policies that it pursued. Imperial policy was shaped and hindered by metropolitan and peripheral pressures. As a consequence, the nature of British rule in the colonies was the product of negotiation between centre and outskirts, colonial rulers and indigenous peoples. Brute force was a vital component in constructing imperial authority, but Britain would have been unable to maintain control without a measure of consent from those it governed.

Approaches that emphasise factors on the periphery examine the way in which indigenous peoples and individuals, such as local officials, affected the nature of imperial rule. Strategies of rule have also been areas of intense debate, much of which relates to the extent to which Britain relied on violence, consent or ideological control in order to dominate colonised peoples.

The traditional approach and interpretation: the importance of metropolitan policy

Key Question:

How has the study of metropolitan policy contributed to our understanding of the way in which factors on the periphery affected imperial rule?

IMPORTANCE OF METROPOLITAN POLICY

Approach:
- ■ an emphasis on the decisions taken in the metropole

Method:
- ■ an analysis of official metropolitan documents

Interpretation:
- ■ imperial rule reflected the decisions taken in the metropole

Approaches that emphasise the importance of metropolitan policy and imperialism

Traditionally, historians tended to focus more heavily on official documents and how metropolitan policy affected imperial rule. In part this was because sources originating in the metropole were more easily available than those which came out of the periphery. Historians working before the 1970s also lacked much of the theoretical framework that more recent historians have been able to utilise. Nevertheless, metropolitan approaches have been useful as a means of subsequently illustrating how the intentions of policymakers in Britain were never matched by the realities of colonial rule on the periphery.

Interpretations of the importance of metropolitan policy

Britain's colonial policy was based around three consistent objectives: security, economic development and trusteeship. The metropolitan authorities appointed officials and provided troops to administer and defend colonies according to these principles. However, the implementation of colonial policy was complicated and hindered by factors such as domestic political pressure and the need to economise.

Security

The protection of imperial possessions from external and internal threats was considered the most important aspect of metropolitan policy. Nevertheless, British politicians devised strategies that prioritised the defence of Britain over that of the colonies. From the late 1840s until the late 1870s, Britain decided to concentrate its armed forces at home, and many troops were withdrawn from the colonies of settlement. Britain also began to cut naval spending in the 1860s and 1870s, and fewer squadrons were deployed outside Europe. However, the threatening international climate of c.1880 caused Britain to change direction and to undertake an expensive programme of naval construction. At around the same time, British policymakers attempted to create a more unified strategy of imperial defence, and settlement colonies such as Australia were increasingly expected to contribute to naval spending; this caused some friction since colonists were initially denied any input into strategy.

Britain's attempts to safeguard the Empire were further complicated by the two major international conflicts of the twentieth century. The First World War was predominantly played out in Europe, but the Second World War was much more global in character. By the early 1940s, it was apparent that Britain was unable to guarantee the security of colonial possessions in the face of a hostile power such as Japan. This significantly weakened the bond between Britain and its colonies.

Policymakers were equally concerned about the internal security of colonies. Britain relied heavily on locally-recruited troops for the maintenance of law and order in the colonies; it was difficult to maintain large numbers of British troops in foreign, particularly tropical, climates. However, the Indian Mutiny (1857–8) revealed that locally-recruited troops were not always reliable and that colonial rule was extremely vulnerable. It was thus important to pursue policies calculated to calm rather than excite local agitation. In general, the British were reluctant to use coercion as a means of maintaining control, since it was believed that this might spark greater resistance. Alongside the use of the stick (i.e. coercion), the British dangled carrots (i.e. incentives) and attempted to exert ideological control over subject peoples.

Development

Britain encouraged the economic exploitation of natural resources in the colonies. This was partly motivated by the fact that the British economy would benefit from rising colonial production. However, the British also believed that economic development would be materially and morally advantageous to local people; it would bring them greater wealth and instil in them a work ethic. The policy of 'development' sometimes provoked tensions with indigenous elites whom the British believed hindered enterprise, either through the promotion of superstitious practices or with the intent of preserving traditional privileges. However, conflict was partly caused by different understandings of European activity. For example, a rebellion in Sierra Leone in 1898 was sparked when Britain attempted to introduce a tax on huts. Local people believed that Britain was asserting ownership of their land and their homes by demanding taxation; Britain had previously promised not to take away their land and, thus, local people believed that they had been betrayed. British ways of thinking, on the other hand, distinguished between taxation (a function of the state) and rent (a function of property ownership). The British introduced taxation in the hope that indigenous people would be compelled to grow cash crops for export; i.e. in order to pay their taxes, local people would have to grow export crops or find some other paid work that contributed to economic development.

The most important figure associated with the idea of colonial development was Joseph Chamberlain, Colonial Secretary from 1895 to 1903. He promoted a development programme for the tropical Empire designed to develop the colonial infrastructure. Although lack of funds limited the impact of this strategy, Chamberlain's involvement 'accelerated and confirmed a tentative trend for greater government responsibility for economic management and development of the Empire' according to E. H. H. Green (in A. Porter (ed.) (1999) *The Oxford History of the British Empire: The Nineteenth Century*, p. 352).

Trusteeship

British policymakers sought to protect indigenous peoples from exploitation and oppressive government. When considerations of economic development and trusteeship were incompatible, it was normally the latter that was favoured. For instance, in early twentieth-century West Africa, respected European companies were refused permission to construct large-scale plantations because the proposals were deemed harmful to the indigenous population. Furthermore, the Colonial Office tended to support the rights of indigenous people over settlers when conflicts between the two groups erupted. The Devonshire Declaration of 1923 (source B) was characteristic of the metropolitan aim to protect 'natives':

Source B Devonshire Declaration

Primarily, Kenya is an African territory, and His Majesty's Government think it necessary definitely to record their considered opinion that the interest of the African natives must be paramount, and that if, and when, those interests and the interests of the immigrant races conflict, the former should prevail.

Quoted in B. Porter (2004) *The Lion's Share*, p. 264

However, in the face of stern settler opposition, it was almost impossible to enforce this policy. For example, the white population in Kenya threatened rebellion in 1922–3 when attempts were made to include Indian immigrants on the electoral register. The idea of using non-whites to suppress the white settlers was not seriously considered, and the colonial authorities were forced to back down. According to Sir Arthur Dawe of the Colonial Office, writing in 1942 (source C), the legacy of the crisis was long-lasting:

Source C Sir Arthur Dawe

The lesson of 1923 is always there… it seems unthinkable that any British government would bring military force to bear upon a community of our own blood who have supported the British cause splendidly in this [World War Two] and the last war [World War One].

Quoted in A. Porter (ed.) (1999) *The Oxford History of the British Empire: The Nineteenth Century*, p. 271

Domestic political pressure

Generally, politicians in the metropole were more concerned with domestic and European issues than complex colonial problems. This was reflected by the concerns of voters. Only rarely did an imperial issue have a significant impact on an electoral result; the **'khaki election'** of 1900 was a distinct exception. Most concerted criticism of imperial policy was aimed at the costs of maintaining Empire. Occasionally, particular issues might arouse concern, such as the violent means used to deal with the Morant Bay rebellion in Jamaica (1865), and the shooting of civilians in the Amritsar massacre in India (1919); there was widespread (but by no means universal) disapproval of the way in which these events were handled. Such criticism reflected wider British values that Empire should be conducted in the right way. This in turn placed pressure on colonial authorities to limit the use of force when dealing with opposition.

The need to economise

Financial accountability in politics was an extremely important concept during the period c.1850–c.1950. Politicians had to make sure that tax-payers' money was well spent. Thus, there were severe restrictions placed on any policy that might require considerable expense, and 'cheap options' were favoured if at all possible. This partly explains the popularity of 'indirect rule', and the extensive use of local **collaborators** in colonial administration.

The significance of factors on the periphery

Key Question:

Why have historians attempted to uncover the way in which factors on the periphery affected colonial rule, and how significant are their findings?

FOR DISCUSSION

Indian immigrants were *not* the indigenous people of Kenya. How might this affect the validity of using the 1922–3 crisis as an example illustrative of the limitations of trusteeship?

QUICK FACT

A **khaki election** is one in which the voters are influenced by wartime or postwar sentiment. In the 1900 election, held during the return of soldiers from the Second Boer War, the Conservatives under Lord Salisbury were victorious over the Liberal Party. The term 'khaki' derives from the colour of the new military uniform of the British army.

Collaborators

A common term used by historians of the British Empire when talking about indigenous people who worked with the colonial authorities.

FACTORS ON THE PERIPHERY

Approach:

■ emphasis placed on the actions of local people and 'men on the spot'

Methods:

■ an analysis of records left by British officials working on the periphery

■ an analysis of memoirs and records left by local people

Interpretation:

■ imperial rule was significantly affected by the actions of individuals and groups
on the periphery

Approaches that emphasise the importance of factors on the periphery

Contemporaries realised that imperial rule depended on the actions taken by colonial officials and indigenous groups on the periphery. However, much of the impetus for studying the significance of these factors occurred in the aftermath of independence when historians from the periphery began to place more emphasis on the ways in which local people dealt with and affected imperial rule. This approach has revealed that indigenous groups were not merely pawns to be moved around but possessed agency in their own right, and were able to influence (to a lesser or greater degree) how imperial rule functioned.

Interpretations of the importance of factors on the periphery

Direct and indirect rule

Britain acquired the right to administer an overseas territory either through signing a treaty with the existing, legitimate ruler of the area, or through military conquest. Once a territory was in British possession, policymakers had to decide whether it would be better to preserve indigenous laws and customs or attempt to export British institutions (e.g. parliament, law courts, an extensive civil bureaucracy). Two-thirds of British India was ruled directly, along the lines of the administration in the metropole. The other third of India was governed by local princes, whose administrations were merely supervised by the British. This was a form of indirect rule, and was often favoured because it was cheaper to implement and less likely to inflame local opposition. In the early twentieth century, Britain also began to adopt a form of indirect rule in the African colonies. This developed in reaction to the growing belief that European interference was detrimental to both African society and colonial authority. Kenneth Bradley, a district officer in Northern Rhodesia (Zambia) and Tanganyika (Tanzania), explained what indirect rule involved (source D):

Source ⒟ Kenneth Bradley

I used to spend a great deal of my time in the bad old days of Direct Rule when the chief was of no account, going round each village hut by hut, exhorting apathetic savages to re-thatch, and sweep and clean. I do not do this anymore […] With, however, the institution of Indirect Rule, the position of the District Officer has altered entirely. He is no longer the ruler of individual lives and the oppressor of the village lazy-bones. The chief is being taught to rule again, and my job is to guide him, and to get him to do the work.

Quoted in J. Samson (ed.) (2001) *The British Empire*, p. 209

'Men on the spot'

Colonial policy was implemented by 'men on the spot' such as governors, generals and various other British officials. It was difficult for metropolitan policymakers to exert authority over these individuals because the distance between centre and periphery hindered effective communications. Colonial governors argued that those in the metropole lacked sufficient firsthand experience of a particular colony to offer suitable advice. Even if advice was sought, it would most likely arrive far too late to be of any use in dealing with local crises. Technological advances such as the introduction of a submarine telegraph system in the 1860s improved the situation. However, this also made it easier for local officials (often with their own agenda) to coerce the centre into making hasty and ill-informed decisions. One prominent example involved Alfred Milner, the High Commissioner of Southern Africa at the time of the Second Boer War. In 1898–9, he used telegrams to hustle the Colonial Office and Cabinet into issuing an ill-considered ultimatum to the Transvaal. Milner had also made the Transvaal question a prominent issue in the British media, thereby placing greater pressure on the British government to act.

Governors, of course, could be recalled. Even this caused problems though. The amateur ethnologist and explorer Mary Kingsley was critical that: 'No sooner does one of [the governors] begin to know about the country he is in charge of than off he is whisked and deposited again, in a brand new region for which West Africa has not been a fitting introduction' (B. Harlow and M. Carter (eds.) (2003) *Archives of Empire Volume II*, p. 441).

Collaboration and the indigenous elite

The use of collaborators underpinned British strategies of rule. **Local** people were used extensively in the administration, **army** and **police force** (source E). This was inevitable because of the difficulties in employing large numbers of **European administrators** in the colonies. Indigenous people also possessed the local knowledge that was essential for effective governance.

Source (E) A group of the newly-organised police force in Bengal, 1864.

QUICK FACT

Local policemen. Generally the colonial authorities favoured the use of an (armed) police force for the maintenance of internal security. Since the majority of policemen were locals, it was hoped that there would be less tension between the civilian populace and the colonial authorities. However, the police often acquired a damning reputation for incompetence and corruption. Mary Kingsley reveals that the strategy of employing policemen may have contributed to the 1898 rebellion in Sierra Leone:

Source Mary Kingsley

There is no manner of doubt that outrages have been committed, disgraceful to England, by the set of riff-raff rascal blacks, who had been turned out by, or who had run away from, the hinterland tribes down into Sierra Leone Colony, and there been turned, by an ill-informed government, into police, and sent back with power into the very districts from which they had, shortly before, fled for their crimes.

Quoted in B. Harlow and M. Carter (eds.) (2003) *Archives of Empire Volume II*, p. 455–6

QUICK FACT

European administrators. Each colony was administered by a colonial civil service. A single administrator often held jurisdiction over a very large number of colonial subjects. For instance, in Nigeria in the late 1930s, there were around 54,000 persons for every colonial official. However, improvements throughout the period in the speed and reliability of transport and communications allowed administrators to respond to difficult situations far more quickly and more effectively than had previously been the case.

Illness was another problem that faced administrators. This was particularly hazardous in the tropical areas of Africa. Despite medical advances, the climate was never hospitable enough for Britain to establish forms of rule which were reliant on a heavy European presence.

British colonial administrators shared a similar background. The majority came from the upper-middle and professional classes, and were products of the public schools. They possessed an authoritarian, hyper-masculine identity and (for the most part) were academically 'capable'. Those who joined the Indian Civil Service were particularly gifted, since this was one of the very few services which held competitive examinations as part of the selection process.

FOR DISCUSSION

The word collaborator often has disparaging connotations in everyday usage. However, it is a common term used by historians of the British Empire when talking about indigenous people who worked with the colonial authorities. Do you think it is a valid term for historians to use, or is it too 'loaded'?

As a result, indigenous elites were courted and involved in the exercise of British power, particularly in areas of indirect rule. These collaborators were sometimes rewarded with material benefits, such as access to investment and technology, or favourable allocations of land and labour. Indigenous authorities gained new legitimacy through association with a technologically-advanced foreign power. However, any relationship with the British placed pressure on indigenous collaborators. They were obliged to uphold metropolitan interests and preserve internal stability. Indigenous elites had to balance the retention of traditional authority with the fulfilment of imperial obligations. The extent to which local people were willing to work with a colonial power was thus a matter of negotiation. In turn, Britain was forced to accept limitations to its power in order to keep collaborators content. Hence, in West Africa some traditional elites managed to maintain and even strengthen their power.

Divide and rule

At other times, however, Britain adopted the strategy of 'divide and rule', and began to alternate patronage between competing elites. Britain also exploited rivalries in order to be seen as an impartial guarantor of the rights of different social groups. For example, when the Indian army was reorganised in the aftermath of the 'Mutiny' (1857–8, see p. 5 and pp. 52–3), a policy of 'divide and rule' was broadly favoured; each 'native regiment' recruited men from different regions, caste and religion. Therefore, soldiers in these regiments lacked a sufficiently strong common identity with which to challenge their British rulers. The success of this policy can be demonstrated by the fact that 'native regiments' subsequently remained loyal to the British authorities.

Collaboration and governance in India

After 1858, the British undertook to build firm relationships with the traditional authorities in India, and in particular the autonomous princes whose territories covered one-third of the subcontinent. There were no further annexations of princely territory after 1858; British authority in these regions was exerted through the influence of the Indian Political Service. In the case of (perceived) Indian mismanagement, the British authorities might temporarily attach the state to British administration, replace the reprobate ruler with a royal relative, or educate a younger prince who would ascend to office when of age.

Meanwhile, in areas of direct rule the Indian Civil Service (ICS), founded in 1861, became the main instrument of imperial administration in the subcontinent. Although there was no official prohibition on Indians joining the ICS, a number of measures were designed to limit their inclusion. Examinations for the ICS were held in London, which for many non-British candidates proved a massive obstacle. Many British officials doubted that Indians possessed the ability to work effectively in the ICS. According to the historian David Gilmour:

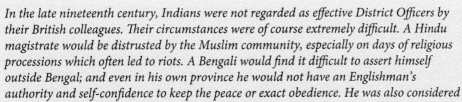

> **Passage** (1)
>
> *In the late nineteenth century, Indians were not regarded as effective District Officers by their British colleagues. Their circumstances were of course extremely difficult. A Hindu magistrate would be distrusted by the Muslim community, especially on days of religious processions which often led to riots. A Bengali would find it difficult to assert himself outside Bengal; and even in his own province he would not have an Englishman's authority and self-confidence to keep the peace or exact obedience. He was also considered – at least by the British – to be less brave and less energetic.*
>
> David Gilmour (2007) *The Ruling Caste*, p. 67

What can you learn from the extract by David Gilmour about the approach and interpretation of the historian? Refer to the extract and your own knowledge to explain your answer.

By around 1900, just 33 out of 1021 ICS officials were Indian. However, by the early twentieth century, rising resentment amongst educated Indians over the inaccessibility of the ICS prompted reforms and partial Indianisation of the service. In 1923, ICS examinations were held in India for the first time. By 1929, there were 367 Indians and 894 Europeans employed by the ICS.

Many more Indians were incorporated within the wider administration. Financial and manpower deficiencies meant that the employment of Indians, who could be paid far less, was necessary. By 1887, over two-thirds of paid government appointments were held by non-Europeans. Indeed, the 1931 census revealed that India had around one million government workers, the vast majority of whom were local people. This clearly demonstrates Britain's reliance on Indian participation in the bureaucracy, and the integration of Indians within the imperial regime.

Britain also possessed a network of informal Indian allies, such as large landholders, whose interests lay in maintaining the status quo. The imperial government would only legislate when it had significant Indian support, but their allies were not the sort who would have wanted radical social change.

'The maintenance of Empire depends on the sword'?

Key Question:

How has the debate about coercion added to our understanding of the nature of colonial rule?

EMPIRE AND COERCION

Approaches:
- the highlighting of particular events, such as the Indian Mutiny and the Morant Bay Rebellion, to support an argument
- an emphasis on military history

Method:
- the use of official and unofficial written and pictorial documents detailing the impact of British rule

Interpretation:
- brutal force was used quite extensively to rule the Empire even though some historians have downplayed this
- some historians have pointed to the use of technology to 'bash' natives although others have rejected this claim by indicating that, in particular conflicts, the British armed forces did not seem to have a technological advantage over their opponents

Approaches that focus on events to emphasise the importance of coercion

The extent to which British power was dependent on the use of coercion has been hotly debated since the inception of imperial rule. Contemporary critics believed that the bloody methods employed by Britain to maintain authority in colonial lands demonstrated the immoral nature of Empire. In 1851, a leading chartist, Ernest Jones, remarked of the Empire that 'on its colonies the sun never sets, but the blood never dries' (quoted in J. Newsinger (2006), *The Blood Never Dried: A People's History of the British Empire*, p. 1). More recently, these sentiments have been echoed by the historian John Newsinger. He has criticised modern-day apologists for Empire, such as Niall Ferguson, for 'their reluctance to acknowledge the extent to which imperial rule rests on coercion, on the policemen torturing a suspect and the soldier blowing up houses and shooting prisoners'. He illustrates his point by examining important instances where Britain reacted violently to indigenous resistance, such as the 'Indian Mutiny' (1857–8), and the Morant Bay Rebellion (1865) in Jamaica. This, he concludes, 'is the inevitable reality of colonial rule' (J. Newsinger (2006) *The Blood Never Dried: A People's History of the British Empire*, pp. 7–11).

Interpretations of events where coercion was used

The Indian Mutiny/First War of Independence (1857–8)

During the early nineteenth century, British territory in the Indian subcontinent expanded rapidly. Endemic political instability in many regions threatened commerce and persuaded the British to intervene and annexe new territory. Under Lord William Bentinck (Governor-General, 1828–35) the British authorities in India adopted a policy of westernisation, in the interests of efficiency and 'progress'. English was made the official language of law, administration and education, and attempts were made to eradicate traditional Indian customs which were deemed backwards and barbaric, such as *suttee:* the burning alive of widows.

A rebellion against British rule erupted in Meerut, in May 1857. The crisis was triggered when a number of Indian soldiers in the East India Company (EIC) army refused to use rifle cartridges which they believed were greased with cow fat (sacred to Hindus) and pig fat (unclean to Muslims). The ringleaders were subsequently sentenced to prison, but their fellow soldiers mutinied and killed a number of British officers. The Mutiny soon spread to Delhi, Oudh, Cawnpore and Lucknow (source G). Traditionally, historians have pointed out that the geographical area of revolt remained relatively restricted; over two-thirds of British India did not actively take part in the rebellion. Britain's Indian soldiers from Bengal, the Punjab, Bombay and Madras remained loyal, as did most Indian princes whose territory was at least nominally independent. Nevertheless, recent research suggests that rebellious sentiments may have been more widespread. Moreover, the rebellion was certainly considered a very serious threat to British rule, and was marked by a great deal of bloodshed. The conflict lasted for over a year, and Britain was only able to defeat the last of the rebels in June 1858.

Source (G) Areas where the uprisings occurred, 1857–8.

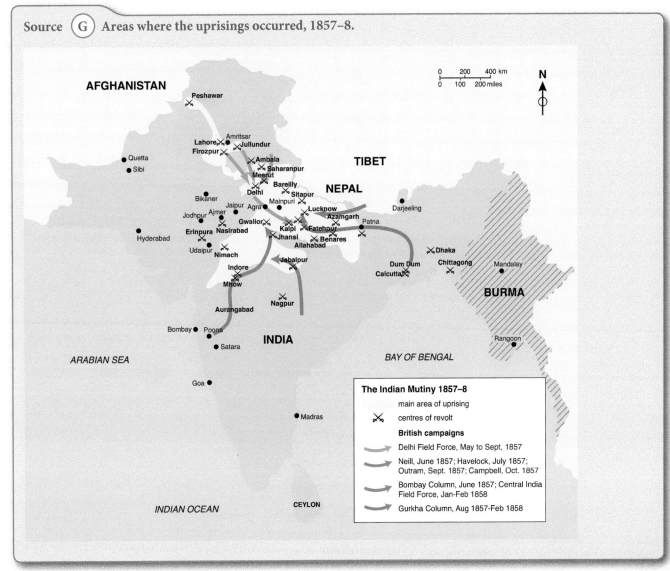

British historians have tended to describe the events of 1857–8 as a 'Mutiny'. Initially, emphasis was placed on the relatively small numbers of rebels involved, the fact that the 'Mutiny' was mainly confined to the army, and the lack of cooperation between rebel groups. In contrast, Indian nationalist historians saw the 'Mutiny' as a revolutionary and nationalist uprising against the British. Subsequent critics of this approach have pointed out that the mutineers were attempting to recreate an idealised vision of the past rather than construct a modern Indian nation-state. Other historians have argued that economic factors contributed to unrest. Peasants were unhappy that an agricultural system involving landlords and rent had been introduced, and artisans were unhappy because they had been adversely affected by British industrial competition. The most significant cause of tension, however, was probably the rapid cultural changes that were imposed on the indigenous population. The policy of westernisation caused a great deal of resentment, particularly in areas that had been recently annexed.

> **FOR DISCUSSION**
>
> How far do you agree with the view that the cultural background and national identity of an historian inevitably affects their understanding of a particular historical event such as the 'Indian Mutiny'. Does this mean that it is impossible to create a completely objective and impartial historical narrative or analysis?

The Morant Bay Rebellion (1865)

In 1865, growing economic and social unrest culminated in a riot in Morant Bay town, Jamaica. Government troops fired on protestors and in the ensuing disorder a number of civilians died. Governor Eyre responded to the 'rebellion' ruthlessly. He imposed martial law and had a local Baptist preacher, George William Gordon, court-martialled and hanged. In the subsequent repression ordered by Eyre, 580 men and women were killed, and around 1000 homes were destroyed.

The Coercion interpretation

It is certainly true that when colonial authority was threatened, the British reacted vigorously and violently. A British Officer wrote to *The Times* describing the reprisals that followed the 'Indian Mutiny':

> **FOR DISCUSSION**
>
> Can history be used to learn lessons, or are such lessons imposed upon the past by people in the present?

> Source (H) A British Officer
>
> *A force of Europeans with guns was sent round the forts, one of which, Meerdan, was held by the 55th Native Infantry in open mutiny; they tried to escape when our force appeared, and some got off to Swat; the others were made prisoners (150 were killed on the spot), tried by drumhead court-martial, and instantly shot. [...] Some of the 200 prisoners of the 55th have been tried, and we blew 40 of them away from our guns in the presence of the whole force three days ago; a fearful but necessary example, which has struck terror into their souls. [...] Such a scene I hope never to witness – human trunks, heads, legs, arms, etc, flying in all directions. [...] Trials are going on, and the mutineers will never forget the lesson taught at Peshawur. It is not my business to contrast or compare with scenes elsewhere. I trust and believe we have done what duty demands.*
>
> Quoted in J. Samson (ed.) (2001) *The British Empire*, p. 172

ACTIVITY

Source I is a photograph of rebels being hanged in the 'Indian Mutiny' of 1857–8.

Why might historians interpret the photograph in different ways? You will need to consider what the photograph reveals about British methods of coercion, and what it fails to reveal. For example:

■ what is the significance of the public and visual aspect of a hanging?

■ who do you think the spectators were, and what do you think their role was?

■ how representative is the photograph, for instance, was the execution an isolated occurrence?

■ did the execution occur as a specific response to the 'Mutiny', or was it a common form of punishment?

You ought to think about the role of written evidence in explaining and validating visual evidence, and vice versa.

Source (I) The hanging of 'mutineers' following the Indian Mutiny of 1857–8.

ACTIVITY

Source J depicts the execution of Indians, who are about to be blown apart by British guns. It was painted by the Russian Vasily Vasilyevich Vereshchagin in 1887. The uniforms of the British soldiers are from the 1880s, implying that such executions continued to be normal practice. In fact, they were peculiar to the reprisals that followed the 'Mutiny' of 1857–8.

Why might historians interpret the painting in different ways? You will need to consider aspects such as:

■ the 'photographic style' employed by the artist

■ the reasons why a Russian in 1887 might wish to depict British rule in India in this way.

Source **J** A painting by Vasily Vasilyevich Vereshchagin produced in 1887 showing the execution of 'mutineers'.

Limitations on the use of coercion

The British authorities, however, were reluctant to rely on coercion as a means of governance since they realised that this would create much resentment amongst the local populace, thereby encouraging serious resistance. Indeed, the British had neither the men nor the resources to govern without the consent and cooperation of those whom they ruled. This was a point keenly emphasised in source K by the Earl of Cromer, British Consul-General in Egypt from 1883 to 1907:

> How could historians who are critical of the coercive nature of British imperialism utilise source K as evidence to support their case?

Source **K** The Earl of Cromer

There is truth in the saying, of which perhaps we sometimes rather hear too much, that the maintenance of the Empire depends on the sword; but so little does it depend on the sword alone that if once we have to draw the sword, not merely to suppress some local effervescence, but also to overcome a general upheaval of subject races goaded to action either by deliberate oppression, which is highly improbable, or by unintentional misgovernment, which is far more conceivable, the sword will assuredly be powerless to defend us for long, and the days of imperial rule will be numbered.

Quoted in A. Porter (ed.) (1999) *The Oxford History of the British Empire: The Nineteenth Century*, pp. 178–9

In India, there was a preference for policemen to be utilised for internal security, most of whom were locals. This policy became even more stringent following the 'Amritsar Massacre' of 1919. Brigadier General Edward Dyer had ordered his (Ghurkha) troops to open fire on a group of unarmed Indians who had disobeyed an order banning public gatherings by congregating near the Sikhs' holiest shrine in the Punjab; hundreds died and more than a thousand were injured. Predictably, there was local outrage, but there was also significant protest in Britain. The General was forced to retire.

To some extent this demonstrates that the ability of colonial authorities to employ coercive tactics was restricted by metropolitan pressures. Political accountability placed limitations on the methods of control that were deemed acceptable. Voters and politicians in the metropole did not wish to see the British Empire maintained through torture, beatings and indiscriminate murder. Moreover, British politicians were not inclined to spend excessive amounts of money on military resources. Thus, the actions of 'men on the spot' were constrained by the numbers of men and weapons at their disposal.

The technology and 'native bashing' interpretation

From the 1860s, it was hoped that technology such as steam ships, the telegraph, and machine guns would allow Britain to retain relatively small military detachments in its colonies. By the twentieth century, developments in air, land and water transport allowed troops to reach crises even more quickly than before. Britain began to place greater emphasis on air power as a tool for reconnaissance, supply and attacking enemies. The most prominent example was when the RAF helped defeat a revolt in Iraq in 1920 by what was termed 'air control'. As a consequence, many troops could be safely withdrawn from certain areas without compromising security. For example, between 1921 and 1928, the garrison of Iraq was reduced from 23 British and Indian battalions to two battalions.

These technological developments have also given rise to charges of 'native bashing'. John Newsinger, for example, believes that 'imperial occupation inevitably involved the use of violence and that, far from this being a glorious affair, it involved considerable brutality against people who were often virtually defenceless' (J. Newsinger (2006) *The Blood Never Dried: A People's History of the British Empire*, p. 8). According to this argument, Britain relied on weapons such as the Maxim machine gun, introduced in 1881, to maintain authority. Hillaire Beloc famously wrote: 'Whatever happens, we have got – The Maxim gun, and they have not' (quoted in A. Porter (ed.) (1999) *The Oxford History of the British Empire: The Nineteenth Century*, p. 265).

However, the historian Robert Kubicek suggests that a 'more revealing assessment of the "little wars" of Empire is perhaps conveyed by Sir Henry Newbolt' (1897) in source L.

Source Sir Henry Newbolt

The sand of the desert is sodden red
Red with the wreck of a square that broke
The Gatling's jammed and the colonel dead
And the regiment blind with dust and smoke

Quoted in A. Porter (ed.) (1999) *The Oxford History of the British Empire: The Nineteenth Century*, pp. 265–6

Indeed, in many cases the 'native bashing' interpretation is demonstrably incorrect. In the nineteenth century, Britain did not always possess a significant technological advantage when engaged in colonial conflict. For example, in New Zealand in the 1860s, the Maori possessed European musketry and used trenches to limit the impact of artillery; their eventual defeat was due to lack of numbers rather than primitive arms. Local groups also had the advantage of fighting in terrain that they knew well.

The military historian Mike Snook has been particularly vociferous in refuting allegation of 'native bashing'. He argues that the 'portrayal of Queen Victoria's enemies as helpless victims of imperialism serves only to demean the often sophisticated indigenous societies of the time. In military terms it belittles their intelligence, their fighting spirit and their capacity for a degree of guile as highly developed, if not more so, that that of their British opponents'. Furthermore, 'in none of [the three most important conflicts in Queen Victoria's reign – the Sikh wars, the "Indian Mutiny", the Second Anglo-Afghan War] did "Tommy" enjoy either a technological or a numerical advantage' (*BBC History Magazine* (2008), January, Vol. 9, No. 1).

THINK LIKE AN HISTORIAN

Historical evidence is often contradictory. One document seems to suggest one thing, and then another suggests the complete opposite. Historians tend to get round this by highlighting certain aspects of the available evidence, whilst concealing others. This can be seen in the way that Newsinger and Snook both treat the siege of Delhi during the Indian Mutiny. According to Newsinger, 'Delhi was finally stormed on 13 September, although fighting continued for another week, as the city was put to the sack'. This mainly consisted of 'looting, rape and murder'. Snook, on the other hand, emphasises that the taking of Delhi was 'another living nightmare for the infantry', many of whom were blown, quite literally, to bits.

Stretch and challenge

How far do you agree with the following statements, and to what extent are they mutually exclusive?

1. 'The Amritsar Massacre demonstrates that British imperialism was based on coercion.'

2. 'The aftermath of the Amritsar Massacre reveals that the notion of political accountability placed limitations on the use violence as a method of control.'

The construction of hegemony

Key Question:

Why have some historians decided to use the concept of hegemony to study Empire, and how significant are their findings?

THINK LIKE AN HISTORIAN

The concept of hegemony assumes that the existing ideology is *clearly* detrimental to a subordinate group. It further assumes that those able to criticise the resulting 'false consciousness' stand outside the ideology (otherwise they would be bound by the same set of 'false' ideas). Some modern political theorists challenge these assumptions, and many have chosen to use an approach based around the concept of 'discourse' instead (see chapter 6).

HEGEMONIC APPROACH

Approach:
- the application of theories developed in other disciplines such as political science

Method:
- the use of a variety of written sources to support and illustrate a theory

Interpretations:
- the British convinced subject peoples that the colonial social order was natural and inevitable, and/or good
- 'colonial knowledge' was accumulated by British imperialists to stereotype indigenous peoples and practices and therefore legitimise certain methods of governance
- hegemony was established through negotiation
- the rulers and the ruled played a kind of game with each other: the rulers knew that they had to *act* in an authoritarian manner to gain respect even though they did not always like doing this. The ruled had to *act* subordinately if they wished to survive
- indigenous peoples often challenged authority by making claims that promises made by rulers had been broken
- hidden transcripts were used to cultivate opposition to authority

Approaches that utilise the theories of hegemony and false consciousness

Sometimes it was clearly in a person's interests to collaborate with the colonial state, either because of the rewards on offer, or from fear of being tortured. However, this was not always the case. In situations where there were apparently few incentives to cooperate with the British, the use of coercion fails to explain why such small numbers of British administrators and soldiers were able to maintain authority over scores of colonial subjects. In this respect, British imperial rule has been described as hegemonic. The term hegemony is derived from Ancient Greek and generally means the dominance of one state, or body, over another. However, the concept also has a more theoretical meaning, often associated with the work of the Italian Marxist **Antonio Gramsci** (1891–1937). He was particularly interested in discovering the reasons why the Russian Revolution of 1917 had not spread across Europe, and why the working classes still lacked class consciousness. In so doing, he began to formulate a theory to explain why subordinate classes were often complicit in, and consented to, their own oppression, even when coercion appeared not to be used. He believed that dominant groups were able to exert ideological control over society, which legitimised existing power relations. He termed this hegemony.

Gramsci's conception of hegemony has subsequently led to the development of ideas about false consciousness. According to these theories, subordinate groups possessed a false conception of their real social conditions. Some theorists argue that dominant values and beliefs became so pervasive that subordinates actively believed that their oppression was just and legitimate. Others believe that the dominant ideology convinced people that the existing social order was natural and inevitable, and therefore could not be challenged.

The colonial knowledge interpretation

Recent historical research had focused quite heavily on how Britain exercised ideological control over indigenous people. The idea of 'colonial knowledge' has been put forward to describe the selective accumulation of information about indigenous societies gathered by the colonial powers. Peoples and customs were classified in order to assist in colonial management, such as tax collection. Significantly, it has also been argued that the knowledge gathered was used to construct skewed stereotypes of natives and to justify the type of rule that Britain exercised. For example, some Indians, such as the Sikhs, were praised as martial races and incorporated into the Indian Army. Educated Bengalis, on the other hand, were ridiculed as effeminate, because they threatened Britain's supremacy as a 'governing race'. Moreover, it has been argued that the colonial state had the ability to reproduce these labels and classifications to such an extent that indigenous people began to believe in them. This was a point emphasised by the African nationalist Edward Wilmot Blyden (1835–83) in source M.

Source (M) Edward Wilmot Blyden

In all English-speaking countries the mind of the intelligent Negro child revolts against the descriptions given in elementary books – geographies, travels, histories – of the Negro; but, though he experiences an instinctive revulsion from these caricatures and misrepresentations, he is obliged to continue, as he grows in years, to study such pernicious teachings. After leaving school he finds the same things in newspapers, in reviews, in novels, in quasi-scientific works; and after a while – saepe cadendo [as it often happens] – they begin to seem to him the proper things to say and to feel about his race, and he accepts what at first his fresh and unbiased feelings naturally and indignantly repelled. Such is the effect of repetition […] And this feeling of self-depreciation is not diminished, as I have intimated above, by the books they read. Women, especially, are fond of reading novels and light literature; and it is in these writings that flippant and eulogistic reference is constantly made to the superior physical and mental characteristics of the Caucasian race, which by contrast suggests the inferiority of other races – especially of that race which is furthest removed from it in appearance.

Quoted in E. Boehmer (ed.) (1998) *Empire Writing: An anthology of colonial literature*, pp. 65–6

How valuable is source M as evidence for British ideological dominance over colonised peoples?

Blyden, however, was referring specifically to black children educated in Europe, America and other Western environments. Most Africans would not have been subject to the same level of Western schooling, or have been avid readers of European literature. Historians have thus pointed out that the spread of legitimising ideas in colonial territories required the assistance of indigenous elites. Recent work has indeed demonstrated that the collection, organisation and distribution of colonial knowledge was a collaborative process. Much knowledge was therefore shaped by indigenous elites, eager to promote their own claims to power and authority. For instance, in India, the Brahmins (the Hindu priestly elite) were able to convince the colonial authorities that caste (religious social status) was an integral aspect of local culture; this made caste even more powerful and rigid under the British than it had been previously.

Colonial knowledge also gave the British insights into local traditions, which could be of use in generating authority. Not only did the British attempt to retain traditional customs, they sought to associate tradition with the imperial enterprise. For example, in Ceylon, the British became custodians of Buddha's tooth, a sacred relic for Buddhists.

ACTIVITY

The historian Peter Burroughs has written that the 'accumulating body of [colonial] knowledge was bound to produce an imperfect grasp of a country's past and social structures. What distorted British understanding most … was the urge to classify information in categories and ordered hierarchies which reflected the preconceptions and purposes of European administrators' (A. Porter (ed.) (1999) *The Oxford History of the British Empire: The Nineteenth Century*, p. 184).

What can you learn from this extract about the interpretation and approach of this historian? Refer to the extract and your own knowledge when answering the question.

The ritual and legitimacy in India interpretation

After 1858, the British monarch replaced the Mughal Emperor as the 'fountain of honour' for India. Attempts to place Queen Victoria as the direct successor to the Mughals were furthered in 1876 when she assumed the title 'Empress of India' on the premise that her Indian subjects held a genuine affection for her. The title was supposed to symbolise Britain's intention to retain a permanent connection with India. In celebration, **Viceroy Lytton** planned an Imperial Assemblage in 1877. This consisted of a grand celebration, procession and presentation of arms to the assembled Indian aristocracy. Lytton wanted to 'place the Queen's authority upon the ancient throne of the Moguls, with which the imagination and tradition of [our] Indian subjects associate the splendour of supreme power!' (quoted in E. Hobsbawm and T. Ranger (eds.) (1992) *The Invention of Tradition*, pp. 187–8).

A further instance of how British authority in the subcontinent was symbolised through ritual and performance occurred in 1861, when a royal order of Indian knights, the Star of India, was created; a second order was also founded in 1877. It was believed that Indians were particularly susceptible to symbolic rituals and that knighthood could function as a reward for loyal service. Its members included important Indian princes and senior British officials. Knights were invested with a robe, medallion and a jewelled pendant (source N).

BIOGRAPHY

Earl of Lytton (1831–91)

Edward Robert Bulwer-Lytton, 1st Earl of Lytton, was educated at Harrow and the University of Bonn. At the age of 18 he travelled to the United States to serve as private secretary to his uncle. He was a keen poet and published poems under the pseudonym Owen Meredith. He became involved with diplomacy before becoming Viceroy of India, a post he held from 1876 to 1880. His tenure coincided with a very severe famine in the subcontinent. In 1887, he was appointed ambassador to Paris.

Source ⓝ The Star of India insignia.

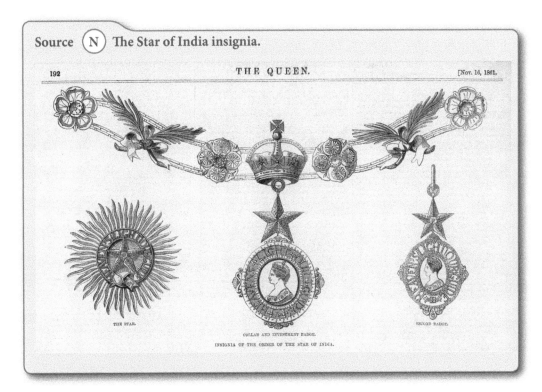

The negotiation interpretation

A number of historians have pointed out that the British were never powerful enough to dictate the terms of the relationship between coloniser and colonised. Thus, if hegemony existed, it was developed through negotiation. This is illustrated in the writings of **Hugh Clifford** (source O) who worked as a colonial officer in the recently-pacified districts of the Malay peninsular.

Source ⓞ Hugh Clifford

Next, [the colonial officer] must study, with the eagerness of Browning's Grammarian, every native custom, every native conventionality, every one of the ten thousand ceremonial observances to which natives attach so vast an importance. He must grow to understand each one of the hints and doubles ententes, of which Malays make such frequent use, every little mannerism, sign and token, and, most difficult of all, every motion of the hearts, and every turn of thought, of those whom he is beginning to call his own people. He must become conscious of native Public Opinion, which is often diametrically opposed to the opinion of his race-mates on one and the same subject. He must be able to unerringly predict how the slightest of his actions will be regarded by the natives, and he must shape his course accordingly, if he is to maintain his influence with them, and to win their sympathy and their confidence. He must be able to place himself in imagination in all manner of unlikely places, and thence to instinctively feel the native Point of View. That is really the whole secret of governing natives. A quick perception of their Point of View, under all conceivable circumstances, a rapid process by which a European places himself in the position of the native, with whom he is dealing, an instinctive and instantaneous apprehension of the precise manner in which he will be affected, and a clear vision of the man, his feelings, his surroundings, his hopes, his desires, and his sorrows, these, and these alone, mean that complete sympathy, without which the white man among Malays, is but as a sounding brass and as a tinkling cymbal.

Quoted in E. Boehmer (ed.) (1998) *Empire Writing: An Anthology of Colonial Literature*, p. 210

BIOGRAPHY

**Hugh Clifford
(1866–1941)**

Hugh Clifford worked as a colonial officer in 'pacified' districts of the Malay Peninsula. On occasions he was the only European in the locality. He employed cultural understanding of the indigenous population in his work but also promoted Westernised progress and civilisation.

Hugh Clifford had arrived in Malaya in 1883 as young cadet in the Civil Service of the Protected Malay States. He developed stories and thoughts about colonial life during his time in the Service. In 1903, he left Malaya and became Colonial Secretary of Trinidad. Thereafter, he assumed the positions of governor in Ceylon, the Gold Coast, Nigeria, and then Ceylon again. In 1927, he became the Governor of Straits Settlements and High Commissioner for the Malay States.

How far would source O support the work of historians who use an approach based on the concept of hegemony? Refer to the extract and your own knowledge when answering the question.

George Orwell (1903–50)

George Orwell was a prolific writer and social commentator. He was born Eric Arthur Blair in 1903 in India (he decided to take the name George Orwell in the early 1930s). His father was a British colonial civil servant. Orwell was educated at Eton in England, but left to join the Indian Imperial Police in Burma. In 1927, he resigned in order to pursue his ambitions as a writer. His political views were left-wing and in 1936 he travelled to Spain to fight against Franco's Nationalists. He returned to England and in the 1940s wrote two of his most famous novels, *Animal Farm* and *Nineteen Eighty-Four*. He died of tuberculosis in 1950.

James Scott uses Orwell's account of Burma to support his idea of a 'public transcript'.

1. What does the extract reveal about Scott's approach, interpretation and method?

2. What are the strengths and limitations of using Orwell's account of his experiences in Burma as evidence of the nature of British imperialism?

Refer to the extract and your own knowledge when answering the questions.

The public transcript approach

The political scientist James C. Scott has adopted a novel approach to power relations and the idea of hegemony. His research is based on an analysis of a variety of relationships between dominant and subordinate groups, which were characterised by economic exploitation, and ideological assumptions about superiority/inferiority. Subordinates understood that dominant individuals possessed the power to punish and reward. Therefore, it was in their interests to preserve the appearance of hegemony and to pretend that they believed in the legitimacy of the existing social order. They strategically adopted a position of deference and concealed their real feelings behind a mask. Scott has described this as a public performance or 'transcript'.

The powerful, on the other hand, attempted to over-dramatise their reputation and mastery. According to Scott, the 'posing of the dominant derives not from weakness but from the ideas behind their rule, the kind of claims they make to legitimacy […] Actions by elites that publicly contradict the basis of a claim to power are threatening' (J. Scott (1990) *Domination and the Arts of Resistance*, p. 11). Thus, the performance of colonial officials had to measure up to claims that the 'sahib' possessed a special, almost magical, ability to resolutely handle crises and difficult situations. Source P is an extract from the writings of **George Orwell**, who had spent some time working as a colonial policeman in Burma in the 1920s. He had been called out to deal with a mad elephant.

Source

But at that moment I glanced round at the crowd that had followed me. It was an immense crowd, two thousand at the least and growing every minute. It blocked the road for a long distance on either side. I looked at the sea of yellow faces above the garish clothes – faces all happy and excited over this bit of fun, all certain that the elephant was going to be shot. They were watching me as they would watch a conjurer about to perform a trick. They did not like me, but with the magical rifle in my hands I was momentarily worth watching. And suddenly I realized that I should have to shoot the elephant after all. The people expected it of me and I had got to do it; I could feel their two thousand wills pressing me forward, irresistibly. And it was at this moment, as I stood there with the rifle in my hands, that I first grasped the hollowness, the futility of the white man's dominion in the East. Here was I, the white man with his gun, standing in front of the unarmed native crowd – seemingly the leading actor of the piece; but in reality I was only an absurd puppet pushed to and fro by the will of those yellow faces behind. I perceived in this moment that when the white man turns tyrant it is his own freedom that he destroys. He becomes a sort of hollow, posing dummy, the conventionalised figure of a sahib. For it is the condition of his rule that he shall spend his life in trying to impress the "natives" and so in every crisis he has got to do what the "natives" expect of him. He wears a mask, and his face grows to fit it. I had got to shoot the elephant. I had committed myself to doing it when I sent for the rifle. A sahib has got to act like a sahib; he has got to appear resolute, to know his own mind and do definite things. To come all that way, rifle in hand, with two thousand people marching at my heels, and then to trail feebly away, having done nothing – no, that was impossible. The crowd would laugh at me. And my whole life, every white man's life in the East, was one long struggle not to be laughed at.

G. Orwell (2002) *Essays*, pp. 46–7

British authority was also entwined with the need for 'respect'. This social act was a symbolic representation of the power of the colonial elite. If it was challenged, then the whole idea of white superiority would be endangered. This is a point made by the novelist Elspeth Huxley, who grew up in Kenya. In her autobiography she writes of an incident involving a Kenyan 'cook-cum-houseboy' called Juma (source Q):

Source (Q) Elspeth Huxley

'No more words,' Tilly said snappily. Juma had a patronising air that she resented, and she doubted if he was showing enough respect. Those were the days when to lack respect was a more serious crime than to neglect a child, bewitch a man or steal a cow; and was generally punishable by beating. Indeed respect was the only protection available to Europeans who lived singly, or in scattered families, among thousands of Africans accustomed to constant warfare and armed with spears and poisoned arrows, but had themselves no barricades, and went about unarmed. This respect preserved them like an invisible coat of mail, or a form of magic, and seldom failed; but it had to be very carefully guarded. The least rent or puncture might, if not immediately checked and repaired, split the whole garment asunder and expose its wearer in all his human vulnerability. Kept intact, it was a thousand times stronger than all the guns and locks and metal in the world; challenged, it could be brushed aside like a spider's web. So Tilly was a little sensitive about respect, and Juma was silenced.

Quoted in J. Samson (ed.) (2001) *The British Empire*, p. 259

ACTIVITY

In 1909, Lord Roberts, a very distinguished soldier in the British army in India, wrote that British colonial authority amounted to 'respect based on fear; remove the fear and the respect will soon disappear' (quoted in A. Porter (ed.) (1999) *The Oxford History of the British Empire: The Nineteenth Century*, p. 179).

1. Does source Q support Lord Robert's views on respect?

2. What are the advantages and disadvantages of using the concept of hegemony to explain British authority in the Empire?

3. What are the advantages and disadvantages of using concepts borrowed from political science as a basis for historical research?

The hegemony and contesting colonialism interpretation

According to theories of hegemony, when subordinates challenge dominant groups, they tend not to contest the underlying principles of rule. Instead, criticism of established authority is mostly based on claims that the dominant group, or specific representatives of that group, fail to carry out their part of the bargain. Every dominant group attempts to justify its position by claiming that it performs an important social function; they are vulnerable to attack if they fail to perform this task adequately. For example, the British claimed that they were a great governing race and would protect indigenous people from various horrible characters such as greedy landlords and exploitative employers. During the Second World War, the British were keen to tell their colonial subjects that Hitler did not like black people. Source R shows the response from the *Nigerian Eastern Mail* in August, 1941:

> **Source** (R) **Nigerian Eastern Mail**
>
> *What purpose does it serve to remind us that Hitler regards us as semi-Apes if the Empire for which we are ready to suffer and die, for whom we poured our blood and drained our pockets in 1914 and for which we are draining the same today, can tolerate racial discrimination against us?*
>
> Quoted in J. Brown and W. R. Louis (eds.) (1999) *The Oxford History of the British Empire: The Twentieth Century,* p. 314

Nigerians were not challenging the legitimacy of the British Empire; indeed they were (or at least claimed to be) willing to die for it. They were, however, challenging the inconsistencies of British rule. On one hand, Britain implicitly promised to protect the world from Nazi racism, but, on the other hand, they continued to allow racial discrimination in their own colonies.

EXAM TIP

When borrowing ideas from other disciplines such as political science, historians are often faced with the unenviable task of having to merge the present tense (often found in the 'foreign' disciplines) with the past tense. For example, either 'dominant groups *hold* ideological power over subordinates', or 'dominant groups *held* ideological power over subordinates'. It is advisable that you remain consistent in using a particular tense when writing essays.

The hidden transcripts and the weapons of the weak approach

According to James Scott, however, 'most acts of power from below, even when they are protests – implicitly or explicitly – will largely observe the "rules" even if their objective is to undermine them' (J. Scott (1990) *Domination and the Arts of Resistance,* p. 8). Thus, the apparent refusal of subordinate groups to challenge the principles of rule is strategic; it is simply the safest way of achieving a particular objective. Indeed, since the 'public transcript' is a 'mask' designed to conceal feelings and thoughts, it is an unreliable record of the opinions of subordinates.

Scott further suggests that resistance is fostered in a 'hidden transcript'. Subordinates share a social existence out of view of the dominant group. They talk with friends and family who are similarly oppressed. This results in the development of a critique of the prevailing ideology. This 'hidden transcript' is spoken openly, but only in a disguised form through, for example, rumours, gossip, folktales, songs, gestures and jokes. It is hidden by 'anonymity or behind innocuous understandings of conduct' (J. Scott (1990) *Domination and the Arts of Resistance,* p. xiii).

The opposition that this critique cultivates is often acted upon using the 'weapons of the weak', such as 'foot-dragging', pretending to be naive and ignorant, pilfering, and gossiping. Thus, local populations resist in ways that are unlikely to provoke an aggressive response. Source S is an extract from George Orwell's account of his time in Burma (published in 1934) which illustrates how less powerful groups chose to challenge perceived oppression.

Source S

In Moulmein, in lower Burma, I was hated by large numbers of people – the only time in my life that I have been important enough for this to happen to me. I was sub-divisional police officer of the town, and in an aimless, petty kind of way anti-European feeling was very bitter. No one had the guts to raise a riot, but if a European woman went through the bazaars alone somebody would probably spit betel juice over her dress. As a police officer I was an obvious target and was baited whenever it seemed safe to do so. When a nimble Burman tripped me up on the football field and the referee (another Burman) looked the other way, the crowd yelled with hideous laughter. This happened more than once. In the end the sneering yellow faces of young men that met me everywhere, the insults hooted after me when I was at a safe distance, got badly on my nerves. The young Buddhist priests were the worst of all. There were several thousands of them in the town and none of them seemed to have anything to do except stand on street corners and jeer at Europeans.

G. Orwell (2002) *Essays*, pp. 42–3

> What difficulties arise when using source S as evidence for local opposition to British imperialism?

ACTIVITY

In a short story entitled *His Chance in Life* (1888) the Anglo-Indian author Rudyard Kipling describes a riot in an Indian town (source T).

Source T Rudyard Kipling

Never forget that unless the outward and visible signs of Our Authority are always before a native he is as incapable as a child of understanding what authority means, or where is the danger of disobeying it. Tibasu was a forgotten little place with a few Orissa' Mahommedans in it. These, hearing nothing of the Collector-Sahib for some time, and heartily despising the Hindu Sub-Judge, arranged to start a little Mohurrum riot of their own. But the Hindus turned out and broke their heads; when, finding lawlessness pleasant, Hindus and Mahommedans together raised an aimless sort of Donnybrook just to see how far they could go. They looted each other's shops and paid off private grudges in the regular way. It was a nasty little riot, but not worth putting in the newspapers.

Quoted in E. Boehmer (ed.) (1998) *Empire Writing: An Anthology of Colonial Literature*, p. 102

1. Some historians use fiction as historical evidence. What are the strengths and limitations of this approach?

2. How useful would this source be for historians using an approach based on hegemony or a public transcript?

6 The experience of Empire: the cultural turn and the impact of imperialism on the periphery

Source (A) **Mary Kingsley, 1901**

In these days the boot of the ubiquitous white man leaves its mark on all the fair places of the earth…It crushes down the forest, beats out roads, strides across the rivers, kicks down native institutions, and generally tramples on the growths of natives and the works of primitive man, reducing all things to that dead level of conventionality which we call civilisation.

Quoted in E. Boehmer (ed.) (1998) *Empire Writing: An Anthology of Colonial Literature*, p. 449

Key Questions:

■ Why are historians so interested in European representations of colonised peoples, and how has the Orientalism debate contributed to our understanding of colonial culture?

■ Why do historians disagree about the impact of imperialism on the periphery, and how does each approach contribute to our understanding of colonial experiences?

■ Why have historians become interested in gender, and how has this contributed to our understanding of colonial experiences?

In a very general sense, *culture* simply means 'way of life'. Since the 1970s, the cultural history of the British Empire has become an area of intense and lively debate. A great deal has been written on the ways in which Europeans described and represented colonies and colonised peoples. British descriptions of indigenous cultures were often uncomplimentary, and critics, mainly from the periphery, have argued that European imperialists manipulated language in order to create a distorted view of indigenous societies. Many of these critics conclude that the development of an 'Orientalist discourse' – a particular way of speaking about the non-Western world – formed part of a nefarious plan to dominate colonial lands through the denigration of local culture.

Another area of controversy surrounds the ways in which colonialism affected the experiences of people on the periphery. Sometimes, the colonial authorities attempted to introduce cultural change. On these occasions, historians tend to see British interference in one of two ways. Either the British were responsible for the development of technological progress in the colonies, or else British civilisation was a sham and destroyed indigenous culture. Meanwhile, on the occasions when the colonial authorities preferred to limit cultural change, the British have either been commended for allowing local customs and institutions to develop at their own pace, or else condemned on the grounds that they were really trying to keep indigenous people in a state of ignorance, which made them easier to control. More recently, historians have attempted to 'reintroduce' women into the historical record, and uncover their role in Empire. This has also served to spark much interest in the relationship between sexuality and imperialism.

Colonial discourse theory

Key Question:

Why are historians so interested in European representations of colonised peoples and how has the Orientalism debate contributed to our understanding of colonial culture?

ORIENTALISM APPROACH AND INTERPRETATION

Approach:
- the use of the concept of discourse to demonstrate that European writings about colonised peoples were not 'objective'

Method:
- the analysis of contemporary works of literature to show the way in which ideas were transmitted

Interpretation:
- Europeans represented indigenous people in a negative light in order to legitimise colonial rule

The discourse approach

In general usage, the term 'discourse' means to converse or to hold forth on a subject. The word has also gained more theoretical meanings. Broadly speaking, when academics talk of discourse, they mean the body of language used to convey particular knowledge about a certain subject. Thus, one might identify a specific discourse of race in the late nineteenth century; when people spoke of different 'races', they used similar language to express and transmit the 'knowledge' that white Anglo-Saxons were racially superior.

Michel Foucault, a French intellectual, has been the most influential figure in developing ideas about discourse. In a general sense, Foucault expanded the definition of discourse to include all meaningful utterances and texts (i.e. linguistic communication) that affect how one perceives and interacts with the external, real world. For instance, imagine a job application form that asks the applicant to tick a box relating to their racial or ethnic origins. Anyone who reads the application form is encouraged to classify people (including themselves) according to the concept of 'race' or 'ethnicity'. The use of such categories conceals the extent to which humans create labels; it is human society which decides whether a biological, cultural or linguistic difference is significant enough to form a new classification. In turn, categories and stereotypes influence how individuals treat each other. Thus, Foucault believed that the real, external world could only be ordered and interpreted through discourse; how one sees the real world is dependent on the linguistic means of describing it.

More specifically, Foucault regarded individual discourses as sets of regulated statements that express a particular viewpoint about a subject. He believed that the knowledge conveyed by a discourse is the result of power relations; only certain points of view

possess the power to be heard. Discursive mechanisms (rules and regulated practices) place limitations on what information is deemed valid, and have the effect of concealing other possible interpretations. Thus, an article that conforms to academic conventions (the inclusion of footnotes, an appearance in an academic journal, the citation of important texts) is considered more authoritative than an article which does not.

Similarly, only certain individuals possess the right to speak authoritatively about a specific matter. For instance, in teaching, the perspective of a teacher carries more weight than the views of their students. These rules and regulations in turn affect how people selectively interpret the world. To demonstrate this, the Marxist linguist Michel Pecheux carried out an experiment with a group of his economics students. He gave each student the same economics text to read, the content of which was relatively impartial in regards to political ideology. However, he told one half of his students that the text was a left-wing interpretation, and the other half that it was a right-wing interpretation. Predictably, the students selectively read the text within the bounds that Pecheux had set them.

Stretch and challenge

Write down the differences between an approach based on discourse and an approach based on ideology/hegemony. What are the advantages and disadvantages of each approach for the historian when attempting to interpret the significance of Empire?

The Orientalism approach

In 1978, the literary critic **Edward Said** published a critique of Western conceptions of the Orient, entitled *Orientalism*. Said identified a discourse of Orientalism in many European, and particularly colonial, texts. He argued that European authors had consistently described colonised countries and colonial subjects in a negative way in order to make their own countries seem civilised. In these writings, the Orient was defined by how it was perceived to differ from the West, and colonised peoples became 'Others'. Hence, Said argued that the 'Orient' was an idea created by Europeans; the portrayal of the East in European texts simply reinforced flawed stereotypes of indigenous peoples and cultures. Colonial stereotypes legitimised exploitation and dehumanised colonial subjects. These negative conceptions of the Orient gained 'truth value' by constant repetition, and because those who authored Oriental texts were supported by the imperial authorities. Furthermore, **Enlightenment** ideas of scientific truth enabled Orientalists to claim that their construction of the East was an objective 'truth', thereby invalidating alternative interpretations.

QUICK FACT

Enlightenment

The Enlightenment refers to the cultural and philosophical movement of the eighteenth century which was characterised by a firm conviction in the power of human reason.

BIOGRAPHY

Edward Said (1935–2003)

Edward Said was born in 1935 in Jerusalem, which was then part of the British Mandate of Palestine. Said came from a Christian family, but he thought of himself as a 'Christian wrapped in Muslim culture'. Much of his early education was conducted at elite colonial schools. When he was fifteen he moved to the United States of America to continue his schooling and he subsequently became a very important academic. He campaigned vociferously for the creation of an independent Palestinian state. This was partly inspired by the fact that members of his family had been made refugees following the 1948 Arab-Israeli War.

ACTIVITY

What does passage 1 reveal about the method and approach of Edward Said? What are the advantages and disadvantages of Said's approach?

Passage 1

My method is to focus as much as possible on individual works, to read them first as great products of the creative or interpretative imagination, and then to show them as part of the relationship between culture and empire. I do not believe that authors are mechanically determined by ideology, class, or economic history, but authors are, I also believe, very much in the history of their societies, shaping and shaped by that history and their social experience in different measure.

E. Said (1993) *Culture and Imperialism*, p. xxiv

The development of colonial discourse theory interpretation

Said's work inspired many other individuals to explore how 'colonial knowledge' was produced, and how it was subsequently used. Some academics began to argue that classifications such as the African 'tribe' and 'Hindoo caste' were in fact European inventions. It was revealed that political and social organisation in Africa varied enormously; for instance, some communities were organised around a central state, whereas many others were not. Meanwhile, it was observed that the hierarchy of caste in India was strengthened under the British; thus, the iniquitous colonial power (Britain) was made responsible for Hindu social inequalities.

Other critics noticed how colonial travel accounts described land in terms of its potential for colonial exploitation. Descriptions of landscapes gave the impression that colonised territories were naturally designed to be exploited by colonial powers. Moreover, it was pointed out that colonised countries were judged according to a British timescale. In comparison to Britain, such countries were described as 'underdeveloped' and 'medieval'. Their progress was limited, and they were therefore 'deficient'. Even sympathetic European figures fell into 'Orientalist' ways of thinking. For instance, **Mary Kingsley**, a traveller to West Africa and an amateur ethnologist, wrote that 'many are found willing to wear out their souls in efforts to convert the thirteenth century into the nineteenth in a score of years', and that 'What we are really attempting [to do in Africa], however, is nothing less than to crush into twenty years the revolution in facts and in ideas, which even in energetic Europe, six long centuries have been needed to accomplish' (B. Harlow and M. Carter (eds.) (2003) *Archives of Empire Volume II*, pp. 449–50).

Furthermore, some texts used an 'ethnographic present' to imply that a 'primitive' practice was continuous and ubiquitous. The third person pronoun 'he' was also favoured, in order to reduce all individuals of a group to a single specimen. These were techniques employed by the novelist **Anthony Trollope** in his writings on Australian Aborigines (source B):

BIOGRAPHY

Mary Kingsley (1862–1900)

Mary Kingsley was an amateur ethnologist who travelled extensively in West Africa. She had a great deal of respect for 'native' West African culture, but retained the belief that Empire based on trade could be a positive development.

BIOGRAPHY

Anthony Trollope (1815–82)

Anthony Trollope was a prolific novelist and travel writer. He was particularly interested in the social and political conditions which were emerging in the colonies during his lifetime.

Gin

An offensive term for an Australian aboriginal woman.

Physiognomy

The idea that a person's outer appearance, particularly the face, gives some insight into the individual's character or personality.

Subalterns

The term subaltern has been used in different contexts to describe a type of subordinate. In the British Army, it refers to a commissioned officer whose rank is below that of captain. However, in a political context, the term has been used, mostly since the 1970s, to refer to social groups who (supposedly) lacked the agency to speak for themselves.

Source (B) **Anthony Trollope**

*The aboriginal walks along erect through the streets of the little town, or more frequently in the forest outskirt, followed at humble distance by his **gin** [...] He does in his heart despise the working white man, and he shows in his countenance the fact that he has resolved to beg, or steal, or eat opossum, and at any rate to be free from toil. This so-called dignity has to me been the most odious part of his altogether low **physiognomy**.*

E. Boehmer (ed.) (1998) *Empire Writing: An Anthology of Colonial Literature*, p. 28

A further consequence of colonial discourse theory has been the move towards studying the history of **subalterns**, a name given to individuals and groups whose voices have been traditionally excluded from historical accounts. Previously, when dealing with colonial subjects, historians tended to concentrate on elite figures and groups, such as Hindu Brahmins, who were taken to represent the entire Hindu community. However, since subalterns were incapable of leaving much of an historical record, it has been very difficult to piece together their story. Hence, cultural theorists have attempted to reanalyse 'ruling class' documents in view of what is omitted. It was hoped that reading elite histories 'against the grain' in this way might shed light on non-elites.

Critical analysis

Said's *Orientalism* and the development of colonial discourse theory has attracted strong criticism.

Variety of Western views

A number of critics have pointed out that there were many different Western conceptions of the Orient, not all of which were critical of indigenous culture. For instance, the European Romantic tradition carried images of the 'noble savage' and 'exotic paradise'. Indeed, memoirs and travel accounts suggest that encounters with

> **QUICK FACT**
>
> **Scientific racism.** During the Victorian period, advances in 'scientific knowledge' began to lend legitimacy to the idea of a (biological) racial hierarchy. In the first half of the nineteenth century, it was widely believed that mankind shared a common human nature. The term 'race' was merely applied to societies that possessed distinct cultural attributes. Gradually though, many people began to believe that the cultural development of societies was due to inherent biological differences. This idea gained impetus following the publication of Charles Darwin's *The Origin of Species* (1859) and *The Descent of Man* (1871), which put forward the idea of 'natural selection' as a means of explaining human evolution. Darwin's theory was adapted by the British social theorist Herbert Spencer, who believed that human development and progress was characterised by the 'survival of the fittest'.
>
> Of course, many people in Britain had always believed that the 'English' were superior to foreigners. But before c.1850, they had defined this superiority in terms of possessing 'free', democratic, political institutions, the origins of which they traced to the arrival of the Anglo-Saxons. Henceforth, however, it was the Anglo-Saxon racial legacy that was celebrated. This idea of racial superiority was to become integral to the culture of New Imperialism which accompanied the expansion of Britain's formal Empire after c.1880.

different cultures often made European travellers question assumptions based on racial superiority. Furthermore, Europeans differed in their response to imperialism; even in the heyday of **scientific racism** in the late nineteenth century, Empire attracted a fair number of critics.

Importance of class

The historian David Cannadine has convincingly argued that the British colonial elite were more concerned with class than race; the Oriental elite held a higher social status within colonial society than many working-class Europeans.

Occidentalism

A number of critics have pointed out that Said's approach amounts to '**Occidentalism**'. Said's work, *Orientalism*, is thus seen as a parody of many of the texts it seeks to criticise. D.A. Washbrook argues that Said 'represents European culture in ways which essentialise, objectify, demean, de-rationalise, and de-historicise it; and he re-evaluates it negatively in the light of its own standards of Reason and Freedom' (R. Winks (1999) *The Oxford History of the British Empire: Historiography*, p. 606). It is therefore claimed that Said has selectively analysed European views of the Orient in order to demonstrate the inferiority of European culture.

> **Occidentalism**
>
> A term which generally refers to stereotypical and unflattering views of the West, particularly Europe, the US and Australia; an inversion of the term Orientalism.

A true conception of the Orient?

Colonial writers have been judged, and metaphorically sentenced to hang, on the premise that they misrepresent the 'true' conditions of colonial society. However, the concept of discourse assumes that all descriptions of the real world are constrained by the 'loaded' (i.e. selective) knowledge encased within language. Therefore, if logic were to be obeyed, colonial writings could only be judged against other discourses, rather than 'truth'. Critics claim that many discourse theorists ignore this logic, and in fact privilege their own work as 'truth', rather than as a separate discourse.

Indigenous elites and classifications

Recent studies have demonstrated that classifications such as caste were altered but not invented by colonisers. Hindu elites had attempted to strengthen inequalities based on caste long before the British became colonial rulers.

Discourse theorists: the colonised elite?

Many discourse theorists originate from the periphery and this seems to have been responsible for their anger towards colonialism. However, critics point out that the vast majority of these angry anti-imperial intellectuals come from families which prospered under colonialism. Many were also educated in Western schools, and have held posts in Western universities. It is thus very tempting to perceive an element of dishonesty in the anti-Western/anti-imperial conclusions that emerge in many discourse theorists' work.

Contemporary politics and selective readings

Much work on colonial discourse has been conducted in the United States of America, where racial and ethnic victimisation remain extremely important political issues. This perhaps explains why such approaches have come to dominate. It is therefore possible that contemporary concerns have created a particularly skewed version of imperial history.

Stretch and challenge

'"Subaltern histories" reflect the angst of the post-colonial intellectual elite, rather than the untold stories of "oppressed locals".'

How far do you agree with this statement?

ACTIVITY

Read source C by Mary Kingsley. To what extent does it support the Orientalist interpretation?

Source Mary Kingsley

Nevertheless, the true negro is, I believe, by far the better man than the Asiatic; he is physically superior, and he is more like an Englishman than the Asiatic; he is a logical, practical man, with feelings that are a credit to him, and are particularly strong in the direction of property; he has a way of thinking he has rights, whether he likes to use them or no, and will fight for them when he is driven to it. Fight you for a religious idea the African will not [...] His make of mind is exceedingly like the make of mind of thousands of Englishmen of the stand-no-nonsense, Englishman's house-is-his-castle type [...] The religious European cannot avoid regarding the races in a different and inferior culture state from his own as more deeply steeped in sin than himself, and the suburban agnostic regards them as "degraded" or "retarded" either by environment, or microbes, or both. [...] My feelings classify the world's inhabitants into Englishmen, by which I mean Teutons at large, Foreigners, and Blacks, whom I subdivide into two classes, English Blacks and Foreign Blacks. English Blacks are Africans. Foreign Blacks are Indians, Chinese and the rest. Of course, everything that is not Teutonic is, to put it mildly, not up to what is; and equally, of course, I feel more at home with, and hold in greater esteem the English Black: a great strong Kruman, for example, with his front teeth filed, nothing much on but oil, half a dozen wives, and half a hundred Ju Jus, is a sort of person whom I hold higher than any other sort of native, let the other form dress in silk, satin, or cashmere, and make what pretty things he pleases [...] In philosophic moments I call superiority difference, from a feeling that it is not mine to judge the grade in these things.

Quoted in B. Harlow and M. Carter (eds.) (2003) *Archives of Empire Volume II*, p. 453

THINK LIKE AN HISTORIAN

Debates about the role of theory in history have at times been marked by a good deal of animosity. In recent years, these arguments have been funnelled into a dispute about the significance of 'post-structuralism' and 'post-modernism' – confusing labels which have been applied to a multitude of different theories and ideas. Many historians argue that 'postmodernists' care little about evidence, use unintelligible jargon to justify assertions, and hold the unsustainable position that there are no absolute truths. On the other hand, some historians have been criticised for refusing, or lacking the capacity, to engage with new ideas. A useful starting place for attempting to unravel the mysteries (and vitriol) of the debate, can be found online. Visit www.pearsonhotlinks.co.uk and enter the express code 2480P.

Colonial experiences

Key Question:

Why do historians disagree about the impact of imperialism on the periphery, and how does each approach contribute to our understanding of colonial experiences?

POSITIVE AND NEGATIVE COLONIAL EXPERIENCES

Approaches:
- an emphasis on how British rule contributed to the political, economic and social progress of colonial countries
- an emphasis on the negative impact of colonial rule

Methods:
- the analysis of contemporary works of literature and memoirs
- the analysis of statistical information relating to economic development

Interpretations:
- imperialism was responsible for 'progress'
- colonised peoples were exploited by imperial rule

European and nationalist approaches

The advantages and disadvantages of colonialism for local people have been discussed since the inception of imperial rule. Generally (but by no means always) Europeans have seen colonialism in a more positive light than have indigenous people on the periphery. Since independence, many people on the periphery have been given greater freedom to challenge imperialism more directly. In part, criticism of colonial rule served to unite people and was a crucial component for the construction of a common identity.

Patterns of work

Colonialism brought important changes to patterns of work on the periphery. Often this involved quite serious disruption to local culture. The British valued hard work and believed that the introduction of more strenuous labour demands would benefit the moral character of indigenous people. Indeed, many Britons were often critical of the perceived laziness of 'natives'. Anthony Trollope, for example, believed that this work ethic was important in distinguishing Africans from Aborigines (source D).

Source (D) Anthony Trollope

Civilisation among the African tribes is not very high, and our knowledge as to the point which it has reached is still defective. But where he has come within the compass of the white man's power, he has been taught to work for his bread, which of all teaching is the most important. The Australian black man has not been so taught, and, in spite of a few instances to the contrary, I think I am justified in saying that he cannot be so taught. Individual instances are adduced, instances which are doubtless true, of continued service having been rendered by aboriginals; but they are so few, so contrary to the life of the tribes as any traveller may see it, that they do but prove the rule. That dignity of black deportment of which one hears not unfrequently [sic] is simply the dignity of idleness.

Quoted in E. Boehmer (ed.) (1998) *Empire Writing: An Anthology of Colonial Literature*, p. 28

Historians nowadays are more aware that groups in subordinate positions are likely to feign laziness and stupidity, since they are relatively safe methods of challenging the powerful.

Subsistence farmers and the global economy

The British wanted to integrate colonial territories into the world economy. Consequently, policymakers sought to encourage local people to produce goods for the global market. This was often accomplished through the introduction of taxation. In order to pay the taxes, subsistence farmers were forced to grow commercial cash crops or to send family members away in search of paid employment. Taxation had the added advantage of making a colony more self-sufficient. Predictably, indigenous peoples often resented the introduction of taxation. In Sierra Leone the imposition of a Hut Tax sparked a rebellion in 1898. Mary Kingsley explained the cultural significance of taxation to local West Africans in source E.

Fetish

In a religious context, a fetish refers to an object perceived to possess supernatural powers. The term *fétichisme* was coined in the eighteenth century by the Frenchman Charles de Brosses in order to distinguish West African religious beliefs from the magical content of Ancient Egyptian religion.

> **Source E Mary Kingsley**
>
> *Direct taxation … to the African means the confiscation of the property taxed […] There is little doubt that there exists a distrustful feeling towards white culture. Up to our attempt to enforce direct taxation it was only a distrustful feeling which a few years' careful, honest handling would have disposed of. Since our attempt there is no doubt there is something approaching a panicky terror of white civilisation in all the native aristocracies and property owners. It is not, I repeat, to be attributed to **fetish** priests. Certainly on a whole it is not attributable to a dislike of European customs or costumes; it is the reasonable dislike to being dispossessed alike of power and property in what they regard as their own country.*
>
> Quoted in B. Harlow and M. Carter (eds.) (2003) *Archives of Empire Volume II*, pp. 443–7

Famine

Another controversial aspect of agricultural life was the occurrence of famines in India and East Africa during the second half of the nineteenth century. There were five major drought-related famines in India from 1860 to 1900, which resulted in the deaths of about 14.5 million Indians. British governments were criticised by post-independence Indian politicians for not doing enough to alleviate famines. Some even blamed British officials for causing food shortages by encouraging and supporting the production of cash crops to the detriment of the supply of adequate staples such as rice. All of this seems a little harsh, as poor harvests were often the result of severe weather conditions. Besides, Famine Commissions (1867 and 1878–80) and a Famine Disaster Fund (1881) were set up in an attempt to plan to cope with famine disaster. This seemed to have a positive effect, since from 1908 to 1942, drought and famine did not really plague India at all. Even the disaster of 1943–4 was rather exceptional, due to the fact that war greatly contributed to and exacerbated it.

Technological progress

In the non-self-governing colonies, especially India, local people were resistant to the coming of technology such as railways and waterways, and more worried about financial costs. They sometimes viewed infrastructural development as an unwanted imposition from greedy businessmen in the metropole. Villains of particular note included investment bankers, railway entrepreneurs and engineers such as Brassey, Lancashire cotton manufacturers looking for a quicker and better supply of yarn, and the Peninsular and Orient (P&O) shipping line. Meanwhile, some contemporaries believed that 'progress' failed to have a positive effect on the periphery because indigenous people were incapable of utilising new technology productively.

The following account from *Letters of a Competition Wallah* (source F), was written in 1864 by George Otto Trevelyan. It describes the situation a traveller was likely to encounter at a station before embarking on a train journey in India:

Source (F) George Otto Trevelyan

A station on an Indian line affords much that is amusing to a curious observer. Long before the hour at which the train is expected, a dense crowd of natives collects outside the glass doors, dressed in their brightest colours, and in a wild state of excitement. The Hindus have taken most kindly to railway travelling. It is a species of locomotion, which pre-eminently suits their lazy habits; and it likewise appeals to their love of turning a penny (gambling). To them, every journey is a petty speculation. If they can sell their goods at a distance for a price which will cover the double fare, and leave a few pice [a coin of small value] over, they infinitely prefer sitting still in a track to earning a much larger sum by genuine labour. A less estimable class of men of business, who are said to make great use of the railway are dacoits [armed robbers], who travel often sixty or seventy miles to commit their villainies, in order to escape the observation of the police in their own district. Every native carries a parcel of some kind, and it often happens that a man brings a bundle so large that it cannot be got in at the door.

Quoted in E. Boehmer (1998) *Empire Writing: An Anthology of Colonial Literature 1870–1918*, p. 5

Source (G) George Otto Trevelyan

There is something very interesting in a first railway journey in Bengal. Never was I so impressed with the triumphs of progress, the march of mind. These two thin strips of iron representing as they do the mightiest and the most fruitful conquest of science, stretch hundreds and hundreds of miles across the boundless Eastern plains – rich indeed, in material products, but filled by a race far below the most barbarous Europeans in all the qualities that give good hope for the future of the nation.

Quoted in E. Boehmer (1998) *Empire Writing: An Anthology of Colonial Literature 1870–1918*, p. 4

Stretch and challenge

Source G is a further extract by Trevelyan from *Letters of a Competition Wallah* (1864).

1. What does Trevelyan mean by 'the march of mind'?

2. Does source G support or refute the claim that the railway was a benefit to the Indian people? Explain your answer by making reference to the source.

3. What does source G tell you about Trevelyan's view of British imperial conquest in terms of the benefits to India?

4. How consistent is this with the observations expressed in source F?

Colonial attempts to improve river and canal transport in India were heavily criticised by the Indian and Pakistani governments following independence (1947).

Achievements were seen as too little, too late. However, lack of progress was understandable given that the financial providers, the Public Works Department of India, was forced to rely on income gained from user fees paid by cultivators. It was not until the Colonial Development Acts of 1929 and 1940 that British governments directly financed colonial projects through subsidies and grants. In addition, technological understanding was still limited, particularly with respect to the collection and storing of the vast amounts of water that Indian irrigation systems required. In fact, 'the fundamentals of hydraulic science and practices of irrigation engineering came out of the great irrigation works of India itself' (quoted in D. Fieldhouse (2001) 'For Richer, For Poorer' in *The Cambridge Illustrated History of the British Empire*, p. 124) and had a positive knock-on effect for other parts of the Empire, as seen by the construction of the Aswan Dam in Egypt (1899–1902).

Finally, it is worth mentioning that road provision before the 1920s was generally poor throughout the non-self-governing colonies. Since a network of roads was mainly of use to locals, this supports the view that the colonial authorities prioritised development which benefited the metropole and British consumers.

Competing with colonial settlers

The arrival of colonial settlers placed further economic pressures on local people. In Southern Rhodesia (Zimbabwe), the Ndebele felt threatened by the arrival of white settlers in 1889. Serious conflict soon erupted in the 1890s, from which the white settlers emerged victorious. Many of the Ndebele lost their land and were forced to labour for colonists on grain and tobacco farms. In Kenya, land was similarly taken away from local people. A Kikuyu chief, Koinange Mbiyu, travelled to London in 1931 and testified to a Parliamentary committee about the situation (source H):

Source (H) **Koinange Mbiyu**

In Kiambu District about 1911, 1912–4 native land called 'Githaka' was taken by the Government and sold to Europeans. The Government promised the natives that it would compensate them – Rs.50,550 – for the land. But they have still not yet been paid [...] The chief trouble is that the country is big enough, but it was divided up without enough forethought, by somebody who did not understand [...] The trouble is that a number of the actual clans who were landowning families had their land alienated over their heads, with them on the land, and eventually pressure was brought to bear to make them leave it, and that is why they have had to go away, far from their own country, as squatters [...] They see that there are cases where a European has 10 square miles, whereas a native is well over 100 to the square mile, while they are being trained and taught to develop their agriculture, and while they are being educated, their cry is 'If we are educated in this way where are we going to develop?'

Quoted in J. Samson (ed.) (2001) *The British Empire*, p. 261

Domestic slavery

Although slavery was illegal in British territory, many African societies continued to practise forms of economic servitude up until the 1920s. This 'domestic slavery' involved various forms of dependency and **clientage**. The British authorities strongly disapproved of the practice. Nevertheless, it was often permitted to continue since it was seen as essential to the mobilisation of African labour; without it, there would have been serious labour shortages. However, the British sometimes suppressed domestic slavery for political reasons. In 1897, a British Mission to the Edo kingdom of Benin (in present day Nigeria) was attacked. In response, the British sent a punitive expedition to

Clientage

The relationship between a patron (master) and a client or servant; dependency.

the Edo capital, which was found deserted on arrival. The British did, though, discover a number of royal slaves who they decided to free as a means of punishing the Edo ruler.

Migration and indentured labour

The introduction of colonial rule caused a great deal of economic migration. Initially this was within countries, and involved individuals moving from the countryside to towns, docks, mines, and plantations in order to earn some money. In India, economic migrants to towns were sometimes induced to accept contracts called indentures, in which individuals agreed to work abroad in return for free passage overseas. Indentured labourers were paid wages and the colonial governments were supposed to regulate their conditions of work in order to protect migrants from exploitative employers. When they had served their time, indentured workers could either remain where they were or return home. Indentured Indians began to emigrate in the 1830s when the abolition of slavery caused massive labour shortages in the Caribbean plantations (source I). Demand for indentured labour was also heavy in South Africa, Fiji, and East Africa during the nineteenth century. There was much contemporary debate as to whether indentured labour was 'slavery by another name'. Certainly, many horror stories were told of the terrible conditions under which labourers worked. On the other hand, mortality amongst Indians emigrants was lower than those who remained in India. Eventually, however, opposition forced the Government of India to ban indentured labour in 1917.

Source (I) Newly-arrived Indian Coolies (labourers) at a sugar plantation in Jamaica.

Disease and medicine

For much of the twentieth century, it was popular to view the spread of Western medical advances as an important colonial achievement. It was argued that Britain had done a great deal to eradicate major diseases in the colonies, and that the colonial subjects were the lucky recipients of Western, scientific knowledge. However, this interpretation began to be challenged in the 1970s and 1980s. It was pointed out that the colonial powers had been responsible for wide-scale migration and the

concentration of indigenous peoples in poor environments such as urban areas. This made many people more vulnerable to diseases such as smallpox, cholera, plague, and malaria. Moreover, advances in medicine and sanitation initially benefited European communities rather than local people. For instance, in Calcutta, sewage disposal schemes and piped filtered water was predominantly delivered to white areas of the city.

ACTIVITY

Passage ② 2

If the industrial revolution had undermined the health of the British working class, there seemed no reason why the same process would not occur in the colonies.

Diana Wylie (1999) 'Disease, Diet and Gender' in the *Oxford History of British Empire, Volume V: Historiography*, p. 281

What can you learn from passage 2 about the interpretation, approach and method of the historian? Make sure you take careful note of the type of book that the quotation is taken from.

The construction of national identities

Colonial nationalism developed in response to imperial rule. The Indian nationalist leader, Jawharlal Nehru, remarked that 'nationalism is essentially an anti-feeling … especially against the foreign rulers in a subject country'. Thus, the Empire became a foreign 'Other', against which subject peoples might unite under a banner of nationalism. Empire was also responsible for exposing Western ideas to members of the indigenous elite, some of whom were educated in England. This provided impetus to theories of nationalism and theories about the creation of modern, secular states.

In the white settler colonies, ties to Britain hindered the construction of a national identity. The continuing flow of emigrants from the metropole meant that many people still felt British. There was also a material obligation for the Dominions to retain a sense of Britishness, since British economic and military support remained essential. It is true that constructive imperialists in the metropole believed that separate national identities could coexist with an imperial identity. However, many of the causes of nationalism in the white settler colonies were not the direct result of Empire. Of greater importance were factors such as the distance from Britain, political unification, the development of railways, the economic integration of colonies and the impact of war. Indigenous culture had a patchy impact on national identities. In New Zealand, the Maori Haka was adopted as a national symbol, but in Australia, Aboriginals were excluded from participating in the project to construct a national identity.

Trusteeship and racism

There is a great deal of debate over the extent to which the British Empire either protected indigenous societies from exploitation, or was responsible for the creation of institutionally racist regimes. Certainly, colonial society was seeped in racial prejudice, and indigenous people were often stigmatised as lazy, backwards, and morally deficient. This severely restricted the opportunities available to local peoples. For example, the first Indian to be made an Anglican bishop was not consecrated until 1912 and no Africans became full diocesan bishops in the Anglican Church between 1890 and 1953, although there were a series of assistant bishops from 1893.

Furthermore, colonial towns began to develop (mostly *de facto*) segregation. In India, Madras (Chennai) and Calcutta (Kolkata) had developed 'white towns' and 'black towns' by the eighteenth century. Segregation became even more pronounced in the nineteenth century. The British feared that unsanitary Indian habits in urban areas would lead to the spread of infections, and, following the Indian Mutiny of 1857–8, many Europeans feared that Indian neighbours might rebel. This prompted the construction of new European urban centres termed 'civil lines'. A military cantonment was located nearby to offer protection in case a rebellion occurred. Even so, there was still much contact with Indians, since servants lived within the civil lines.

Most Europeans in India lived in bungalows, partly because the thick walls and high ceilings lessened the impact of the heat. However, the layout of bungalows also contributed to the creation of a separate social space, which allowed Europeans to distance themselves from the Indian community (source J). Business with traders was discussed outside on the veranda and only 'social equals' were allowed into the interior. Some Europeans also became members of all-white clubs which similarly served to preserve social distance from the locals.

Source **J** A typical colonial bungalow in India. A British family is seen here in the garden of their home, being attended by Indian servants, c. 1900.

Meanwhile, in Fiji, the British created a system called 'Benevolent Apartheid'. Fiji – a set of 320 islands in the South Pacific – had become a British colony in 1874. The British wanted to protect Fijian society from outside interferences and introduced legislation designed to uphold the authority of the traditional chiefs and prevent the alienation of land. However, many Indians had migrated to Fiji as indentured labourers and the British treated the Fijian and Indian societies separately. Thus, Indians and Fijians lived under different legal and political systems. 'Benevolent Apartheid' was still in place in 1959 when the British declared that their intention was to 'intervene to reinforce the moral and customary sanctions which in earlier times bound Fijians together in a communal fold'.

To what extent does Hyam's interpretation of racism help or hinder attempts to understand the experiences of indigenous people who lived in Britain's colonies?

The historian Ronald Hyam has defined racism in a political context as 'the abnormal systemisation of racial prejudice into institutionalised (legalised) discrimination or exploitation [and that] by this tight definition it is clear that certain states are undoubtedly "racist" by deliberate intent: the United States before the victory of civil rights, Australia in the days of "White Australia" immigration policy, South Africa in the era of Apartheid, Nazi Germany, Rhodesia between 1965 and 1979' (Ronald Hyam (2006) *Britain's Declining Empire: The Road to Decolonisation*, pp. 38–9). But *not*, crucially, colonial territories directly controlled by the British. On the contrary, the idea of 'trusteeship' (i.e. protecting indigenous people) was very important to British policymakers. This was made clear in a number of statements such as the 1923 Devonshire Declaration, which emphasised that the rights of African 'natives' were paramount.

In spite of these good intentions, Britain was often unable to enforce a policy of trusteeship when it conflicted with settler interests. The British simply lacked the power to protect minorities. In Kenya, settlers resisted attempts at increasing indigenous political participation by threatening rebellion. Nevertheless, in some cases, the policy of trusteeship did reap positive rewards. In the interwar period, Britain was able to prevent the High Commission territories of Basutoland, Bechuanaland, and Swaziland from falling into the hands of the Union of South Africa. The indigenous people were keen to remain under the British sphere of influence rather than be subjected to the racist policies of the South African state.

Religious beliefs

Missionary activity had given much impetus to early imperial expansion, but it is difficult to evaluate its impact on indigenous culture. In the Indian subcontinent, Christian missionaries encountered established religions based on official texts, such as Islam and Hinduism. This made it difficult to gain converts because Christianity had to compete with resilient belief systems that were firmly set in local society. Most Christian converts were drawn from the margins of society (such as slaves, victims of war and famine, and debtors) and were those who had benefited least from existing belief systems which justified their low social position.

However, evangelical activity in the subcontinent still had a significant impact on relations between Europeans and locals. The influence of missionaries in India has been carefully studied and it is now known that they brought about a major change in attitudes during the first half of the nineteenth century – bringing to an end the previously common practice of British soldiers, administrators and merchants marrying Indian women and adopting Indian customs to varying degrees.

It is sometimes suggested that Christianity was used to strengthen British authority. It was certainly an alien belief system imposed on indigenous people by a colonial elite. However, the Christian message given to local people was often hostile to aspects of colonial rule; most missionaries emphasised that everyone was equal in the eyes of God, and this conflicted with the views of many colonial settlers. It is possible to see the relationship between religion and society in a more subtle light though. Emile Durkheim (1858–1917), a French anthropologist, noted how religions tend to reflect social organisation. If one applies this to colonial rule, the results are interesting. Christianity is a hierarchical, monotheistic religion: there is one God (as part of a Trinity), a number of saints, and a great many earthly priests who are responsible for various rituals. Similarly, colonial society had a hierarchy of white officials leading all the way up to a governor, and ultimately the British monarch. In contrast, existing indigenous religious beliefs in many colonies, particularly in Africa, were often based on numerous spirits and deities. Thus, Christianity can be seen as a cosmological reflection of colonial rule. According to this view, converts were essentially worshipping the new social organisation, thereby helping to legitimise and naturalise it.

However, converts often integrated Christian beliefs and practices into existing religious frameworks, thereby creating a **syncretic** form of Christianity. Since religion was more fluid in many parts of Africa, missionaries found it easier to adapt existing beliefs to the Christian faith. It has also become clear that indigenous people began to pick and choose which aspects of missionary activity to accept. Missionary education and scientific knowledge were often keenly sought, only for the wider message of Christianity to be rejected. Local responses to Christianity also depended on the attitude of the missionary. Those that were dismissive of indigenous beliefs were less successful in gaining converts.

Subsequent generations of converts have sometimes found it difficult to integrate modern Christian beliefs with the desire to retain parts of their heritage. The Nigerian novelist Chinua Achebe has explored many of these themes. One of his novels, *Things Fall Apart* (1958), is about the Igbo tribe and the difficulties in melding tradition with colonial modernity.

> **Syncretism**
>
> Syncretism is the fusion of two different practices or belief-systems.

ACTIVITY

Chinua Achebe has been a great critic of what he claims to be racist fiction. In particular he has been outspoken in his attacks on the work of Joseph Conrad. To find out more about his views, go to www.pearsonhotlinks.co.uk and enter the express code 2480P.

1. Obtain and read a copy of *Heart of Darkness* by Joseph Conrad.

   a) Write an imaginary letter to Achebe that defends the writing of Conrad.

   b) Working with a partner, get them to respond to your letter on behalf of Achebe. (Your partner should also have read *Heart of Darkness*.)

2. How valid and useful are Achebe's writings as evidence about the effects of Empire on indigenous peoples? To help you answer these questions it would be useful to read some of the original works by Achebe. Also, make reference to your own contextual knowledge.

> **FOR DISCUSSION**
>
> How can one judge whether attempts to convert indigenous people to Christianity were successful, or whether a particular conversion was authentic?

Education

Initially, indigenous people were reliant on mission schools for the provision of Western education. Literacy was integral to Protestant beliefs, since it allowed Christians access to the 'word of God', i.e. the Bible. However, particularly in India, indigenous communities often reacted violently when attempts to convert children were mixed with their education. Gradually, colonial states began to take on the burden of education. However, throughout the period (1850–1950) access to education remained limited. For example, in the Gold Coast in 1921 just 3.9 per cent of children under the age of 16 attended a government-financed school.

Source (**K**) **Mr Mackay teaching at his school in Uganda, 1876.**

Indigenous people generally found Western education to be positive since it enabled them to understand white culture and further themselves in the colonial state. For example, an Indian soldier wrote the following letter (source L) during the First World War.

Source (**L**) **An Indian soldier**

My own eyes have been opened since I came to Europe, and I have entirely altered the views which I held before. I wring my hands with regrets that I did not set myself to acquire learning, but regrets are of no avail now […] Please God I will give them a good education, whether they be sons or daughters […] I used myself to say 'these people lose their religion and return as Christians'. Now that I have come here, I realise how wrong I was in my ideas. There is no question at all of religion – it is education alone which makes them wise, and teaches them to hate and abandon those habits and customs in our country which are improper, and to live according to their new ideas.

Quoted in J. Samson (ed.) (2001) *The British Empire*, p. 231

[Handwritten margin note: Indian soldier – wouldn't have other reason to support West]

[Handwritten note below: 'abandon habits' might seem like own culture being squashed out of them]

ACTIVITY

Source L could be classified as a non-official, written account. Some historians have focused on official, written primary sources when considering the impact of British rule on the education of indigenous peoples. Explain the shortcomings of this approach. What other sources would be useful to the historian researching the impact of British rule on the education of indigenous peoples? What is the value and limitation of using each of the sources you mention?

In contrast, Western reactions to 'educated natives' were diverse. Missionaries, of course, encouraged education. The colonial authorities on the other hand were more wary. In early nineteenth-century India, Westernisation was mainly encouraged, but this policy was reversed after the 'Mutiny'. Educated Africans, on the other hand, were increasingly marginalised in the late nineteenth century. This was partly because of rising racial intolerance, but also because medical advances were making Africa less dangerous to white men and therefore colonial administrations were not so reliant on educated Africans.

The erosion of indigenous culture

Sometimes the British were keen to get rid of certain indigenous customs and habits. Predatory ways of life and 'piracy' were particularly frowned upon. However, these terms were often ambiguous. **Isabella Bird**, while travelling in the Malay peninsular, reveals in a letter from 1883 that:

> 'In this four Malay policemen and a corporal have dwelt for three years to keep down piracy. 'Piracy,' by which these rivers were said to be infested, is a very ugly word, suggestive of ugly deeds, bloody attacks, black flags, and no quarter; but here it meant, in our use of the word at least, a particular mode of raising revenue, and no boat could go up or down the Linggi without paying black mail to one or more river rajahs.'

> (Quoted in E. Boehmer (ed.) (1998) *Empire Writing: An Anthology of Colonial Literature*, p. 81)

Stretch and challenge

1. How far was the idea of 'piracy' a case of colonial ethnographers stigmatising a legitimate indigenous practice?

2. To what extent does this view ignore the position of those who had to pay the blackmail money?

3. Was 'piracy' much different from the imposition of colonial taxes?

Europeans were also eager to eradicate 'native vice'. However, some local people contested the assumption that these practices were traditional, and instead blamed their prevalence on foreign influences. Chinese nationalists, for instance, believed that it was the British who were enticing young Chinese girls into vice dens, and that this was not a 'native practice'. Indians, on the other hand, were reluctant to get rid of high status cultural practices such as female infanticide, pre-pubescent marriage, and *suttee* (burning widows alive); it was felt that the British ought not to interfere with traditional culture, especially when it was fused with religious belief.

The British also chose to attack aspects of indigenous culture for political reasons. British and French troops destroyed the Chinese Summer Palace in 1860 during the

BIOGRAPHY

Isabella Bird (1831–1904)

Isabella Bird was a renowned Victorian traveller. In the 1850s she visited North America, but it was not until the 1870s that she began to travel extensively, particularly in Asia. Her writings reveal that she was open-minded in relation to new cultures and ideas.

Second Opium War in retaliation for the brutal torture of a number of Western prisoners, including two British envoys and a *Times* journalist. The decision to destroy the Palace was taken by Lord Elgin, the British High Commissioner to China, and was much criticised by European contemporaries. However, it was felt that it would appropriately symbolise China's inability to challenge the foreign powers. Furthermore, whereas a fine would have hurt the populace at large, no ordinary Chinese person had ever been allowed in the Summer Palace, which was a residence for the Chinese Emperors.

Westernisation

At various times, plans were formulated to bring the perceived benefits of Western civilisation – religion, morals, education, material and technological progress, political development – to colonial subjects. However, these inclinations never hardened to become a definitive 'cultural project'. By the late nineteenth century, it was often believed that either indigenous people were incapable of becoming Westernised (they were too backwards), or else that Westernisation was detrimental to indigenous culture.

These developments are illustrated by the case of Sierra Leone, a colony set up by the British on the west coast of Africa in 1787 as a place for former slaves to settle. The inhabitants were given a Western education, and they gradually began to adopt the values of the British middle class and develop a **Creole** culture. However, following the development of pseudo-scientific racism in the late nineteenth century, black people in Sierra Leone began to encounter increasing discrimination. For example, in 1902, the colonial authorities made British doctors senior to Sierra Leoneans, irrespective of qualifications. More generally, Europeans began to see the Creole lifestyle as a perverse mimicry of European culture.

Many Britons believed that attempts to civilise indigenous people were doomed to failure. Trollope wrote of the Australian Aborigines that 'for years, probably for many centuries, they have made no progress, and the coming of the white man among them has no tendency to civilise, only a tendency to exterminate them' (E. Boehmer (ed.) (1998) *Empire Writing: An Anthology of Colonial Literature*, p. 26). Often these attitudes were accompanied by the belief that the 'savages' were conspiring against Europeans. Mary Kingsley criticised those who 'go about sagely referring to "a general antipathy to civilisation among the natives of West Africa," "anti-white-man's leagues," "horrible secret societies," and such figments of your imagination' (B. Harlow and M. Carter (eds.) (2003) *Archives of Empire Volume II*, p. 444).

However, there was certainly indigenous resistance to 'Western civilisation', partly because it was seen as a threat to local cultural identity. In 1862, the Maori chief Te Waharra wrote to another chief that the British were attempting to '[introduce] schools so that we may be taught the European language; this will also tend to our subversion as a race as at present constituted (our likeness will be destroyed)' (J. Samson (ed.) (2001) *The British Empire*, pp. 174–5). Even non-Europeans who embraced Western civilisation were keen to retain links with their traditional culture. In Singapore, the extremely rich Chinese businessman Whampoa sent his son to be educated in England; he was, however, horrified when his son returned calling himself a Presbyterian, and having chopped off his pigtails.

Indeed, young people seemed most susceptible to the attractions of Western culture, and this was the cause of much tension. Kingsley revealed that '[the elders in West Africa] know that the young men of their people who have thoroughly allied themselves to white culture look down on their relations in the African culture state. They call the ancestors of their tribe "polygamists", as if it were a swear-word … and they are ashamed of their mothers […] it is a factor in the formation of anti-white-

QUICK FACT

Creole (Krio)

The term Creole refers to locally-born people who possess foreign ancestry (usually European). In Sierra Leone, the 'Krio' developed a way of life that incorporated elements from European and West Indian (slave) cultures. The surrounding African population of Sierra Leone had far less of an impact on the 'Krio' way of life.

culture opinion among the mass of the West Africans' (B. Harlow and M. Carter (eds.) (2003) *Archives of Empire Volume II*, p. 448).

The African nationalist Edward Wilmot Blyden offered a different reason why Western civilisation ought to be rejected. He believed that Africans did not excel while studying at Western schools because most of the material they were obliged to study was critical of 'backwards' Africans. Blyden believed that Africans ought to progress along their own lines: 'We must show that we are able to go alone, to carve out our own way. We must not be satisfied that in this nation, European influence shapes our polity, makes our laws, rules in our tribunals, and impregnates our social atmosphere' (E. Boehmer (ed.) (1998) *Empire Writing: An Anthology of Colonial Literature*, p. 67).

ACTIVITY

What can you learn from passage 3 about the effect of Westernisation on the periphery? Refer to the extract and your knowledge to explain your answer.

Passage 3

There were many important Asians whose cultural encounters with the West were positive and creative. The remarkable Calcutta polymath Raja Ram Mohan Roy (d. 1833) was proficient in Greek, Latin, Hebrew, and English, as well as Bengali, Sanskrit and Persian. He debated the concept of Christ's incarnation with Christian missionaries, and berated British officials in 1823 for being slow to instruct their Indian subjects in the 'useful sciences'. The so-called Young Bengal radicals of the 1830s and 1840s went even further in embracing novel ideologies imbibed from their Western-style schooling, denouncing the Hindu scriptures in favour of Tom Paine and the French positivists, and shocking their cow-revering teetotal elders by publicly consuming beef and brandy.

Susan Bayly in A. Porter (ed.) (1999) *The Oxford History of the British Empire: The Nineteenth Century*, p. 459

The preservation of indigenous culture

In place of 'Westernisation', many Britons believed that it was best to preserve indigenous culture and institutions. For example, Chinese businessmen were encouraged to dress like Confucian **mandarins**, and the Hong Kong Secretariat for Chinese Affairs used official documents based on imperial China's bureaucracy. Furthermore, indigenous languages were retained in the colonies for low-level administration. Often, certain dialects and languages were favoured over others, and this strengthened the position of particular tribes and communities. In the region around Lake Victoria in East Africa, the Luganda language became the principal language of church and state. The Ganda people who spoke this language gained power over neighbouring peoples who did not.

In order to gain knowledge of local peoples and culture, the British attempted to record and translate indigenous languages accurately. However, the historian Andrew Porter makes the point that 'the transcriptions and translations made by British people inevitably had British preconceptions imposed on them, and that these indelibly marked the outlook and thought-patterns of Non-European societies. Scottish missionaries in the Niger delta, for example, struggled with the local Efik language, which lacked the means to express concepts such as "resurrection", "temptation", "individual responsibility" and "human sinfulness"' (P. J. Marshall (ed.) (1996) *The*

Mandarins

High-ranking public officials in the Chinese Empire.

Cambridge Illustrated History of the British Empire, p.191). The sermons of the missionaries show that Christian beliefs were imprecisely linked to existing Efik beliefs, and that Efik terms were stretched to apply to Christian concepts.

Sport

Sports such as cricket were used to instil a moral code and a particular set of values. Integral to this was the necessity to abide by rules, whether formally or more informally set down. This created a sense of 'fair play' and an obligation to play the game in the right spirit.

In areas of the Empire where climate and landscape allowed, such as the West Indies, cricket became very popular. Many historians, particularly those from the periphery, have viewed the introduction of cricket as a means of social control. The great Caribbean historian, C. L. R. James was critical of the way cricket was used to create a process of **cultural reproduction**, which was used to control local people. Cricket forced participants to accept the judgements of umpires; to 'walk' when the player knew he was out even if the umpire did not make a decision; and to generally behave in a manner that was dignified, courteous and respectful, regardless of circumstance. Respect for authority was therefore ingrained. Interestingly, James was educated at Queen's Royal College, Trinidad, which was akin to a minor English public school. Despite his anti-imperialist views, he maintained a sense of 'fair play', and claimed that 'colonial radicals were products of an educational system, which stressed the virtues of classical learning and cricket practice … and who did not see any contradiction in supporting the British forms of recreation, whilst denouncing British forms of exploitation.'

> **Cultural reproduction**
>
> This refers to attempts to impose or reproduce one set of cultural values in place of another.

> **Stretch and challenge**
>
> Obtain and read a copy of *Beyond the Boundary* by C. L. R. James. In about 500 words, write a review of the book, focusing on the value and limitation of it as evidence about the impact of cricket on Caribbean culture.

The use of the stick

It has been frequently argued that excessive forms of coercion were an inevitable aspect of colonial rule; the only reason indigenous people would consent to being governed by alien overlords was because they feared being beaten up. This is an argument that has been used at various times both by those on the political right and the political left. Conservatives sought to show that the use of the stick was necessary for the maintenance of law and order. Meanwhile, left-wing critics of Empire pointed to the bloodshed and brutality of events such as the 1865 Morant Bay rebellion and the 1919 Amritsar massacre, as reasons to abandon or modify colonial rule.

At first glance, British brutality seems a fairly clear impact of Empire. However, there are important arguments against such an interpretation. For one thing, Britain has had a long history of beating up various peoples who were *not* in their Empire. Violence was a weapon used between states, and not simply one used within colonies. Some international disputes clearly had an imperial angle, such as when Britain used 'gunboat diplomacy' to forcefully open up markets. But the same does not hold true for Britain's participation in the two world wars, the main causes of which were European rather than imperial in origin.

Moreover, it is clear that coercion was, and is, used by political authorities against their own people, and not just against colonial subjects. For instance, in 1819, British cavalry charged a crowd at a public meeting in Manchester, killing eleven individuals and injuring over 500. Almost a century later, in 1910, troops were sent to South Wales to quell striking miners. Similarly, following decolonisation, nationalist governments began to deal quite roughly with their own miscreants and internal enemies. One recent example might be found in the disturbances that have occurred in Zimbabwe under the former anti-colonial leader, **Robert Mugabe**.

There is also a strong case for suggesting that British colonial rule was a good deal better than that of other colonial powers. Moreover, if Britain had not colonised some regions, particularly in Africa, it is more than likely that other, competing European powers would have gobbled them up instead. A particular example of a really brutal colonial regime is the Belgian Congo, which became the personal possession of King Leopold II of Belgium in the 1870s. The inhumane treatment of Africans there caused an international scandal.

Finally, it is clear that dangling carrots and negotiating hegemony were also important in the creation of colonial authority.

> ### ACTIVITY
>
> Source M is a proclamation issued by Lord Roberts during the Second Boer War.
>
> > **Source (M) Proclamation by Field Marshal Lord Roberts, British Commander-in-Chief in South Africa, 1900**
> >
> > *Whereas small parties of raiders have recently been doing wanton damage to public property in the Orange River Colony and South African Republic by destroying railway bridges and culverts and cutting the telegraph wires, and whereas such damage cannot be done without the knowledge and connivance of the neighbouring inhabitants and the principal civil residents in the districts concerned ... Now; therefore, I ... Commander in-Chief of Her Majesty's Troops in South Africa, warn the said inhabitants and principal civil residents that, whenever public property is destroyed or injured in the manner specified above, they will be held responsible for aiding and abetting the offenders. The houses in the vicinity of the place where the damage is done will be burnt and the principal civil residents will be made Prisoners of War.*
> >
> > Quoted in J. Samson (ed.) (2001) *The British Empire*, p. 228
>
> 1. What does the proclamation reveal about the impact of British colonialism on the periphery?
>
> 2. The proclamation can be classified as an 'official' source as it was issued by Field Marshal Lord Roberts. What are the strengths and weaknesses for the historian of using official sources such as this when attempting to assess the impact of British colonialism on the periphery?

Law and order

Law and order is often considered the reverse side of the coercive coin. The frequent use of the stick to punish unruly locals contributed to the creation of internal stability, in which indigenous civil and property rights might be respected (so the argument goes). For example, before Britain assumed control of India there was endemic civil instability in which the peasantry were cruelly exploited by the ruling classes. This was a line of reasoning that the British authorities continually used in order to justify colonial rule.

More recent apologists for Empire have pointed to the terrible violence that occurred in post-colonial countries as evidence that British rule was harsh but necessary, bringing peace and stability not matched before or since. In 1947, partition between India and Pakistan sparked horrific chaos and lawlessness in which at least half a million people died and twelve million were made homeless. However, it should be remembered that the British authorities believed that they themselves were incapable of maintaining order at this point in time. In 1946, the minutes of the Cabinet record: '[T]he Indian Army … could not fairly be expected to prove a reliable instrument for maintaining public order in conditions tantamount to civil war' (J. Brown and W. M. Louis (eds.) (1999) *The Oxford History of the British Empire: The Twentieth Century*, p. 332). According to this line of reasoning, if Britain was to avoid being dragged into a long and vicious civil war that it would not be able to prevent or stop, it had no choice but to partition India and leave.

Another reason for treating the 'law and order' argument with suspicion is that indigenous rights were often poorly protected by law. Sometimes legislation was introduced that was detrimental to locals. At other times, indigenous people found themselves incapable of using laws that had been designed to protect them. The novelist Anthony Trollope wrote that 'there seems to be an idea prevalent with many that the black [Aborigine] is not defended by the law. This is an erroneous idea. The black man has been treated with all possible tenderness by the law; but his life is such that the law can hardly reach him either to defend or to punish.'

In India, English was the official language for administrative purposes, and few people had access to effective legal support. It was always dominant groups that had the advantage and possessed the power to bend law to support their own interests. Indeed, many Britons in India were loath to lose the protection of a legal system that was loaded in their favour. Thus, when the Liberal Viceroy Lord Ripon proposed in the 1883/4 Ilbert Bill to allow senior Indian magistrates the right to try British subjects in the Raj, there was a huge outcry; it was argued that Indians might be prejudiced against British individuals.

British constitutional practices and the development of modern states

A particularly forceful argument is that British rule was responsible for the development of modern political ideas and structures in the colonies. Before the British, political power was concentrated in the hands of unrepresentative elites. Under colonial rule, however, regions such as India developed democratic institutions that allowed an electorate to choose their own political representatives; thus, the interests of ordinary people were better served. British rule also provided an administrative framework around which the post-colonial states were built. Furthermore, after independence, these countries were run by an educated elite who had been trained by Britain.

Nevertheless, this argument needs to be qualified. The development of democratic institutions was often a slow process. In India, even after the Morley-Minto reforms (1909), the electorate was mainly confined to the privileged few, and there were many groups of society who were not represented. And despite the development of a broad-based electorate in the twentieth century, politics continued to be dominated by a small, educated elite.

Secondly, critics point out that Britain was also responsible for the creation of artificial states. Each of Britain's colonies in Africa covered regions inhabited by a number of different, and often antagonistic, ethnic groupings. Kenneth Bradley, a district officer in East Africa wrote: 'such was the habit of our fathers when the scramble of Africa was at its height, [that the region has] been cut in a dead straight line for a hundred miles or more regardless of all natural landmarks or tribal boundaries. [This has caused] endless

THINK LIKE AN HISTORIAN

The British were often horrified at 'native' practices such as 'piracy', which seemed to have operated in some regions as giant 'protection-rackets'. However, historians have to be careful not to take sources at face value. It is very difficult to discover whether indigenous people would have seen piracy as less legitimate than British forms of rule. Were British tax-collectors 'pirates' of a different kind?

disputes about trespass by the poor bewildered natives on either side' (J. Samson (ed.) (2001) *The British Empire*, p. 208).

Post-independence was subsequently marred by infighting, as different groups vied for dominance within an artificially-created political region. However, to hold the British Empire *solely* responsible for this requires two assumptions. The first is that without colonial rule, there would have been no subsequent, ethnic conflicts. The second assumption requires one to believe that if Britain had constructed administrative areas more in tune with ethnic groupings, then the subsequent states would have coexisted as peaceful neighbours. Since many states squabble over issues such as borders this seems unlikely.

Thirdly, the imposition of modern political ideas on indigenous peoples was not greeted with universal joy. Many locals resented Britain making changes to traditional ways of running society. Taxation was particularly (and predictably) resented. It was imposed in order to support fledgling administrations and fund social and economic development. In Sierra Leone, the imposition of a Hut Tax sparked a war in 1898, partly from fears that Britain intended to take possession of African property. Taxation also caused changes in patterns of work, as subsistence farmers had to begin growing cash crops or seek paid work in the mines and cities. Thus, a political impact (the imposition of taxation) had a social and economic impact.

> **Stretch and challenge**
>
> How far do you agree with the following statements?
>
> 1. 'The further in time one is from an event, the more difficult it becomes to measure the consequences of that particular event because other variables occur to blur the picture.'
>
> 2. 'The historian is always influenced by the times within which he/she lives and works.'
>
> With this in mind, how accurately can the effects of Empire be measured?

Indirect rule

A further qualification to the 'constitutional development' argument lies in the fact that, in many areas, Britain pursued a policy that deliberately held back political change. In Africa, a system known as 'indirect rule' was implemented in the early twentieth century. Britain delegated much authority to so-called traditional chieftains, who ruled according to custom. This policy was mainly adopted because it was cheap and because the British believed that it would not disrupt or damage local society. However, in some African regions there was no tradition of a 'head man' or chieftain; the British were thus forced to 'invent tradition' and impose an often unpopular ruler on bewildered locals. A further criticism is that the system of indirect rule was not designed to help African peoples develop a progressive political system based on democracy. Western educated elites were ignored, and little was done to help Africans develop a sense of nationhood. Colonial rule is thus open to the charge that it failed to prepare Africans properly for independence.

However, there is evidence that contradicts this thesis. For instance, Kenneth Bradley paints a positive picture of indirect rule and the development of education (source N).

Source (N) **Kenneth Bradley**

The first thing the Angoni did with their money when they achieved a Native Treasury was to start a school. The Ngoni father may be reactionary and tiresome about windows in his hut, rubbish-pits, latrines, or selling his cattle, but he differs not a whit from his Chewa cousin in his enthusiasm for education. Let my son be educated, he says, and then he will be able to get a better paid job, and my rake-off from his salary will be correspondingly greater […] no English history is taught until the children have been thoroughly grounded in the history of their own tribe and of Northern Rhodesia. One of the chief's Elders comes once a week to teach the children Ngoni law and custom, they learn tribal dances, and we hope before long to arrange for the teaching of Ngoni handicrafts. We are trying to be very practical in our policy of bringing the children up to be good Angoni as well as educated citizens of a British Commonwealth of Nations.

J. Samson (ed.) (2001) *The British Empire*, pp. 209–10

ACTIVITY

Indirect rule has attracted both support and criticism.

1. What would influence an historian to pick one approach (i.e. for or against the benefits of Empire) over another?

2. To what extent do historians on the periphery *need* to see 'bad' in imperial rule?

ACTIVITY

Divide the teaching group into mini 'expert' groups consisting of at least three members. Each group researches the political impact of Empire on one particular country of their choice and structures their results under the following headings. (Each member should focus on one heading.)

- Coercion
- Law and order
- The imposition of a constitutional model

Once the research is completed, the groups should re-form to compile their material, check that they understand the political impact of Empire on their chosen country and standardise an approach to be used to convey their findings to other members of the class. The class then 're-jigs' so that newly-formed groups each have experts on particular countries who then take turns to present their findings to the rest of the re-jigged group. Those not presenting should take notes and be prepared to ask questions to clarify understanding once the micro presentation is complete.

The whole class can then be brought back together to compare what they have learned about the political effect of Empire on the periphery, with the political effects on the metropole. To consolidate understanding the following question should be answered using extended writing. It should be about 750 words in length.

> To what extent was the political impact of Empire on the periphery negligible and insignificant? Illustrate your response with reference to a range of countries.

Gender and sexuality

Key Question:

Why have historians become interested in gender, and how has this contributed to our understanding of colonial experiences?

In the last thirty years, many (particularly female) historians have begun to pay a good deal more attention to the role of women in Empire. This is partly due to the obvious reason that historians tend to be interested in individuals and groups from the past with whom they can identify. A further reason is that historians have become increasingly aware that gender is an important component of identity, and therefore open to manipulation as a means of controlling and dominating individuals and groups. Thus, the significance of gender in colonial lands potentially sheds light on the way in which imperial power was exercised.

GENDER AND SEXUALITY

Approach:
- a focus on the role of women in colonial society

Methods:
- the use of case studies
- the analysis of contemporary written sources such as diaries and newspapers

Interpretations:
- the image of a woman was used to symbolise nationhood in many colonies
- the British portrayed threatening indigenous males as feminine
- male European sexual jealousies caused fears about a 'black peril'
- in the late Victorian era, sexual relationships between Europeans and colonial subjects were increasingly condemned; this had a negative impact on relations between colonisers and colonised
- women were responsible for worsening relations between colonisers and colonised; this contributed to the loss of Empire

> **THINK LIKE AN HISTORIAN**
>
> Gender refers to the sexual identity of a person. Although much work on gender relates to the role of women, it is important to remember that the terms 'gender' and 'women' are not synonymous.

The restoration of women to historical visibility: work and gender

Passage Rosalind O'Hanlon

> *Nowhere has the restoration of women to historical visibility within the British Empire been clearer than in the field of labour [...] Changes in women's productive and reproductive labour lay at the heart of ... processes of economic 'development'. From the southern states of Africa to the Indian Punjab, colonial pressures to draw labour out of the subsistence economy into production for the market helped to create a 'feminisation of subsistence agriculture'.*
>
> J. Brown and W. M. Louis (eds.) (1999) *The Oxford History of the British Empire: The Twentieth Century*, p. 380

> What can you learn from passage 4 about Rosalind O'Hanlon's interpretation and approach? Refer to the extract and your knowledge to explain your answer.

Throughout the Empire, indigenous women were involved in work such as subsistence agriculture, petty commerce and craft activity, and domestic and sexual services. Although historians have begun to reveal more details about the relationship between

women and labour, much of this economic activity is still invisible (or semi-visible) to the historian, so it is difficult to identify how significant the work of women was, and how this affected women's lives. The integration of colonies into the world economy caused many men to migrate in search of paid work. In consequence, greater responsibility was placed on women to continue subsistence agriculture in the absence of male family members. Sometimes women became economic migrants, but this tended to be discouraged. In India, female migration was often a response to family rejection and entailed the dissolution of family ties. In contrast, male migration was a strategy for family survival, and family ties were thus retained.

In urban areas, the colonial state offered economic opportunities for women. A local study in Kenya has demonstrated how Nairobi prostitutes were able to save money in order to buy houses or support other family members. Further south, in the 1920s Zambian copper belt, the Northern Rhodesian mining companies encouraged women and families to reside in mining compounds. This opened up economic opportunities for activities such as beer brewing, selling food, and offering sexual services. However, the mobility of women in Northern Rhodesia (Zambia) upset many traditional chiefs and elders, who were the allies of the British authorities. In response, regulations were put in place to limit such mobility. Women were subsequently required to possess a marriage certificate issued by the indigenous authorities in order to reside in an urban area. Laws against divorce and adultery were enacted and limits placed on female earning potential. This example shows how female mobility affected family life, and how traditional authorities used the colonial state in order to limit the impact of change.

Gender and nationalism

Female historians have been keen to emphasise the role that women played in nationalist movements. Some women joined specifically-female organisations such as the All-India Women's Conference in India. However, female support for nationalist movements often meant that women had to sacrifice the interests of their sex in favour of those of their nation. For instance, women in India did not feel able to criticise nationalist conceptions of womanhood because this would have implicitly supported British views about Indian backwardness and uncivilised habits.

The image of the ideal 'woman', sometimes in the guise of a 'mother', was often a potent symbol in nationalist movements. **Gandhi**, for example, saw women as representative of the Indian nation – those who were able to bear suffering and self-sacrifice. Opponents of nationalist projects were denigrated as violators of the sanctity of womanhood. The identity of these violators was flexible depending on the political situation. In the 1920s, it was Muslim men rather than the colonial state that became the gravest threat to Hindu womanhood.

British conceptions of indigenous males: effeminate Bengalis and martial races

In 1841, Thomas Macaulay wrote that the Bengali male was 'feeble even to effeminacy'. He lives, 'in a constant vapour bath. His pursuits are sedentary, his limbs delicate, his movements languid. During many ages he has been trampled upon by men of bolder and more hardy breeds.' Bengalis were contrasted to the 'martial' (manly) races, such as the Sikhs. This reputation was long-lasting and the Raj recruited its soldiers primarily from the warrior peoples of the north and north west. Recently, historians concerned with imperialism and gender have recognised that there was 'an intimate relationship between sex and racism' (passage 5).

Passage 5

This pairing, for example, showed itself in the portrayal of some colonised men as feminine. This was a strong theme in British depictions of some Indian men, and the critique was often internalised by Indians: Gandhi observed in 1938, when discussing European doctors, 'we have become deprived of self-control and have become effeminate'. Imperialism was, in short, so powerful that it could make some men feel as if colonised men had lost their gender.

Diana Wylie in R. Winks (1999) *The Oxford History of the British Empire: Historiography*, p. 287

What can you learn from passage 5 about the interpretation, approach and method of the historian Diana Wylie? Refer to the extract and your knowledge to explain your answer.

The 'myth of the destructive female'

According to the historian Margaret Strobel, writing in 1991, 'Histories of the nineteenth- and twentieth-century empires virtually ignore European women. If they are mentioned at all, their arrival is seen to have contributed to the deterioration of the relationship between the European administrator and those he governed' (J. Samson (ed.) (2001) *The British Empire*, p. 147). Strobel and a number of other feminist historians were keen to reverse this trend. In particular, they sought to challenge what was termed the 'myth of the destructive female', a prevalent belief that the 'insular whims and prejudices' of European women in the colonies had contributed to the loss of Empire. According to this interpretation, European women were the custodians of British moral virtues and dominated the domestic sphere, the segregated space of the white family. This heightened the social distance and soured the relations between the British and their colonial subjects. On the one hand, European women disapproved of European men taking indigenous concubines or wives, a practice which had previously served to unite coloniser and colonised. On the other hand, the introduction of European women served to cause jealousies between white men and black men, thereby creating a hostile atmosphere.

Few historians now believe that women can be held responsible for racial tensions. The arrival of women coincided with a greater European presence and the development of pseudo-scientific racial beliefs; these factors are now considered the most likely cause of rising racial tensions. It is also argued that many women were merely playing the role that society expected them to play.

More positively, women contributed to the colonies through helping with charitable and voluntary work. However, although some women became involved in helping indigenous causes, such as Annie Besant who supported Indian Home Rule in 1917, many women did their utmost to uphold the imperial ideology.

Indigenous sexuality: the traditional approach

Supporters of Empire have pointed out that Britain did much to protect indigenous girls and women from various ordeals that had previously been inflicted on them. The British authorities clamped down on child sexual activity in India, and forbade forced marriages in Africa. Both of these measures were controversial at the time, as indigenous societies resented colonial interference.

The British authorities attempted to tamper as little as possible with indigenous culture, which was one reason why they were suspicious of missionaries. Sometimes, however, certain indigenous customs caused such controversy that the British were obliged to intervene. In the 1890s, there was a very controversial debate about the age of sexual consent in Indian child marriages. Social reformers believed that young girls lacked the physical and mental maturity to engage in sexual relations. Many Indians, however, resented colonial interference with traditional customs. An Act was passed in 1891

FOR DISCUSSION

Why would the British believe a 'feminine, educated native' man was more dangerous than a 'violent savage'?

93

setting the age of sexual consent for girls in marriage at 12 years. The colonial authorities argued that before the age of 12 few girls had begun menstruation. This was important, since those who defended early sexual relations believed that conception ought to be attempted as soon as a girl began to menstruate.

FOR DISCUSSION

Did questions about the age of female consent encourage conservatism amongst Indians, thereby holding back the development of a 'progressive' nationalism?

A subsequent debate about the age of marriage in India erupted in the 1920s. The previous legislation had been difficult to enforce since sexual relations were (in the majority of cases) a private act between two people, and there was often little accurate information as to a girl's date of birth, thus making it difficult to know her age. In 1929, an Act was passed that meant girls had to be above the age of 14 in order to marry. Unlike the previous legislation, this interfered with the religious ceremony of marriage, and hence sparked opposition from religious leaders. Moreover, those in favour of child marriages argued that families had to marry girls off early in case elders died and girls were left without material support. Additionally, since girls and boys were supposed to marry within the same caste, there would be few marriageable candidates left if a family waited too long.

In the early twentieth century, there was a great deal of British opposition to forced African marriages. Officials protected women by making them legal individuals, thereby giving them some protection under the law. Different ideas of sexuality operated amongst indigenous societies. In Southern Rhodesia, individual members of the Shona people were answerable to their family in regards to sexual activity. Sexual acts such as masturbation were not judged bad in themselves, but gained meaning depending on how they affected the family. For instance, family heads desired compensation if adultery was committed. This horrified colonial officials who believed that the act was inherently bad, and therefore needed to be punished. Hence, in 1916, a law was brought in for the colony that criminalised adultery.

Missionaries were particularly critical of indigenous sexual practices. Sometimes, this provoked a great deal of tension. In Buganda (in modern Uganda) in the 1880s, the ruler enjoyed sodomising his page boys. However, some of the boys were converted to Christianity by missionaries and were encouraged to refuse their master his sexual pleasures. In response, the Bugandan ruler castrated and burned alive a number of these recalcitrant page boys. Another practice of which missionaries disapproved was clitoridectomy (female circumcision) which caused conflict with the Kikuyu people in Kenya in the 1920s. Members of the colonial service tried to persuade reformers to show restraint, for fear of angering local people. Matters were made worse when locals allegedly raped and circumcised a 70-year-old female missionary in 1930.

The British were also very fearful of what was termed the 'Black Peril': black men ravaging white women. In the second half of the nineteenth century, greater numbers of European women travelled to the colonies and this served to intensify fears, well illustrated in E. M. Forster's *A Passage to India* (1924). In Papua New Guinea, Sir Hubert Murray introduced a White Women's Protection Ordinance in 1925, following a number of complaints about black men sexually assaulting women and young girls. Most of these assaults were supposedly carried out by black servants whose offences ranged from being a 'peeping tom', to various forms of groping. European men seemed keener than European women on introducing the Papua New Guinea Ordinance, which promised the death penalty for rape. However, the 'Black Peril' was not simply the result of fears and jealousies on the part of British men. As Lady Mary Anne Barker, reveals, European women feared such encounters (source O):

Source (O) Lady Mary Anne Barker

The scene was laid in Jamaica, where my father then held the office of 'Island Secretary' under Sir Charles – afterwards Lord Metcalfe – the Governor. It was Christmas day, and I had been promised as a great treat that my little sister and I should sit up to late dinner. But the morning began with an alarm, for just at breakfast-time an orderly from one of the West Indian regiments, then stationed in Spanish Town, had brought a letter to my father which had been sent upstairs to him. I was curled up in a deep window-seat in the shady breakfast-room, enjoying a brand-new story-book and the first puffs of the daily sea-breeze, when I heard a guttural voice close to my ear whispering, 'Kiss, missy, kiss.' There stood what seemed a real black giant compared with my childish stature, clad in gorgeous Turkish-looking uniform with a big white turban and a most benignant expression of face, holding his hand out, palm upwards.

I gazed at this apparition – for I had only just returned to Jamaica – with paralysed terror, while the smiling ogre came a step nearer and repeated his formula in still more persuasive tones. At this moment, however, my father appeared and said, 'Oh yes, all right; he wants you to give him a Christmas-box. Here is something for him'. It required even then a certain amount of faith as well as courage to put the silver dollar into the outstretched palm, but the man's joy and gratitude showed the interpretation had been quite right. I did not dare to say what my alarm had conjured up as the meaning of his request, for fear of being laughed at.

Quoted in E. Boehmer (ed.) (1998) *Empire Writing: An anthology of colonial literature*, pp. 304–5

The historian Margaret Strobel believes that 'Black Peril' threats 'resulted from the contradictory feelings of racial superiority and vulnerability and the sexual projection of white males on colonised men' (J. Samson (ed.) (2001) *The British Empire*, p. 150). To what extent does the extract by Lady Mary Anne Barker (source O) support this interpretation?

Subsequent critics have suggested that Britain did not go far enough, or that intervention was motivated by the desire to strengthen colonialism. For instance, it has been argued that the opposition of Bengali men to the 1891 Age of Consent Act diverted energy away from the nationalist movement. However, there is little evidence to suggest that the colonial authorities enacted social reform with any ulterior motive in mind; it was understood that interference in local customs caused hostility that might endanger colonial authority. Thus, colonial officials tried to dissuade Scottish missionaries from conducting campaigns against clitoridectomy (female circumcision) in Kenya in the 1920s.

European sexuality

Sexuality interests historians primarily for the same reason that it interests everybody else: it deals with a person's innermost desires, and often involves much secrecy, fear, and repression. The work of Ronald Hyam has been particularly important in mapping out the significance of European sexual activity in Britain's Empire. He has argued that empire-building allowed European males to relieve sexual frustrations generated in the repressive atmosphere of British society. However, from the latter half of the nineteenth century, campaigns for sexual purity placed restraints on British sexual activity in the colonies. This was intimately linked with the growth of racism. Hyam further suggests that the rigid boundaries placed on acceptable British and indigenous sexual behaviour were detrimental to individuals and to society. For example, interference in local sexual customs in Buganda and Kenya caused some unsavoury results. Meanwhile, up until the 1880s in India, the colonial authorities tolerated regulated prostitution, because this ensured sex workers were relatively clean from venereal disease. Moral purity campaigners eventually forced the abandonment of this policy. In consequence, cases of syphilis in 1895 rose 25 per cent in the Indian Army. It was thus decided to reintroduce regulated prostitution.

In Africa, sexual activity between white and black people was initially widespread. A colonial official in London remarked that 'cohabitation with native women is extremely

common throughout west and east Africa: indeed I am informed that of the unmarried white officials, there is only a small percentage who abstain entirely from the practice.' However, these relations became more heavily curtailed at the beginning of the twentieth century. In 1909, the Crewe circular forbade colonial officials from taking concubines (i.e. mistresses), since it was argued that this lowered respect for white people in the eyes of the indigenous population.

Predictably, Hyam's views have come under considerable attack. Since Hyam treats the individuals of his study with sympathy, he has been accused of defending sexually exploitative and abusive relationships. John Kelly criticised Hyam for a 'faulty premise: that his audience wishes for a world organised for the maximum sexual opportunity for European men' (J. Kelly (1992) 'Review' in *Journal of the History of Sexuality*, Vol. 2, No. 3., p. 476). Kelly was further disappointed that Hyam failed to address the issue of sadism, which apparently characterised British sexual relations in the colonies. The historian P. J. Marshall is also convinced that, in many cases, sexual relations between coloniser and colonised were 'highly exploitative'. Marshall points out that the offspring of mixed relationships were rarely recognised and that when European men returned to Europe they left indigenous women to fend for themselves. Thus, the relationship between European men and their concubines was one of unequal power. Whereas European men could forego sexual relations without serious damage, indigenous women were obliged to offer sexual services because of economic necessity and colonial exploitation. In contrast, others have claimed that many sexual relationships were conducted according to local norms and were classed as legitimate. For example, a 'bride price' was sometimes paid for marriage or concubinage in Africa and South East Asia. Furthermore, it is argued that indigenous women were often treated better by British men than they would have been by indigenous men.

> ### Stretch and challenge
>
> How useful is the concept of sexual exploitation for understanding sexual relations between colonial officials and indigenous people?

Another criticism of Hyam surrounds his 'naïve' view about natural sexual urges:

> ### Passage ⑥ Lesley Hall
>
> *Hyam appears to hold the [view] that ('normal') men need to be 'regularly despunked' and while they may prefer this to happen with a socially acceptable partner of the opposite sex, in case of necessity anything with a hole will do. (However there are no accounts of sexual congress with 'lower animals' – in spite of the good old Colonial joke 'female camel – nothing queer about Carruthers' – or melons.) The possibility that sexual desire may be acted on by surrounding social beliefs and norms in ways which are not simply about 'repression' or taboo is unfortunately not explored.*
>
> *To see this in full, go to www.pearsonhotlinks.co.uk and enter the express code 2480P.*

The apparent lack of interest shown in sexual matters by a number of famous nineteenth-century imperialists such as Rhodes, Gordon, Kitchener and Baden-Powell, has also attracted controversy. It has been argued that these 'asexual males' translated sexuality into daring deeds done for Empire. However, Dennis Judd points out that this 'did not mean that they did not lead sexual lives of some sort. **General Gordon** derived considerable pleasure from scrubbing down dirty urchins in bathtubs; Baden-Powell

BIOGRAPHY

General Gordon (1833–85)

Charles Gordon was commissioned into the Royal Engineers in 1852. He served in the Crimean War (1853–6), and then in China (1860–5) where he was given command of a militia force raised to defend Shanghai, an important European trading city. 'Chinese Gordon' returned to England and was then posted to the Sudan in 1873 where he rose to become Governor-General. Ill health caused Gordon to resign in 1880 and move back home. However, in 1884 he returned to the Sudan on a mission to evacuate Egyptian forces from Khartoum, which was under threat from Sudanese forces led by Muhammad Ahmad al-Mahdi. During the siege of Khartoum, Gordon was killed, two days before a British relief force arrived.

enjoyed seeing youthful naked bodies'. Moreover, according to Judd, it was apparently 'inevitable' that relief was found in masturbation (passage 7).

> Passage 7
>
> *It is obvious that the historian will never know whether most of these self-proclaimed celibates, misogynists or asexuals masturbated or not, but it is beyond belief that none of them engaged in the classical 'solitary vice' that so perturbed the moralists and puritans in the nineteenth and twentieth centuries. Indeed, the intensity and passion with which men like Baden-Powell sought to discourage and stamp out the sin of masturbation is in itself worthy of comment, and may well be evidence of the disgust and self-loathing felt by the moralist himself for his own masturbatory activities and fantasies.*
>
> D. Judd (1997) *Empire*, p. 175

ACTIVITY

> Passage 8
>
> *Critics of what was alleged to be the prudery of later generations have assumed that liaisons were conducive to good race relations. Some well-documented instances do indeed leave no doubt of deep mutual affection, but in many cases such relationships were highly exploitative of the women involved.*
>
> P. J. Marshall (ed.) (1996) *The Cambridge Illustrated History of the British Empire*, p. 247

What can you learn from passage 8 about the interpretation and approach of the historian?

ACTIVITY

What can you learn from passage 9 about the interpretation, approach and method of the historian Margaret Strobel? Refer to the extract and your knowledge to explain your answer.

> Passage 9
>
> *If concubinage enhanced the relationship of coloniser and colonised, then why should not voluntary sexual liaisons between European women and indigenous men do the same? Because they confounded the fundamental belief that women should be subordinate to men, and a wife from the racially superior group threatened that subordinate status.*
>
> Margaret Strobel in J. Samson (ed.) (2001) *The British Empire*, p. 150–1

The experience and impact of imperialism on Britain

> **Source** (A) **Alfred, Lord Tennyson, 1886**
>
> *Sons, be welded each and all,*
> *Into one imperial whole,*
> *One with Britain, heart and soul!*
> *One life, one flag, one fleet, one Throne!*
>
> Quoted in E. Boehmer (ed.) (1998) *Empire Writing: An Anthology of Colonial Literature*, p. 64

> **Key Questions:**
>
> - Why have historians disagreed about the cultural impact of Empire in the metropole?
> - How significant are approaches that focus on the political impact of Empire?
> - How significant are approaches that focus on the economic impact of Empire?

The approach emphasising the cultural impact of Empire

> **Key Question:**
>
> Why have historians disagreed about the cultural impact of Empire in the metropole?

IMPERIAL CULTURE IN BRITAIN

Approach:
- an emphasis on how imperialism affected popular culture in Britain

Methods:
- an analysis of written and pictorial sources relating to popular culture
- interviews with people who remember Britain before the loss of Empire

Interpretations:
- Hobson: masses manipulated into imperial frenzy
- Revisionists: most people were apathetic about Empire
- MacKenzie: Empire was a significant element of metropolitan culture
- the British public still supported Empire at the time of decolonisation

The New Imperialism interpretation: jingoism or indifference?

From c.1880, the British Empire expanded rapidly in response to the acquisitive and competitive tendencies of other European powers. Much debate surrounds the extent of popular enthusiasm for Empire during this period of 'New Imperialism'. J. A. Hobson, a prominent contemporary critic of the nature of British imperialism, assumed that popular jingoism (an excessive form of patriotism) was widespread. He claimed that the masses became 'jingoistic' because they were easily manipulated by those in power, particularly Conservative imperialists and greedy businessmen such as Joseph Chamberlain and Cecil Rhodes.

In the twentieth century, historians began to challenge the view that popular jingoism and uncritical support for the Empire were prevalent during this period. It was argued that the 'new enthusiasm' was brief and intermittent. The working classes were more concerned about unemployment and the price of bread. Instead, it was the lower-middle class that was most prone to jingoistic tendencies. Recently, historians such as John MacKenzie have begun to re-emphasise the pervasive nature of 'Empire' in British culture. Ideas and images of the colonial world appeared in art, architecture, exhibitions, adult literature, school texts, comics and juvenile novels, advertising, plays, music hall performances, radio, television and film. The Empire was also promoted through organisations such as the Imperial Institute and the Empire Marketing Board. Historians who approach the study of Empire from this angle have done much to further our understanding of the relationship between imperialism and metropolitan society.

Source B A lithograph from 1851 showing the huge interior of the Crystal Palace Exhibition in Hyde Park, London.

The development of exhibitions

The growing importance of Empire to Britain in the second half of the nineteenth century was reflected by the development of imperial exhibitions. In 1851, a Great Exhibition was held in Hyde Park, London (source B). On view were industrial products from around the world, including the Empire. The exhibition was designed to flaunt Britain's industrial and commercial dominance and technical achievements. It was a great success and received around six million visitors. A subsequent exhibition was held in 1862 in South Kensington, in which even greater prominence was placed on the imperial content of the exhibits. By the 1880s a number of specifically imperial

exhibitions began to be staged, such as the London 'Colonial and Indian' Exhibition (1886). Ethnic artefacts were put on display to illustrate various stages of social development, and 'native villages' were recreated to give an insight into the cultures found throughout the Empire. Some historians have seen the rise of imperial exhibitions as symbolic of Britain's decline in world affairs. Britain had become reliant on the economic contribution of its Empire, and hence, the Empire gained more prominence in Britain.

ACTIVITY

Source C is a verse of a poem written by Alfred, Lord Tennyson to mark the opening of the 1886 Colonial and Indian Exhibition. How useful is the poem as evidence for changes in British imperialism during the nineteenth century?

> Source Alfred, Lord Tennyson
>
> *Sharers of our glorious past,*
> *Brothers, must we part at last?*
> *Shall we not through good and ill*
> *Cleave to one another still?*
> *Britain's myriad voices call,*
> *Sons, be welded each and all,*
> *Into one imperial whole,*
> *One with Britain, heart and soul!*
> *One life, one flag, one fleet, one Throne!'*
> *Britons, hold your own!*
>
> Quoted in E. Boehmer (ed.) (1998) *Empire Writing: An Anthology of Colonial Literature*, p. 64

ACTIVITY

Construct a table with two headings, as below.

Significant impact of Empire on popular culture	Limited impact of Empire on popular culture

As you read the rest of the section, write down evidence which supports each interpretation under the appropriate heading in the table.

School texts, race and the construction of a national identity

The content of late-Victorian school texts reveals that ideas of Empire were significant in the state's attempts to create model citizens. In 1870, the British government passed a law that was intended to provide elementary (primary) education for every child in Britain. Subsequent legislation in 1880 made elementary education compulsory for children between the ages of 5 and 10. Ideas of race and images of Empire were prominent in the students' reading material. Early Victorian school history texts had focused on the Norman Conquest (**1066**) and the Glorious Revolution (**1688**) as the pivotal moments in British history; it was believed that these events had been crucial in the development of the English constitution, which was characterised by parliamentary democracy and a limited monarchy. However, towards the end of the nineteenth century, more space in texts began to be devoted to the Elizabethan Age of 'Merry England', the period in which England's spirit of imperial adventure had first been unleashed through the actions of heroes such as Sir Francis Drake.

From around 1890, texts also began to place more emphasis on the 'Anglo-Saxon' racial origins of English children. It was increasingly believed that inherited racial characteristics had enabled constitutional progress to occur – only a race such as the English could have developed an ideal political system based on parliamentary democracy and a limited monarchy. These beliefs about race were intimately connected to Empire. English racial superiority ensured that British colonialism would be successful; some people even argued that racial superiority made it Britain's *duty* to colonise uncivilised parts of the world. Thus, it seems clear that the promotion of an Anglo-Saxon racial identity in schools served to legitimise and encourage Britain's imperial mission.

Moreover, the concept of race was inclusive and was used to promote domestic harmony. Although outsiders such as 'blacks' were excluded, marginalised groups such as women and the working class were able to share in an identity of Englishness. Children were taught that they must not 'let the race down'. If Britain was to succeed in its mission, domestic conflicts about political ideology, gender or class must be given up. Although much of the imperial administration was run by those from the middling and upper ranks of society, the labouring classes could still contribute to Britain's Empire. Working-class children were encouraged to see themselves as pedestals on which great imperial heroes such as General Gordon could stand and fight Britain's enemies. In other words, the role of the working class was vital; it was their duty to fight or labour in the imperial enterprise, even if (as individuals) they might not get due recognition. To reinforce this message, children were reminded in history texts of the past victories won by 'honest' English yeoman, many of whom had lost their lives defeating wicked enemies such as the French. The imperial mission demanded similar sacrifices, as was illustrated by General Gordon's death (1885) which was immediately turned into a national symbol.

Stretch and challenge

Passage 1 is an extract from a satirical 'textbook' entitled *1066 and All That* (1930).

 Passage **1**

> *It was in the eighteenth century that Indian History started. Indian History is a great number of wars in which the English fought victoriously against the Waratah Confederacy and various kinds of potentates [...] Many of these victories were due to an Englishman named Robert Clive, a typist in the East India Coy Ltd, who, after failing to commit suicide three times, made the famous raid on Arcos [... In 1857] an outbreak of very serious Meeruts occurred at Cawnpore and elsewhere and a descendant of the Great Mohawk was set up as Emperor at Dulwich (the old capital of India). Most terrible among the Indian leaders was a native Pundit called the Banana Sahib who by means of his treacherous disguise lured famished British regiments to destruction. [...In other parts of the Empire, during a Wave of Justifiable Wars] Spheres of Interference were discovered; these were necessary in all countries inhabited by their own natives.*

W. C. Sellar and R. J. Yeatman (1985) *1066 and All That*, pp. 93, 111, 114

1. What criticisms are Sellar and Yeatman making about the way in which imperial history was traditionally represented in school textbooks by 1930?

2. What does it reveal about the problems facing historians who use the material in school textbooks as evidence about attitudes towards Empire?

Literacy and ideas of Empire

As more individuals became literate, ideas about the Empire were increasingly circulated through the written word. Between 1870 and 1900, literacy in England and Wales had risen from 80 to 97 per cent, and in Scotland from 90 to 98 per cent. Meanwhile, the development of printing techniques did much to lower the price of written texts and increase their distribution. Individuals also had greater opportunities to borrow books; since 1850, municipal councils had possessed the authority to impose local rates (taxes) for the purpose of building public libraries. Newspapers were also a widely available source of information on imperial developments. However, historians are aware that just because people *could* read, does not mean that they necessarily *did* read. Many people were too tired to read extensively since they worked very long hours. This problem was made worse because Victorian text was printed in very small type.

Young people were often the keenest readers of Empire-related texts, such as novels, schoolbooks and, from the end of the nineteenth century, Empire annuals. Autobiographies of individuals who grew up in the Edwardian era emphasise the importance of juvenile novels in developing their personal outlook on life. Many of these books dealt with imperial themes. A particularly prominent author was G. A. Henty who wrote a great many books with titles such as *With Clive in India* and *True as Steel* (source D).

Source (D) The cover of 'True as Steel' by G. A. Henty – an example of the type of popular fiction which promoted the idea of Britain's pre-eminent place in the Empire.

Other historical novels described times when England had been 'under the cosh' but had emerged victorious, such as when King Alfred had defeated the Danes. These stories reinforced the message that the English nation had heroic origins and required valiant, military characters to carry on defending the homeland and the Empire. Some stories also involved girls, most of whom were portrayed as dutiful subordinates.

ACTIVITY

Passage 2 is taken from *Culture and Imperialism* by Edward Said. What can you learn from the extract about Said's interpretation, approach and method? Refer to the extract and your knowledge to explain your answer.

> Passage 2
>
> *Since my exclusive focus here is on the modern Western empires of the nineteenth and twentieth centuries, I have looked especially at cultural forms as the novel, which I believe were immensely important in the formation of imperial attitudes, references and experiences. I do not mean that only the novel was important, but that I consider it the aesthetic object whose connection to the expanding societies of Britain and France is particularly interesting to study […] Narrative is crucial to my argument here, my basic point being that stories are at the heart of what explorers and novelists say about strange regions of the world; they also become the method colonised people use to assert their own identity and the existence of their own history. The main battle in imperialism is over land, of course; but when it came to who owned the land, who had the right to settle and work on it, who kept it going, who won it back, and who now plans its future – these issues were reflected, contested, and even for a time decided in narratives. As one critic has suggested, nations themselves are narrations.*
>
> E. Said (1993) *Culture and Imperialism*, pp. xii-xiii

Empire Day and youth organisations

From 1902, school students began to celebrate Empire Day (May 24). Children saluted the Union Jack, sang patriotic songs and listened to pro-imperial speeches and stories. They were sent home from school early so that they could take part in marches, maypole dances, concerts and parties. The day was officially recognised as an annual event in 1916 and during the interwar years it was consistently observed in schools under the leadership of the Empire Day Movement. However, not all children appear to have been as enthusiastic about Empire as it was hoped. The schoolboys in **Rudyard Kipling**'s book, *Stalky and co.* (1899), contemptuously described an overly patriotic M.P. as 'a jelly-bellied Flag-flapper'. Although fictional, the story implies that children were able to resist some of the ideas directed at them.

Nevertheless, young people did respond positively to various youth groups that were implicitly connected to Empire, such as the Boys Brigade (Glasgow, 1883), and most famously the Boy Scouts (1907), which was formed by Robert Baden-Powell, an imperial hero. He intended to teach boys outdoor skills and instil a sense of independence and duty in them. Scouting became popular throughout the Empire, and subsequently spread to other parts of the world. An equivalent organisation, the Girl Guides, was introduced in 1910. Some historians suggest that it was camping that attracted children to the scouts, and that the imperial nature of the organisation was minimal. Nevertheless, the link between Empire and scouting was clear to many, and certainly helps to explain its popularity with the authorities.

BIOGRAPHY

Rudyard Kipling (1865–1936)

Rudyard Kipling was an Anglo-Indian writer born in Bombay. He wrote a great many stories and poems about colonial life in India, including *The Jungle Book* and *Kim*.

ACTIVITY

What does Orwell's description of Kipling in passage 3 reveal about changes to the meaning of imperialism in metropolitan culture?

> ### Passage (3)
>
> *[Rudyard Kipling's] popularity was, of course, essentially middle class. In the average middle class family before the [First World] War, especially in Anglo-Indian families, he had a prestige that is not even approached by any writer to-day. He was a sort of household god with whom one grew up and whom one took for granted whether one liked him or not. For my own part I worshipped Kipling at thirteen, loathed him at seventeen, enjoyed him at twenty, despised him at twenty-five and now again rather admire him [...] What is more distasteful in Kipling than sentimental plots or vulgar tricks of style, is the imperialism to which he chose to lend his genius. The most one can say is that when he made it, the choice was more forgivable than it would be now. The imperialism of the 'eighties and 'nineties was sentimental, ignorant and dangerous, but it was not entirely despicable. The picture then called up by the word 'Empire' was a picture of overworked officials and frontier skirmishes, not of Lord Beaverbrook and Australian butter. It was still possible to be an imperialist and a gentleman, and of Kipling's personal decency there can be no doubt.*
>
> G. Orwell (2002) *Essays*, pp. 38–9

Imperialism and societies

Adults also joined societies and groups linked to the Empire. The exploits in far-off lands of Christian heroes such as Gordon and Livingstone helped to inspire the formation of Christian organisations such as the Salvation Army (1878). At around the same time, local geographical societies began to spring up in the provinces, many of which were concerned with exotic, imperial lands. They gave lectures and offered prizes for exploration. Most societies declined in popularity during the years prior to the First World War, and were then disbanded.

Paintings and photographs

Paintings continued to depict imperial scenes (source E), and the introduction of photography in the late nineteenth century gave people in Britain the chance to view real-life images of the Empire. Some of these pictures were circulated widely through the newspaper press, the increasingly popular illustrated magazines, postcards, cigarette cards, and advertising (source F).

Source (E) 'The Last Effort and Fall of Tippoo Sultaun', by Henry Singleton, c.1800.

Source (F) A postcard commemorating the contribution of the British Colonies during the First World War.

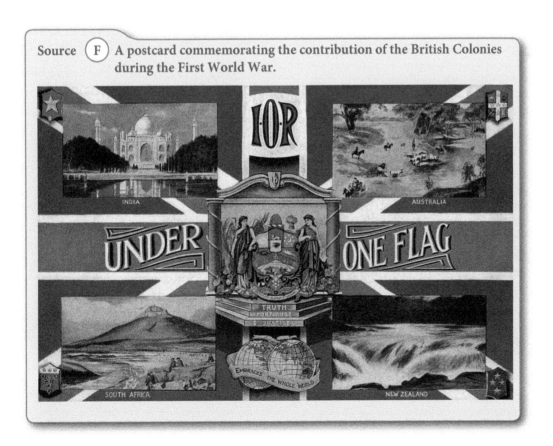

Plays and the Music Halls

Stories about Empire remained a popular choice for theatrical productions. In London and the provinces, plays were shown that involved British imperial conflicts such as the Indian Mutiny (1857–8), the Zulu War (1879), and the death of General Gordon (1885). Meanwhile, from c.1870, entertainment at Music Halls, in which patriotic songs were often sung, became all the rage. Recent research has demonstrated that such entertainment was popular in working-class and wealthier areas alike. A number of contemporaries satirised these flag-waving goings-on. However, some historians argue that this merely demonstrates the popularity and fame of the original Music Hall productions.

The Boer War and afterwards: jingo exaggerated?

Popular hostility towards the Afrikaners during the Boer War has also been used to support the argument that the working classes had been successfully seduced by imperial minded governments. In 1900, the Conservatives gained victory in the 'khaki election', in which the Liberals were stigmatised as pro-Boers. When the siege of Mafeking was relieved in 1902 there were popular celebrations in Britain. However, it has since been pointed out that during the 1900 election the Conservatives received only 400,000 more votes (out of a total of 4.5 million) than a fragmented Liberal Party. Some jingoistic candidates were rejected, and in many instances it was opposition to Irish Home Rule that prompted the urban working class to vote Conservative. By 1902, the Conservatives had begun to lose by-elections, and in 1906 the Liberals won a landslide election victory.

The Empire in interwar Britain

What can you learn from the John MacKenzie extract (passage 4) about the interpretations, approaches and methods of this historian? Refer to the extract and your knowledge to explain your answer.

> **Passage ④ John MacKenzie**
>
> *It seems to be one of the apparent curiosities of British imperial history that, when the Empire encountered the economic, political, and constitutional crises that would ultimately bring it down, British domestic culture came to emphasise colonial relationships as never before.*
>
> J. Brown and W. M. Louis (eds.) (1999) *The Oxford History of the British Empire: The Twentieth Century,* p. 230

MacKenzie provides evidence that the Empire gained increasing visibility during the interwar period through public exhibitions, consumer propaganda, popular literature, the newspaper press, radio and film. Furthermore, increasing numbers of people had a personal connection to the Empire: some had been employed in colonial lands, working as civil servants, teachers, missionaries, engineers, or soldiers; others had relatives who had either worked temporarily in the colonies, or emigrated permanently to one of the Dominions such as Australia. MacKenzie's thesis has important ramifications for theories of decolonisation. Some historians had previously suggested that a groundswell of public opinion developed in opposition to imperialism in Britain, and this contributed to decolonisation. If MacKenzie is right, then this argument can be discounted.

The Wembley Exhibition

Following the First World War, it was suggested that an imperial exhibition would restore imperial confidence and illustrate the continuing economic importance of the Empire to Britain. Plans were made to stage an exhibition at grounds in Wembley, north London. A national sports ground was also constructed on the exhibition site, and in 1923 it hosted the famous 'White Horse' F. A. Cup Final between Bolton Wanderers and

West Ham United. It was hoped that associating Wembley with a popular working-class sport would raise awareness of the British Empire Exhibition, which was finally inaugurated on 23 April, 1924. Pavilions for the various imperial territories, as well as technical and medical displays which emphasised imperial progress, were dotted around the site (sources G and H). The exhibition was certainly popular. In the two years it was open – 1924 and 1925 – it received over 27 million visitors. Another (and ultimately the last) Empire exhibition was staged in Glasgow in 1938; its aim was to stimulate Scottish trade and foster imperial sentiments.

Source (G) A poster featuring the Malaya Pavilion at the British Empire Exhibition at Wembley.

How might visual evidence such as posters and photographs mislead an historian who is trying to discover the nature of popular attitudes towards Empire?

Source (H) **The Indian Pavilion, Wembley Exhibition.**

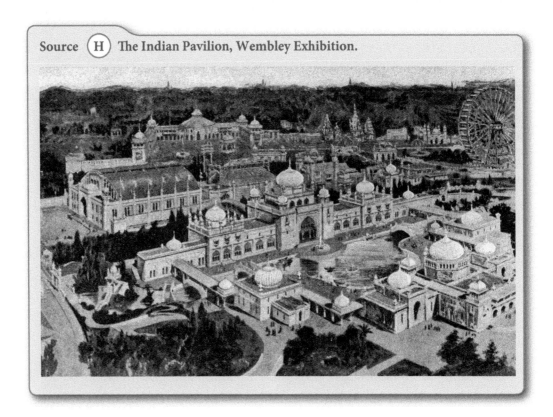

Source (I) **The Imperial Institute in South Kensington, London.**

The Imperial Institute and the Empire Marketing Board

The Imperial Institute (source I) had been founded in the late 1880s through public subscriptions. Its objective was to obtain and exhibit material relating to the Empire and give lectures on imperial themes. However, it only really gained popularity after 1914. By the early 1930s, it was receiving around one million visitors a year. Many of these, though, did not necessarily attend out of choice. Many school children, for instance, were compelled to visit as part of school trips. The Institute closed in 1955.

Other organisations were keen to stimulate interest in imperial economic relations; the most important of these was the Empire Marketing Board. This was set up by the British government in 1926, and lasted until 1933, when government economies forced its closure. The Board published booklets, pamphlets and postcards, showed documentaries, and gave public lectures in order to persuade people to buy imperial goods. However, although families were encouraged to buy such products, it is likely that price was the overriding concern when shopping for groceries.

The BBC and cinema

The British Broadcasting Corporation (BBC) was founded in 1922. It broadcast radio programmes, some of which were concerned with Empire. Many of the talks and features about the Empire emphasised colonial economic development, and promoted the idea that all was peaceful. The BBC broadcast Empire Day programmes and, from 1932, began a tradition of Christmas programmes which included contributions from the colonies. Furthermore, in the last years of the Second World War, festivals of Empire were broadcast from the Royal Albert Hall. Since 9 million people possessed wireless licences in Britain in 1939, it is likely that broadcasts on Empire had a wide audience.

The growing popularity of cinema was another significant development. Although the origins of cinema can be found in the 1890s, it was only in the interwar period that it began to gain real popularity. In 1926, there were 3000 cinemas in Britain, and by 1938, nearly 5000. Policymakers realised that the cinema was potentially very useful for propaganda purposes and, in particular, the positive portrayal of Empire. Documentaries were shown in schools, to youth organisations and at the Imperial Institute cinema, and newsreels told viewers of important developments in the Empire. However, it was feature films on imperial themes, such as **Gunga Din** (1939) (source J), which were probably most influential in conveying ideas of Empire. Since the government realised that cinema was an extremely powerful tool for manipulating the minds of the audience, tight controls were put in place to regulate the content of films. Those which showed the denigration of white officials, or indigenous resistance such as the 'Indian Mutiny', were not allowed.

> ### QUICK FACT
>
> **Gunga Din (1939)**
>
> This motion-picture film was very loosely based on Kipling's poem *Gunga Din*, but included elements from another of Kipling's works, the novel *Soldiers Three*. The film's plot revolves around three British sergeants and their Indian water-carrier, all of whom stumble upon a group of *Thugees*, members of an Indian religious group which sought to attack and strangle travellers as sacrifices to the goddess Kali.

Source J A poster advertising the feature film, *Gunga Din*, released in 1939.

FOR DISCUSSION

How did documentaries and feature films differ in the ways in which 'truth' about the Empire was conveyed?

ACTIVITY

1. Construct a line graph according to the following labels:

   a) vertical axis: 0 (limited impact) to 10 (large impact)

   b) horizontal axis: 1850 to 1950.

2. Complete the graph according to how significant you perceive Empire to have been in metropolitan culture throughout the period.

3. Perhaps you have relatives who were at school before the 1950s. If so, try to discover how important Empire was in school and at home for them. What are the difficulties in using this evidence?

The political impact of Empire

> **Key Question:**
>
> How significant are approaches that focus on the political impact of Empire?

IMPERIALISM AND METROPOLITAN POLITICS

Approach:
- an emphasis on how Empire affected domestic politics

Methods:
- an analysis of a variety of contemporary written sources relating to political opinion
- analysis of election results

Interpretations:
- Empire had a negligible effect on British politics
- Empire sparked European competition

Metropolitan politics

On balance, the impact of Empire on domestic politics was negligible. The position of Secretary of State for the Colonies was relatively unimportant and obscure until the arrival of Joseph Chamberlain, who held office from 1895 to 1903. He tried to emphasise the importance of the colonies to the wider public and wanted Britain to develop a closer relationship with the Dominions. However, 'constructive imperialism' failed to gain much support (see chapter 1). Most people in Britain were more concerned with domestic issues such as unemployment and the price of food. Occasionally though, a particular imperial issue such as the Second Boer War stirred patriotic feelings and affected politics. Anti-Boer feelings certainly contributed to the Conservative victory in the khaki election of 1900, while Chamberlain's imperial preference proposals helped them to lose the 1906 election .

International relations

Broadly speaking, there are two particular issues that relate to the impact of Empire on international relations. The first deals with 'New Imperialism', and whether Britain's Empire made other European nations jealous, thereby sparking a 'scramble for Africa'. This claim is difficult to substantiate. Although rivalry was an issue, there were a number of other more important factors involved, such as the need to find new markets for European goods.

The second issue concerns the strategic importance of Empire, and the extent to which imperial resources helped Britain dominate its rivals. For much of the time, Britain could draw on the Indian army as a relatively cheap military force to be deployed across the globe. The Dominions also contributed financial and military aid, which was crucial to Britain's success during the two world wars. Britain was also able to make use of the strategic naval bases that were spread across the Empire, such as Trincomalee in Ceylon (Sri Lanka), Singapore and Hong Kong.

The economic impact of Empire

Key Question:

How significant are approaches that focus on the economic impact of Empire?

IMPERIALISM AND THE ECONOMIC IMPACT ON THE METROPOLE

Approaches:
- counter-factual: what would have happened if Britain had not built an Empire?
- a survey of the costs and benefits

Method:
- an analysis of statistical material

Interpretations:
- the development of infrastructure on the periphery facilitated trade and therefore benefited Britain
- Britain benefited from the import of colonial produce
- mining made some individuals very rich

The counter-factual approach

This approach looks at what benefits would have accrued to the colonial countries and Britain if there had *not* been an Empire. A lot of the work in this area has been carried out by the economic historian, Michael Edelstein. Using complex statistical techniques, he has attempted to calculate the gains and losses to Britain in terms of trade, investment and, more generally, national income. His findings can be summarised as follows.

- 'If Empire territories had remained independent of Empire rule, they would not have participated in the international economy to the same extent. This was especially true of India where the British Raj *probably* brought a more peaceful, unified, and commercially orientated political economy than would have been the case in its absence' (Edelstein, (1981) 'Foreign Investment and Empire' in *The Economic History of Britain since 1700: 1860–1939*, p. 92).

- If territories in the Empire had remained independent, British exports to these lands from 1870 to 1913 would have been just 45 per cent of what they actually were. In other words, as totally independent countries, they would have diversified and looked across the world to import goods, not just from Britain. In 1870, colonial exports were actually worth 7.9 per cent of national income, and in 1913, 11.9 per cent. Without Empire, exports to the same regions would have been 3.6 per cent and 5.4 per cent respectively; a significant difference.

- A similar situation would have occurred with investment (though less so in relation to settlement colonies). Without the Empire, the same areas would only have yielded between 0.3 per cent and 0.5 per cent of national income over the period from 1870 to 1913.

- Thus, through the export trade and investment opportunities, 'the Empire made a significant contribution to the growth in the income and output of Britain in the nineteenth and early twentieth centuries.' (Edelstein, (1981) 'Foreign Investment and Empire' in *The Economic History of Britain since 1700: 1860–1939*, p. 92.)

What do you think are the advantages and disadvantages of using a counter-factual approach when examining the economic impact of Empire?

The cost-benefit analysis approach

The creation of infrastructure certainly supported the expansion of trade. For the period up to 1914, imports from the Empire hovered between 22 and 25 per cent of total imports. There was a notable increase in heavy, bulky, low-cost food items such as grains, but also perishables such as butter and meat, which is a clear reflection of the benefits of steam-powered transport (coupled with the introduction of refrigeration and canning). After the First World War, the Empire played an even greater role in Britain's trade, with the percentage share of imports rising to nearly 36 per cent by 1939. The Empire also provided an important market for exports; before 1914 it accounted for about 37 per cent of the total on average and this increased to 44 per cent by 1939. The main beneficiaries were the old staple industries and, again, the transport of manufactured goods to imperial markets was greatly aided by advancements in shipping.

ACTIVITY

Given that imperial trade policy centred around 'free trade' until the interwar period, how exactly did the creation of infrastructure in the periphery support the expansion of trade?

Source **K** Ships in Calcutta Harbour loading goods from the Empire.

More important with respect to wealth creation was income earned through invisibles. By the outbreak of the Second World War, over 60 per cent of all British overseas investment was in the Empire, although the vast proportion (41.4 per cent) was in the Dominions. The attraction of imperial investment was in the high rate of return; the railway was a good example of the gains to be had. The economic historian, Avner Offer, has demonstrated that, on average, an investment in colonial railway was likely to provide a return of 4.5 per cent compared with 3.8 per cent for a domestic railway project. Interestingly, the returns for overseas railways (i.e. non-Empire) are estimated

THINK LIKE AN HISTORIAN

What other reasons might there have been for investment in colonial railways?

to be 5.7 per cent, which partly suggests that Britons chose to invest in colonial railways for reasons other than to maximise profit.

Another crucial benefit resulting from better transport and communications was the ability to maintain (and restore) law and order more effectively. Officials and the military could now quickly move to trouble spots to quell rebellion. A good example of this was the suppression of the Indian Mutiny in 1857. It is difficult to see how the metropole was disadvantaged in any way by improvements to colonial infrastructures. However, this was not the case when it came to changes in agricultural practice.

The cost-benefit approach: agriculture

By the 1930s Britain still relied heavily on the Empire for imports of food and raw materials. This is supported by the figures in source L which show that the percentages of these imported goods were mostly high, adding weight to the argument that the Empire was a reliable and stable supplier of raw materials and foodstuffs. However, the information does not reveal some of the 'costs' that had emerged as a result of dependency.

Source (L) Empire share of major British imports, 1934.

Goods imported from the Empire	£m	% of imports
FOODSTUFFS		
wheat		63.3
tea		88.9
cocoa		90.7
spices		77.6
sugar, raw		64.2
meat, etc.		32.1
butter		53.5
cheese		88.9
RAW MATERIALS		
copper, ore		80.0
copper, smelted		47.4
tin, smelted		60.3
lead		89.4
mineral oils		5.9
cotton, raw		17.1
wool		83.4
jute, raw		98.8
oilseeds		60.5
rubber, raw		79.7
Imports from the Empire	257	35.3
Total imports (from everywhere)	727	100.0

From: D. K. Fieldhouse (2001) 'The Metropolitan Economics of Empire' in *The Oxford History of the British Empire: The Twentieth Century*, p. 101

- The increase in imports from the Empire was mainly the result of trade agreements and policies in the 1930s:
  - *The Import Duties Act* (1932) imposed a general 10 per cent duty on all imports and signalled the end of free trade. It was hoped this would protect British industry and cushion the impact of the severe economic depression of the 1930s. Permanent exemption of payment was given to the colonies and conditional exemption to the Dominions (i.e. Britain expected preferential treatment in Dominion markets).
  - *The Ottawa Conference* (1932) attempted to clarify what 'preferential treatment' involved, but what emerged was a very complicated set of proposals. Basically, the Dominions were allowed to keep tariffs high (up to 10 per cent) on a specified list of foreign goods, and promised that 'all British dependencies would give the Dominions whatever preferences they gave to Britain'.
- On the plus side, 'imperial preference' strengthened the economic and political unity of the Empire.
- The minus side was that increased dependency on imports from Dominions through trade restrictions increased prices in Britain (as by definition, foreign competition was restricted). This was especially hard on those with fixed incomes, such as the low paid and the elderly.
- Also, Britain found it difficult to match the cost of imports by increasing exports, especially at a time when there was a world slump in international trade. This resulted in a worsening balance of payments deficit and the choice between borrowing and/or making expenditure cutbacks.

Overall, until the 1930s, the metropole seemed to gain from the specialisation in agriculture adopted by the Dominions. However, the laissez-faire approach to agricultural industry in other parts of the Empire resulted in accusations by humanitarians of negligence that were difficult to defend. In other words, Britain could have helped farmers in non-Dominion countries to develop their livelihoods but chose not to do so. The result, as far as the critics were concerned, was poverty and exploitation.

The cost-benefit approach: industry

Investors in gold and diamond mines based in Britain stood the chance of making substantial gains, although such investment was a risky business. Some 'claims' were not profitable and the market for gold and diamonds could be volatile. For example, the Rhodes and Judd Gold Fields Company was registered in February 1889 and immediately sold 70,000 £1 shares; by the end of the year the total share allocation of 250,000 had been distributed. However, the Gold Fields mines contained low grade gold ore and shareholders dividends were in theory likely to be low. Their investments were only protected by Rhodes' decision to divert shareholders' money into diamond mining. In comparison, the Corner House Company reported profits of £860,000 in a five-month period from August to December 1889, based on the higher quality of their gold. In fact, there were over 400 individual companies in a similar situation to that of Corner House by 1890, and the Standard Bank claimed that the market value of the shares of all of these businesses stood at around £100 million. Much depended on how painstaking the originators of companies were when researching discoveries, and how willing they might be to invest in technology to improve the grade of gold if it was difficult to extract. Thus, companies that invested heavily in the new cyanide process for heating gold ore introduced in the 1890s found that they could extract an extra 6,000 ounces of pure gold per 10,000 tons of ore. The result was an increase in the value of gold production from £1.7 million in 1890 to £4.2 million in 1892. By 1900, the Transvaal was the world's leading producer of gold, with output reaching £1.7 million per month in July.

Investment in the Rand mines had reached £75 million and two-thirds of this was British. The Second Boer War, the unification of South Africa in 1910 and the two World Wars caused some disruption and dislocation, but up until 1950, many of those in the metropole who invested in gold and diamonds made a lot of money.

Another 'industrial' benefit to Britain came through the adoption and maintenance of free trade. Without substantial financial investment directly from London, colonies were never in a position where they could set up industries to compete with British manufacturers. Some colonial governments even saw this as a conspiracy between British governments and entrepreneurs. Indian rulers viewed it as an attempt to deindustrialise their **proto-industries** (cotton textiles, iron and steel). It is evident that British politicians went out of their way to protect British manufacturers by insisting that colonies allowed an 'open door' to British manufactured goods. However, this did not really apply to the self-governing colonies and it was not always easy to implement in the dependent colonies. For example, in 1917, India was forced by the British government to make payments towards mounting war debts, but in return was allowed to increase import duty on cottons. In 1921, further assistance was given through a 'fiscal autonomy convention, which left India free to protect any industry it wished, provided that a Tariff Board, set up in 1923, was convinced that the industry concerned had natural advantages, could eventually do without protection, and would not need government support' (D. Fieldhouse (2001) *For Richer, for Poorer* in *The Cambridge Illustrated History of the British Empire*, p. 140). On balance, though, British politicians put British industry before colonial industry right up to the time of independence.

Proto-industries

These were small-scale versions of industries that had the potential for growth. They were usually organised under the domestic or home-based production system.

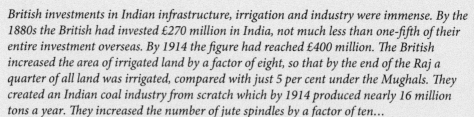

> **Passage** (5)
>
> *British investments in Indian infrastructure, irrigation and industry were immense. By the 1880s the British had invested £270 million in India, not much less than one-fifth of their entire investment overseas. By 1914 the figure had reached £400 million. The British increased the area of irrigated land by a factor of eight, so that by the end of the Raj a quarter of all land was irrigated, compared with just 5 per cent under the Mughals. They created an Indian coal industry from scratch which by 1914 produced nearly 16 million tons a year. They increased the number of jute spindles by a factor of ten…*
>
> *It is true that the average Indian did not get much richer under British rule… But for the majority of Indians it was far less clear that their lot would improve under independence. Under British rule, the village economy's share of total after-tax income actually rose from 45 per cent to 54 per cent. Since that sector represented around three-quarters of the entire population, there can be little doubt that British rule reduced inequality in India. And even if the British did not greatly increase Indian incomes, things might conceivably have been worse under a restored Mughal regime had the Mutiny succeeded.*
>
> N. Ferguson (2004) *Empire: How Britain made the Modern World*, pp. 216–8

Other costs

Given the size of the Empire it would be easy to assume that it was costly to administer and govern. In purely financial terms this was not really the case. Until 1914, expenditure on defending the Empire averaged 3 per cent of national income per year, a relatively small amount. The British kept about 315,000 military personnel under arms, which was low compared with other great powers, such as Germany (600,000) and Russia (900,000). Much emphasis was placed on the use of 'native' troops (about 140,000 in India alone). Costs did increase with the naval arms race. Between 1906 and 1913, 27 modern dreadnought battleships and turbine engines were constructed, to the tune of £49 million. But this was a small price to pay given the protection the navy provided to commercial shipping, the decline in the need for land forces, and the deterrence to other 'competitor' countries. As Ferguson has aptly stated, 'this was world domination on the cheap'.

This all changed after the First World War. Britain's expenditure on the war was in the region of £106 billion. This debt was soon to be exacerbated by costs of reconstruction and the upkeep of territories newly acquired from Germany and the Turks. The war had also led to the liquidation of overseas investments and damage to the old staple industries, which were overstretched and in need of modernisation. The cost of running the Empire suddenly became of major concern, although it was really the opportunity cost rather than the financial one that bothered politicians most; that is, the cost of not being able to spend government money on the implementation of policies not connected with the Empire. For most of the interwar period, orthodox economic thinking prevailed. Governments constantly looked to balance the books. If expenditure increased in one area it had to be reduced in another, depending on what was considered to be a priority. Therefore, as increasing amounts were spent on cushioning the effects of unemployment, on implementing social policy (especially with respect to housing), and coping with a balance of payments deficit, expenditure was reduced elsewhere, most notably on defence. Policing the Empire became increasingly challenging, particularly at a time when some regions were witnessing the rise of nationalism and protest groups demanding independence.

8 The experience and impact of Empire: area studies

AREA STUDIES

Approach:
- the analysis of a particular historical question through focusing on a small area

Method:
- detailed research relating to a small area

Interpretations:
- informal Empire existed in Argentina, but there were significant limits to British power
- indirect rule in Nigeria had a negative impact on large sections of indigenous society
- nationalism contributed to decolonisation in India, but British interests in the region were also in decline

The completion of local and area studies as a means of approaching British imperialism has become increasingly popular in recent years. In part this is because it allows postgraduate students the opportunity to complete theses by testing a theory over a manageable area. Significantly, the production of area studies has allowed historians to identify how imperialism differed in various parts of the globe. Thus, a more nuanced picture of British imperialism is beginning to emerge.

Informal Empire in Argentina

Source A

George Canning, Secretary of State for Foreign Affairs, 1824	British Ambassador in Buenos Aires, 1929
Spanish America is free and if we do not mismanage our affairs sadly, she is English	*Argentina must be regarded as an essential part of the British Empire*
Quoted in A. Porter (ed.) (1999) *The Oxford History of the British Empire: The Nineteenth Century*, p. 122	Quoted in J. Brown and W. M. Louis (eds.) (1999) *The Oxford History of the British Empire: The Twentieth Century*, p. 633

Historical overview

British politicians and businessmen believed that the collapse of the Spanish Empire in Latin America in the 1820s presented an opportunity to open up hitherto closed markets to British commerce and capital. In the first half of the nineteenth century, these hopes were mainly unfulfilled; there was little demand in Latin America for British goods since local populations were small, dispersed and did not have much disposable income. Commerce was also hindered by poor transport links and endemic political instability. However, in the latter half of the nineteenth century, Britain became very important to Argentina as the main source of financial credit and as a market for Argentine goods. By the early twentieth century, British financial and commercial hegemony in Argentina began to be challenged by US and German competition. Britain also faced opposition resulting from the rise of nationalist sentiments directed against foreign control of the Argentine economy. Yet it was not until after the Second World War that Britain's position of financial and commercial dominance was eclipsed.

The Anglo-Argentine economic relationship

From c.1850 to c.1950, Britain became Argentina's major foreign creditor and was the most important market for Argentine goods. According to Cain and Hopkins, 'the ability to borrow on a massive scale and to make repayment through exports of primary products became the basis of power and prosperity of the 400 or so wealthy landed families who formed the Argentine elite, and also of their allies in banking and commerce' (P. J. Cain and A. G. Hopkins (2001) *British Imperialism*, p. 254).

Thus, it was vital for the Argentine government to retain the confidence of British creditors. In particular, this meant a commitment to the repayment of government debt, even in times of financial crisis such as the 1870s and 1890s. President Avellaneda claimed in 1873 that Argentina would 'willingly suffer privations and even hunger' to retain its credit reputation. In the financial crisis of 1890, the Argentine government was compelled by Britain to adopt unpopular deflationary policies in return for the advancement of a government loan. This allowed the value of Argentine government bonds to remain stable and helped alleviate the problems which faced (the British-owned) Barings Bank, which had acquired a great many government bonds. By 1892, the Argentine president Pellegrini had fallen amidst much anti-British feeling.

At the beginning of the twentieth century the Unites States began to threaten Britain's commercial and financial hegemony in Argentina. However, in the 1930s, British influence revived. The Great Depression prompted the United States to introduce prohibitive agrarian protection, and since Argentine exports, such as grain and beef, competed with US products, this meant Argentina relied even more heavily on the British market. Moreover, since Argentina had been excluded from the Ottawa trade agreements, which had been conducted amongst Commonwealth states, there was a real threat that Britain would apply similarly prohibitive tariffs. It was in this context that the controversial Roca-Runciman Pact was signed in 1933. Britain promised to allow Argentine goods access to the British market in return for tariff reductions for British goods, and the retention of a British stake in the meat industry. Argentine nationalist historians have subsequently maligned the treaty; they claim that it was designed to preserve Argentina as a giant cattle ranch for British consumers.

Metropolitan interference

Metropolitan interference in defence of Britain's interests in Latin America was greatest in the first half of the nineteenth century. However, attempts at political coercion often proved counterproductive. For example, in the 1840s, Britain became displeased with the Argentine dictator Rosas. This led to a haphazard military expedition against Buenos Aires. Many British expatriates were unhappy with these actions and some even volunteered to man shore batteries against the Royal Navy. The expedition also revealed the difficulties in implementing metropolitan directives. The British minister at

Buenos Aires (Mandeville) disobeyed Whitehall; in turn, the Commander of the British flotilla in the River Plate (Purvis) disobeyed Mandeville.

From c.1850 to c.1950, the metropole interfered far less. Political pressure was exerted by representatives of British economic interests residing in Argentina ('men on the spot'). Moreover, by the second half of the nineteenth century, Argentina possessed a political elite who were willing to collaborate in creating hospitable conditions for British commerce and capital. Therefore, there was little need for metropolitan interference.

'Men on the spot'

'Men on the spot', such as resident business representatives, encouraged Argentina to adopt policies favourable to British investment and commerce; in particular, they demanded 'order', and protection of foreign property and contract. To achieve these aims, 'men on the spot' lobbied local politicians, supported rival political factions and used bribery. They were able to influence economic policies that dealt with tariffs, economic treaties and labour unrest. The opposition to the Argentine Radical Party which came to power in 1916 illustrates how 'men on the spot' were often more effective than the metropole in exerting pressure. The radicals under Hipolito Yrigoyen supported working-class interests against those of 'big business'. In response, British officials threatened to boycott Argentine ports and end Argentine grain purchases. Yet the radicals were only forced to capitulate after local British interests joined forces with Argentine businessmen to create strike-breaking organisations.

Collaboration

The collaboration of the Argentine elite (generals, ministers, lawyers, businessmen, judges, officials etc.) was vital in creating the conditions for British economic interests to thrive. Elites collaborated due to:

- self-interest: collaborators would receive a share of the profits
- economic logic: policies that favoured British capital and commerce might also benefit the Argentine economy
- ideology: the Argentine elite had adopted British cultural values and practices (source B), including a commitment to laissez-faire capitalism.

Dependency theory

In the 1960s and 1970s, the historical Anglo-Argentine economic relationship began to be described in terms of 'dependency'. It was argued that whilst the British market had been vital to Argentina, the Argentine market had merely been important (but not crucial) to Britain. Hence, Britain had been in a position to manipulate Argentine economic policy to the latter's disadvantage. The main points of the theory are as follows:

- British intervention: British officials intervened frequently on behalf of British business interests
- Specialisation: British financiers dictated the type of goods that Argentina would produce. These were developed towards the export market and lacked diversity. Hence, if international (and particularly British) demand for beef fell, then Argentina would face an economic crisis. The results of international economic crises would have been less devastating if Argentina had produced a greater range of goods for different markets
- Local industry: Britain's cheap exports prevented the development of local industry.

Source B A polo match in Buenos Aires – a game originally derived from the Tibeto-Burman kingdom of Manipur, but popularised and spread by the British worldwide in the late nineteenth century.

A number of historians have since questioned the conclusions of 'dependency'.

■ Limited British intervention: D. C. M. Platt, an Oxford historian, demonstrated that metropolitan interference was infrequent and limited. There was a significant gulf between the British government and business interests; the former did not act at the whim of the latter.

■ Argentine autonomy: A number of historians argue that the Argentine elite freely collaborated. Moreover, surviving railway company archives suggest that the Argentine government had the ability to act against British business if it was in Argentina's best interests to do so.

■ Economic logic: Cain and Hopkins have argued that 'If South America's economic prospects came to rely on a narrow range of exports, it was because specialisation followed the logic of comparative advantage, and not because imperialist forces imposed deviations from the "natural" path of development' (P. J. Cain and A. G. Hopkins (2001) *British Imperialism*, p. 244).

> What are the advantages and disadvantages of using the term 'informal Empire' to describe Britain's relationship with Argentina?

Indirect rule in Nigeria

Origins of British involvement

British involvement along the coastline of Nigeria stemmed from Britain's commitment to suppress the slave trade in the mid-nineteenth century. The West African coast subsequently gained commercial importance as a source of primary products, in particular palm oil, cocoa and tin. In the 1880s, French expansion prompted Britain to make treaties with indigenous rulers and establish protectorates along the coast and into the interior, sometimes through the use of force. This sphere of influence was united in a single colony and protectorate on 1 January 1914. The new colony of Nigeria

contained many different ethnic groupings, which operated under different political systems.

Indirect rule

Frederick Lugard is regarded as the man responsible for introducing the idea of indirect rule to West Africa. Lugard justified the introduction of indirect rule on a number of counts.

- Retention of indigenous social structures: it was believed that colonial interference often had a very negative impact on indigenous societies. Lugard argued that it was far better to retain traditional forms of authority, such as tribal chiefs, than to impose a foreign, colonial administration. The local populace were less likely to rebel, and would be happier living and working according to the norms and values that they were accustomed to.

- Impossibility of European settlement: white settlement in significant numbers was impossible due to the climate and propensity of Europeans to catch local diseases. Hence, there was little opportunity for Britain to impose a system of colonial government reliant on European administrators.

- Economics: indirect rule was a cheap form of colonial rule, since the administration of the colony was mainly undertaken by existing rulers.

However, nationalist historians of West Africa, working in the aftermath of independence, have subsequently criticised indirect rule. There are a number of reasons for this.

- Propaganda: it is argued that Lugard's vision of indirect rule was idealised because his wife, Flora Shaw, was a well-connected journalist, adept at promoting the work of her husband. Furthermore, Lugard's protégé and biographer, Margery Perham, was the foremost **Africanist** of her generation, and did much to endorse the idea of indirect rule.

- Marginalisation of southern Nigeria: the north of Nigeria was ruled by an autocratic Islamic sultanate that Lugard favoured. In 1914, northern and southern Nigeria were joined together, mainly because the financially-solvent south could subsidise the north. According to a number of historians, Lugard imposed an alien, hierarchical system onto the more progressive south. Southern Nigeria was more advanced in finance, trade, industry, education and public health, and had no tradition of chieftainship. In 1929, the imposition of 'chiefs' in south-eastern Nigeria sparked a number of uprisings.

- Hindrance of local political development: in the late nineteenth century, Britain relied on a number of educated, Westernised Africans to assist in colonial government. Lugard's insistence on indirect rule marginalised this group of people. In their place, too much power was placed in the hands of unrepresentative 'chiefs'. The spread of Western education to local peoples was discouraged. Consequently, Nigeria had no experienced, political class able to assist in the transition towards independence and democracy.

BIOGRAPHY

Frederick Lugard (1858–1945)

Frederick Lugard served in the British Army in India before arriving in Africa in 1888. In 1894, he became a special commissioner for inner Nigeria, and in 1900 was appointed High Commissioner for Northern Nigeria, a position he held until 1906. He subsequently spent five years as governor of Hong Kong before returning to West Africa and serving as Governor-General of Nigeria from 1912 to 1918.

Africanist

Someone who studies the cultures and/or languages of Africa.

ACTIVITY

Source C is a selection of diary entries written by Frederick Lugard in 1894, while he was working for the Royal Niger Company. He was later to become the Governor-General of Nigeria and a firm advocate of indirect rule.

What do the entries reveal about the exercise of imperial rule in West Africa? You might wish to consider the following:

■ How did Europeans attempt to deal with West African chiefs?

■ What do Lugard's entries reveal about the difficulties in working with indigenous elites?

■ How might Africans have perceived the European presence? What, for instance, do the refusal of European gifts, and the prophecy of a potential royal death mean?

Source (C) Frederick Lugard

17th (November 1894)

In the afternoon a summons came from the King about 4 P.M. Went up with Watts, who is still very shaky with fever, and we were kept waiting in the sun for nearly half an hour. I got terribly out of patience. It is a radical mistake, this abasement of the European before very petty African chieflets. I would not be treated so at any Government Department in England. I brought the scarlet coat emblazoned with gold lace and stars and foolery, but I wrapped it up in a towel and only put it on at the door. I detest this mummery, it is more irksome to me to dress myself up like a Punch and Judy show than to visit a dentist. The King of all the Bussas turned out to be a specially dirty and mean-looking savage, seated on a filthy and greasy carpet and Musnud, surrounded by a group of ordinary savages. The door-ways were blocked with gazing crowds of naked girls and semi-nude women – sheep, goats and fowls wandered about. And this man is subsidised by the Royal Niger Company to the tune of £50 a year. And on his whim the representative of the Company has to stand in the sun and wait, with fever on him! etc. At Rome, we must do as the Romans do, but my heart sinks at the thought that I must submit to such customs and indignities for another year!

19th

I asked if Macdonald was treated like this, for he came as a government official and put on full uniform, with Ferryman as a Lieutenant, and hundreds of porters carrying every conceivable luxury, and with large presents. Watts replied that Bida refused to see him in a hurry thereupon M. said he would go, and would not give him his present. Bida replied that he could keep the present for he did not want it! The king of Yola was even worse, and refused to see Macdonald at all! [...] The 'intrepid French explorers' who have succeeded in penetrating these countries with a handful of men and no goods or rifles, and have brought back packets of treaties, are roundly accused here of never having translated the real contents of these treaties. Facts seem to point to this conclusion. To secure a treaty with Sokoto, [the Briton] Thomson spent £500... – how then could Frenchmen secure important treaties for nothing at all? Again they say here...[that] if the French want to come into the country with which they have made a treaty they invariably have to fight, which shows that the treaty was Nil [...] Bida threatened to cut off Wallace's head and he [is] Agent General when [Flint] is at home. Nothing was done; MacTaggart was tied to a tree and shot at – and another agent was flogged! [...] There is a report in camp that the King has given orders that no provisions are to be sold to us. I trust it may not prove true – for 415 rations are daily wanted. Borgu is a trying country to travel in! [...] I found out...that the real obstacle is that the King – or rather the people – are possessed by this prophecy that if the King sees a European he will die within 3 months.

B. Harlow and M. Carter (eds.) (2003) *Archives of Empire Volume II*, pp. 388–401

BIOGRAPHY

Jinnah (1876–1948)

Muhammad Ali Jinnah was born in Karachi (now part of Pakistan) in December 1876. He was the son of an affluent Muslim merchant. After receiving a basic education in India, Jinnah spent a few years in England where he studied law. He became increasingly involved with politics, joining the Indian National Congress in 1896, and promoting Hindu and Muslim unity. In 1913, Jinnah decided to join the All India Muslim League (founded in 1906) and became its leader in 1916. During the interwar years, he campaigned to ensure that Muslim political rights would be safeguarded in an independent India. In the immediate years before independence, he began to believe that partition and the creation of a separate Islamic state was the most appropriate way of dealing with decolonisation.

India and Pakistan: case study

Independence (1947): an overview

The 1935 constitutional changes effectively granted India provincial self-government within an overall framework of imperial rule. However, nationalists wanted complete self-government and the acquisition of Dominion status. At the outbreak of the Second World War, the Viceroy declared war on behalf of India without consulting Indian politicians; this angered many nationalists, and the provincial governments headed by the pro-independence Congress Party resigned. In 1942, Sir Stafford Cripps was sent to India to strike a compromise with nationalists. He proposed that in exchange for cooperation and no major political advances during war, India would be granted full Dominion status after the war and the option of seceding from the Empire-Commonwealth. Congress refused this offer and launched a 'Quit India appeal' demanding complete independence and the immediate withdrawal of the British. Since the Indian contribution to the war effort was absolutely vital, the British authorities responded swiftly, suppressing civil disobedience (source D) and arresting 90,000 supporters of Congress.

Source **D** *Satyagrahis* being tear-gassed during the 'Quit India' movement, Bombay 1942.

Nevertheless, after 1945, Britain did not stand in the way of Indian independence. However, decolonisation was complicated by the question of Muslim participation in a Hindu-dominated Indian state. The Muslim leader **Jinnah** feared the creation of a unified state dominated by Hindus. Eventually, it was decided that the partition of India was the course of action least likely to lead to bloodshed. The British left in 1947 and the separate states of (Hindu) India and (Muslim) Pakistan came into existence. This was unfortunately accompanied by much violence.

Source **E** Muslim refugees flee from New Delhi to Pakistan, crowding onto the roof and between the carriages of a train, 26 September 1947.

FOR DISCUSSION

To what extent does the violent nature of partition in India indicate that Churchill was right in suggesting that British rule was essential for peace and good government?

Erosion of imperial interest in India

A number of historians have pointed out that British interests in India were being eroded during the interwar years. Judith Brown argues that 'by the later 1930s almost all [of the] facets of the Imperial interest were in decline because of shifts in the world economy or of repercussions to British political decisions made to elicit Indian co-operation in Imperial governance' (J. Brown and W. M. Louis (eds.) (1999) *The Oxford History of the British Empire: The Twentieth Century*, p. 439). Thus:

■ indentured labour had been banned in 1917
■ the Indianisation of the military, police, and civilian services meant that there were fewer opportunities for expatriate service
■ from the early 1920s, Britain (responding to Indian opinion) agreed not to use the Indian army as a cheap source of troops
■ by the 1940s, trade and investment with India was far less important than it had been in 1914
■ the position of India was strategically important to Britain for defence purposes; this would not be endangered if a self-governing India subsequently signed defence treaties with Britain and remained within the Commonwealth.

However, many British politicians still felt that India was vital to British interests. Winston Churchill, for example, believed that 'The loss of India… would be final and fatal to us. It could not fail to be part of a process which would reduce us to the scale of a minor power… The British Empire would pass at a stroke out of life into history' (R. Hyam (2007) *Britain's Declining Empire*, p. 63).

Nationalism

Nationalism was an important force in Indian politics during the interwar years, despite society being fractured along regional, linguistic, religious, caste and class lines. Nationalist leaders held different conceptions of the Indian nation. Jawarharlal Nehru, who was to become the first Prime Minister of an independent India, wanted to create a secular, socialist, national identity. His key ally Gandhi, on the other hand, was keener to emphasise the moral, and religious foundations of 'traditional India'.

Source **F** Mahatma Gandhi in traditional dress outside No. 10, Downing Street in London on a visit to attend the Round Table Conference on Indian constitutional reform, 3 November 1931.

FOR DISCUSSION

Gandhi's life became the subject of an award-winning biopic film in 1982. To what extent do you think modern films affect the way in which major historical figures are remembered?

The Indian National Congress, founded in 1885 as a vehicle to articulate nationalist grievances, continued to be dominated by a small, educated elite. The British were keenly aware that Indian nationalism was unrepresentative of the population at large and they often emphasised this point when legitimising the role of the colonial state. However, the interpretation that India was not 'a nation' overlooked the fact that nationalism was powerful as an 'anti-feeling', directed against colonial oppression. Moreover, the image of the colonial state as the protector of minorities concealed the extent to which Britain exploited and intensified divisions in Indian society as a means of strengthening its own power. Classifying the Indian population by religion was a policy introduced by the British and one that, thereafter, only encouraged increasing tension and division.

Meanwhile, Britain's decision to work with nationalist moderates was significant and paved the way for independence. The Indianisation of the civil service and army weakened British authority, and the increasing power given to Indian politicians gave nationalists a legitimate platform on which to challenge the colonial state. The British felt compelled to continue making concessions to moderates in order to prevent extremists and agitators gaining popular support.

By November 1946, it was clear that Britain was incapable of maintaining control of India. The Labour Prime Minister Clement Atlee explained the reasons why Britain would have to pull out (source G).

> **Source G Clement Atlee**
>
> (a) In view of our commitments all over the world we have not the military force to hold India against a widespread guerrilla movement or to reconquer India.
>
> (b) If we had, public opinion especially in our Party would not stand for it.
>
> (c) It is very doubtful if we could keep the Indian troops loyal. It is doubtful if our own troops would be prepared to act.
>
> (d) We should have world opinion against us and be placed in an impossible position at UNO.
>
> (e) We have not now the administrative machine to carry out such a policy either British or Indian.
>
> R. Hyam (2007) *Britain's Declining Empire*, p. 108

The Viceroy of India, Lord Wavell, confirmed these fears (1947): 'The really fatal thing for us would be to hang on to responsibility [in India] when we had lost the power to exercise it, and possibly to involve ourselves in a large-scale Palestine' (J. Brown and W. M. Louis (eds.) (1999) *The Oxford History of the British Empire: The Twentieth Century*, p. 332).

> **Stretch and challenge**
>
> Obtain and view a copy of the feature film 'Gandhi' (Attenborough, 1982).
>
> 1. To what extent does the film accurately portray the role played by Gandhi in the Indian independence movement?
>
> 2. How far does it reinforce the 'celebrity status' that was attributed to Gandhi?
>
> 3. How far does the celebrity status afforded to Gandhi create an illusion that nationalist movements were responsible for independence?

QUICK FACT

The Indian National Congress

Britain's cultivation of traditional elements in Indian society alienated many Westernised Indians. In response, a number of malcontents formed the Indian National Congress in 1885. They had several grievances.

- The Council of India was out of touch.
- The ICS was too inaccessible to Indians.
- Indian councils required more Indian representation.
- The army and administration were too expensive.

Before the First World War, nationalist strategy encompassed the use of constitutional methods and bouts of terrorism. The return of Gandhi in 1915 heralded the beginnings of a new strategy, *satyagraha* (peaceful resistance to perceived injustice). The British were made to look aggressive, and the nationalist struggle elicited international sympathy. Congress subsequently alternated between constitutionalism and direct non-violent opposition. Nationalists were hindered by lack of money and the tendency of some activists to favour acts of violence. The local nature of many grievances also failed to contribute to the construction of a national consciousness.

Decolonisation

> **Source** Ⓐ
>
> **Winston Churchill, 1946**
>
> *'Scuttle' is the only word that can be applied.*
>
> **Mohandas Karamchand 'Mahatma' Gandhi, following Indian independence, 1947**
>
> *The noblest act of the British nation.*

> **Key Questions:**
>
> ■ How has the metropolitan approach contributed to our understanding of decolonisation?
>
> ■ How has the international approach contributed to our understanding of decolonisation?
>
> ■ How has the periphery approach contributed to our understanding of decolonisation?

After the Second World War, many British imperial territories acquired formal independence. The two main periods of decolonisation occurred in 1947–8 (India, Pakistan, Burma, Ceylon, Palestine/Israel), and from 1957 to the late 1960s (Malaya, most of the African colonies, the West Indies). The significance of this constitutional transfer of power has caused a great deal of controversy. Some historians believe that the act of decolonisation allowed imperialism to continue through informal means. This thesis suggests that Britain voluntarily handed over power to moderates in the belief that these allies would become post-colonial collaborators, allowing Britain to continue exerting influence over former colonial territories. However, such an interpretation tends to conceal the important changes that occurred once colonies gained independence. In light of this, the historian John Darwin believes that decolonisation ought to be seen more broadly as the breakdown of the 'global colonial order', the dissolution of the ideas and institutions that had provided the foundation for European imperialism. Historians tend to use one (or indeed a mixture) of three approaches to explain the causes of decolonisation. The first approach emphasises metropolitan attitudes and suggests Britain lost either the will or the economic strength to maintain its colonial possessions. The second approach focuses on international relations and Britain's inability to retain an Empire in the face of a hostile, international climate. Finally, the third approach considers the periphery and the impact of anti-colonial movements on decolonisation.

Approaches that focus on metropolitan influences

> **Key Question:**
>
> How has the metropolitan approach contributed to our understanding of decolonisation?

METROPOLITAN INFLUENCES

Approach:

■ an emphasis on how metropolitan factors affected the dissolution of the Empire

Methods:

■ an analysis of official documents
■ an analysis of sources relating to popular culture in Britain

Interpretations:

■ Britain had accomplished its original purpose, and therefore there was no reason to retain an Empire
■ British public opinion forced the authorities to grant the colonies independence
■ the retention of the Empire ceased to be seen as vital to British interests
■ after the Second World War, Britain lacked the financial capacity to retain control of the Empire

The 'a task well done' interpretation

Some British contemporaries attempted to make sense of decolonisation by claiming that it represented the successful completion of 'a task well done'. It was argued that Britain had originally assumed control of colonial territories with the express intention of allowing self-government when the local inhabitants proved sufficiently competent to rule themselves. By the middle of the twentieth century, the colonies had supposedly reached such a stage of political maturity. According to this interpretation, decolonisation was not the result of a loss of will in the metropole, or Britain's declining standing as an international power. The idea of 'a task well done' was a convenient means of soothing conservative opinion, but very few modern historians are convinced by the argument. There is no evidence that, prior to 1939, Britain desired or intended to accelerate the process by which the dependent colonies would receive full self-government. For instance, even after India had been granted provincial self-government in 1935, Britain did not set a clear timetable for when the subcontinent might receive Dominion status. Hence, it seems unlikely that British policymakers believed that their task of governing an Empire had come to a successful end. Even after the Second World War, Britain seemed in little hurry to divest itself of colonies, unless a quick withdrawal was necessary to prevent a serious local crisis, such as in India.

The public opinion and imperialism interpretation

In contrast, some historians have argued that public opinion became hostile to imperialism in the twentieth century, and this forced the British government to give up its colonies. It is certainly true that conservatives criticised their contemporaries for lacking the will to sustain an Empire. Meanwhile, there were many on the Left who were critical of the blood-letting that seemed to be an integral part of colonial administration. In 1945, a Labour government was elected, which seemed intent on allowing colonial self-government. Three years earlier (1942), the Labour Party had promised to abolish 'imperialist exploitation' (source B).

> **Source (B) The Labour Party**
>
> *This Conference considers that the time has arrived for a restatement of the principles of the Labour Party as applied to the government of the colonies and to the status of colonial peoples.*
>
> *This should be a charter of freedom for colonial peoples abolishing all forms of imperialist exploitation and embodying the following main principles:*
>
> *(1) All persons who are citizens of the colonial commonwealth should be considered to possess and be allowed to enjoy equality of political, economic and social rights in the same way as the citizens of Great Britain.*
>
> *(2) The status of colony should be abolished and there should be substituted for this that of States named according to the country in which they are situated and having an equal status with the other nations of the commonwealth.*
>
> *(3) In all colonial areas there should be organised a system or democratic government, using the forms of indigenous institutions in order to enable the mass of people to enter upon self-government by the modification of existing forms of colonial administration in conformity with these principles.*
>
> *(4) In all colonial areas, in Africa and elsewhere, where the primitive systems of communal land tenure exist, these systems should be maintained and land should be declared inalienable by private sale or purchase. All natural resources should be declared public property and be developed under public ownership.*
>
> *(5) A commonwealth council of colonial peoples should be set up on which each former colonial state should be represented in accordance with the number of its population, but giving also special attention to the representation of national groups within each State.*
>
> Quoted in J. Samson (ed.) (2001), *The British Empire*, pp. 210–1

Stretch and challenge: counter-factual question

If Labour had not won the election of 1945, how far might decolonisation have been delayed?

However, while Labour was in office (1945–51), decolonisation occurred in response to tensions on the periphery, rather than as part of an intentional strategy of rapid withdrawal. Up until the late 1950s, the Labour Party favoured gradual, constitutional change as the means through which colonial self-government ought to be attained.

Moreover, it has been demonstrated that there was very little sustained popular anti-imperialism during the interwar years. Contemporaries certainly did not believe that domestic opposition to Empire would force decolonisation; it was far too small-scale. The Labour Secretary of State for India, William Wedgwood Benn, remarked in 1930 that the working classes were 'a mixture of ignorance … and idealism, always with racial prejudice ready to be excited, so that the ground is indeed clear for any argument' (J. Brown and W. M. Louis (eds.) (1999) *The Oxford History of the British Empire: The Twentieth Century*, p. 199). Indeed, if anything, popular enthusiasm for Empire was growing during these years.

The British interests in the post-war world interpretation

Another metropolitan interpretation points out that Britain's interests in the post-war world were changing. The Empire was ceasing to be of vital importance and instead was becoming somewhat of a nuisance. After 1945, Britain's economic prosperity was increasingly dependent on partnership with the industrialised European and North American states, rather than on the exploitation of colonial commodity producers. Similarly, Britain's strategic priority moved away from the defence of its various imperial territories, to the protection of Europe from the threat of Soviet Russia. It is argued that this explains why Britain lacked the will to resist nationalist moves for independence. The loss of the colonies was only really significant because people feared that Britain might become a second-rate nation. The British government assured the electorate that decolonisation would not place Britain's position as a world power in jeopardy. In this respect, the idea that the Empire would be replaced by a Commonwealth of Nations was important, since it served to remind the British people that their imperial status had been retained, albeit in a different form.

The Second World War and economic weakness interpretation

A closely-related thesis contends that, even if Britain had wanted to retain its Empire after the Second World War, it lacked the economic strength to do so. Britain's post-war economic recovery was too slow for it to remain the leading market, supplier and investor for the Empire. Furthermore, Britain lacked the resources necessary to gain local collaborators, and thus Britain's ability to rule was eroded. Indeed, in the immediate years after 1945, policymakers in the metropole consistently refused to use force to deal with the crises in India and Palestine, primarily because of the costs involved.

> Explain why historians differ in the significance they place on the role of public opinion in the process of decolonisation?

ACTIVITY

1. What can you learn from passage 1 about the interpretations, approaches and methods of the historian Dennis Judd? Refer to the extract and your knowledge to explain your answer.

> **Passage** **1**
>
> *There were, beyond question, manifestations of Labour's apathetic colonial and imperial policies during these years (1945–51). Sometimes these were reflected in the turn of events, sometimes in the choice of personnel. When the genuine reforming and committed Creech Jones lost his seat at the general election of 1950 and a replacement at the Colonial Office had to be found for him, the Prime Minister's choice fell upon James Griffiths. Griffiths was a former coal miner, viewed with both affection and trust by the Labour Party. He possessed, however, very little expert knowledge of the colonies, and had the habit of demonstrating his sincerity 'by beating his chest while talking'. Whether this latter habit was considered to be an important quality in a Colonial Secretary is not clear. What is evident is that, for all his virtues, Griffiths was not a politician or statesman of the first rank. Perhaps the colonies deserved better than that.*
>
> D. Judd (1997) *Empire: The British Imperial Experience, from 1765 to the Present*, pp. 344–5

2. Some historians have accepted the conservative critique that Britain was losing the will to maintain an Empire. Assess the extent to which this critique was an accurate reflection of contemporary opinion, or whether it might have been a device to frighten public opinion into adopting conservative attitudes towards Empire.

> **Stretch and challenge**
>
> Assess the reasons for the change in Britain's strategic priority, that is, from the defence of its various imperial territories to the protection of Europe from the threat of Soviet Russia. To answer this question you may have to carry out some background reading and research on the changing nature of international relations in the interwar period and the establishment of communist rule in Russia.

Approaches that focus on international influences

> **Key Question:**
>
> How has the international approach contributed to our understanding of decolonisation?

INTERNATIONAL INFLUENCES

Approach:
- an emphasis on how international factors influenced decolonisation

Methods:
- the application of Marxist theory to decolonisation
- an analysis of official documents

Interpretations:
- large, international businesses favoured decolonisation since this ensured friendly relations with increasingly-powerful local politicians and leaders
- Britain was bullied into allowing decolonisation by two (supposedly) anti-imperial superpowers, the USSR and the USA
- international opinion viewed imperialism as illegitimate, and this forced Britain to allow decolonisation

The international capitalism interpretation

In 1957, the Marxian-Socialist economist Paul Baran put forward the idea that changes in international capitalism had led (and was leading) to the dissolution of the European empires. He argued that 'big business' had become more international in outlook and organisation, and that it increasingly came to look upon colonial forms of government as a threat and a hindrance. According to this view, commercial interests favoured decolonisation because it allowed them to make an accommodation with nationalist politicians. If the colonial authorities tried to hang on to power, then nationalists might adopt an anti-capital and anti-foreign attitude, regarding foreign business as an ally of the colonial state. In contrast, self-government would establish a new political elite willing to work with foreign capital.

However, there are strong arguments against this thesis. The type of economic interests across the Empire varied enormously; in some places business still relied on the colonial state, and in other places commercial interests were not significant enough for decolonisation to matter much. And yet despite these differences, the vast majority of Britain's colonies achieved independence at roughly the same time. This suggests that other factors had a greater influence on the timing of decolonisation. Furthermore, there is no evidence that important areas of policy were affected by capitalist pressure. Indeed, a number of regional studies, which have investigated the cases of India and West Africa, suggest that commercial interests had little influence on policy in the metropole and on the periphery.

The British decline as an international power interpretation

One of the most widely held 'international' arguments views decolonisation as the result of the rise of the USA and the Soviet Union as the two world superpowers. On the one hand, neither of these powers wanted a rival, rather archaic, imperial power (i.e. Britain) on the world scene. On the other hand, both the US and Soviet Union were opposed to Empire on specific, ideological grounds. As part of the American national myth, imperialism was viewed as an inherently oppressive system; American independence had involved throwing off the imperial shackles. The Soviet Union similarly disliked the idea of formal Empire, since Marxist theory held it to be the result of capitalist iniquity. Thus, it is argued that, since Britain lacked the economic clout to compete with the two superpowers, it was bullied into giving up its Empire. Certainly, the United States was in a position to affect British policy. In 1946, a gigantic US loan of $3.5billion proved vital in enabling the British government to avoid bankruptcy. Hence,

1. How far does Paul Baran's interpretation of decolonisation appear to have been influenced by Marxist views about historical development?

2. What are the advantages and disadvantages of using an approach based on regional studies?

Britain was reliant on American support, and any policy in regards to the colonies had to take into account the USA's anti-imperial attitude.

However, it has been demonstrated that American hostility to the British Empire declined after the Second World War. The United States was more concerned with tackling the Soviet threat, and Britain was an important ally. This tacit support for the British Empire was not publicised, since the British did not wish to appear reliant on US support and the Americans did not want their reputation as strident anti-imperialists tarnished. Eventually, though, Britain was encouraged to decolonise since it was feared that nationalists might adopt communism if colonial governments refused to allow them independence. In spite of this, it is surprising that Britain was incapable of resisting these international pressures for longer; a relatively weak nation such as Portugal was able to maintain its imperial possessions until 1975.

The United Nations and the legitimacy of Empire interpreation

A slight variant of the international thesis emphasises that colonial rule over indigenous peoples in the interests of the 'civilised powers' ceased to be considered legitimate after the Second World War. This international climate was exemplified by the creation of the United Nations in 1945 and the strong international reaction against the Anglo-French seizure of the Suez Canal in 1956. In the phrase of Ronald Hyam, Britain was 'booed off the field'.

ACTIVITY

What can you learn from passage 2 about the interpretations, approaches and methods of the historian Ronald Hyam? Refer to the extract and your knowledge to explain your answer.

> Passage (2)
>
> *Historians have offered four main options for explaining the end of Empire. These may be put in the form of a cricketing analogy. Either the British were bowled out (by nationalists and freedom fighters), or they were run out (by imperial over-stretch and economic constraints), or they retired hurt (because of a collapse of morale and 'failure of will'), or they were booed off the field (by international criticism and especially United Nations clamour) [...] My particular angle of vision leads me to the conclusion that the international dimension was the most important of all. It may be objected that an account based mainly on British government records is likely to be skewed, and to underestimate the role of colonial nationalism. In fact, the documentary record takes us deep into the heart of complex policy-making processes, and, as has been rightly argued, it is 'certainly an authentic slice of the past, even if it is not the whole of the past'.*
>
> R. Hyam (2007) *Britain's Declining Empire*, pp. xiii-iv

Approaches that focus on influences from the periphery

Key Question:

How has the periphery approach contributed to our understanding of decolonisation?

INFLUENCES FROM THE PERIPHERY

Approach:
- an approach that focuses on how peripheral factors contributed to decolonisation

Methods:
- an analysis of official documents
- an analysis of sources relating to popular culture in the periphery

Interpretations:
- anti-colonial movements forced Britain to relinquish control
- the Second World War provided the impetus for anti-colonial movements

The nationalism and anti-colonial movements interpretation

It is unsurprising that many historians from Britain's former colonies have emphasised the importance of nationalist and anti-colonial movements in the achievement of independence. The defeat of a 'tyrannical' power and the realisation of 'freedom' are often integral to the creation of a national myth, a common story that unites inhabitants and roots their identity to a founding event in which they can take pride.

In support of the anti-colonial thesis is the fact that many contemporaries anticipated or feared the triumph of nationalism. Marxist-Leninists believed that colonial independence was inevitable, and would mark the beginnings of the collapse of capitalism in the imperial metropoles. These beliefs were strengthened in the interwar years by the effects of global depression and the political unrest in dependent territories such as India. Meanwhile, conservatives were keen to magnify the dangers of nationalism in order to justify taking a 'hard line' over subversives.

It was common for the British authorities to respond to the growth of nationalism by denying that the people of a particular colony constituted a nation. India, for example, was described as an area populated by many different social groups, and divided by religion, caste, region and language. Winston Churchill remarked that India was 'an abstraction… a geographical term… no more a united nation than the equator'.

Educated, local elites provided the main impetus for nationalism. However, such ideas gained popular support because there was a strong underlying resentment against colonial rule. Some anti-colonial movements were fronted by charismatic leaders who inspired support, such as Gandhi in India and Aung San in Burma (source C). Many important British politicians were wary of these figures. Churchill particularly disliked Gandhi: 'It is alarming and also nauseating to see Mr Gandhi, a seditious Middle Temple lawyer, now posing as a fakir of a type well-known in the East, striding half-naked up steps to the viceregal place … to parley on equal terms with the representative of the King-Emperor' (1930) (R. Hyam (2007) *Britain's Declining Empire*, p. 63).

Assessing the importance of anti-colonialism is far from simple. Historians have found it difficult to access archival evidence in the ex-colonial countries, many of which have suffered political instability and financial crises since independence. This has meant that very few documents relating to decolonisation from the perspective of the periphery have been published or are available for research. In consequence, historians tend to rely on published sources from the metropole.

FOR DISCUSSION

Was violence the most effective strategy for resisting colonialism?

Source C General Aung San (right of centre, wearing national costume) leads a demonstration from Bandoola Square through the streets of Rangoon, Burma, to the Secretariat where the first meeting of the Constituent Assembly was held, 27 June 1947.

The minutes from a meeting of the cabinet held in 1946 recorded that: '[T]he Indian Army… could not fairly be expected to prove a reliable instrument for maintaining public order in conditions tantamount to civil war' (J. Brown and W. M. Louis (eds.) (1999) *The Oxford History of the British Empire: The Twentieth Century*, p. 332). Such evidence suggests that anti-colonial movements made colonial rule unworkable. However, many historians believe that this was not the case. They argue that the success of nationalist movements was mostly due to metropolitan and international pressures that had weakened Britain's power. Ronald Robinson believes that nationalism was an effect of colonial breakdown, rather than the cause of it. He suggests that the colonial authorities had ceased to be able to find enough local collaborators willing to help in colonial governance. Instead, it was nationalist movements that began to attract 'collaborators', diverse groups that could be united against Britain. In this scenario, Britain lacked the strength in the post-war world to recreate the collaborative mechanisms of rule that had been employed in the past.

The impact of the Second World War interpretation

Some historians believe that the Second World War was the key event in the creation of successful nationalist movements. Britain's humiliating retreat from Japanese forces in 1941 (and in particular the fall of the Singapore naval base in 1942) demonstrated to its colonial subjects that Britain was not invincible; indeed, far from it. Secondly, many colonial subjects who participated in the Second World War developed a 'political consciousness', an awareness that colonial rule was unjust. This feeling was often strengthened when locals were subjected to allied propaganda which explained that the war was being fought for 'democracy'; in many parts of the Empire, locals questioned why equality and self-government did not apply to them.

What are the strengths and weakness of using an approach that focuses on the role of nationalist movements on the periphery?

Stretch and challenge: counter-factual questions

1. If the Second World War had not occurred, how long would decolonisation have been delayed?

2. What are the advantages of using a counter-factual approach when attempting to explain decolonisation?

10 And finally: the British Empire, c.1950 to the present

'Take down the Union Jack. It clashes with the sunset.'

(Billy Bragg)

The development of the Commonwealth of Nations

In 1926, the Balfour Report defined Dominions as 'autonomous communities within the British Empire, equal in status, in no way subordinate to one another in any aspect of their domestic or external affairs, though united by common allegiance to the Crown, and freely associated as members of the British Commonwealth of Nations'. The idea of a Commonwealth gained further ground when the British Empire began to break up. In 1949, a conference of Commonwealth leaders decided that an allegiance to the Crown was no longer a necessary requirement for Commonwealth member states. Instead, it was agreed that the British monarch was to be recognised as the Head of the Commonwealth. This was called the London Declaration. It was significant since it allowed newly-independent countries such as India the opportunity to retain links with Britain and the rest of the Empire.

In the 1950s and the 1960s, many former colonies chose to join the Commonwealth. The increasing importance of the association was reflected by the establishment of an independent civil service in 1965, the Commonwealth Secretariat. In its present form, the Commonwealth is defined as 'an association of sovereign nations that support each other and work towards international goals'. The association consists of 53 member countries with a combined total of 1.8 billion citizens. Meanwhile, all that remains of the British Empire is a handful of very small dependent territories such as the Falkland Islands.

The legacy of Empire

The British Empire has left a lasting impact on the former colonies in many areas of life.

Sport

British sports such as football, rugby and cricket have flourished in the ex-colonies, whose inhabitants have often gained the upper hand in recent sporting contests against England, Wales, Scotland and Northern Ireland.

Education

The Empire promoted learning and was fundamental for the development of schools and universities. Nowadays, English has become a widespread medium of communication, allowing scholars from the periphery a greater opportunity to participate in international projects and debates.

Politics

British ideas about the rule of law and democracy have more or less been retained. However, in some former colonies, such as Zimbabwe, more dubious forms of government have been adopted.

The Commonwealth

The Commonwealth has developed into a forum for discussion in which less powerful nations are given a political voice.

In Britain, the dissolution of Empire caused relatively little disquiet. Britain was beginning to focus more on Europe and the United States of America, and the Empire ceased to be seen as vital to national interests. The most significant legacy of Empire after the Second World War was the influx of ex-colonial subjects into Britain, many of whom were used as unskilled labourers. In subsequent decades, immigrants increasingly faced racial prejudice, as racism began to be transferred from the colonies to the mother country.

ExamCafé
Relax, refresh, result!

Relax and prepare

Preparing for the exam

Eva

At the start of my AS year, my history teacher kept going on about the need to revise right from the beginning of the course. He made the point that revision means filling in the gaps in our knowledge and understanding after each lesson. I didn't believe this was worth it at the time, but now I've completed my AS exams I fully understand what he meant. I knew what I had to write to get a good grade but didn't have all the evidence to fully back up my ideas.

Dave

I was in Eva's class and thought the same way. Our teacher also told us about reviewing our work about a month before the exams and making revision notes on index cards. I did this and it made it so much easier to break down the mass of information we were given.

Paulo

There's nothing wrong with being stylish in the way you approach reading your handouts and books. Use different colour highlighters to mark key points on handouts and annotate them in the margin (i.e. write your own summaries of what you have read). When making notes from books, use different kinds of headings, abbreviations, numbering, bullet points, colour and formats. I particularly like using spider diagrams and charts as they are a neat, tidy and visual way of presenting information. I know some people think it's not cool to be careful and conscientious with their note-taking, but it pays off in the end.

Cassie

I know I can be a bit of a pain when it comes to classroom discussions as I get a bit hot under the collar when I disagree with someone. My mate Bill has helped me with this by teaching me to actively listen to what people say before making comments. It's quite easy, really. What you do is listen carefully to every word but also observe **how** other people speak. It's also important to show that you are listening by making slight nods of the head, keeping eye contact and using words such as 'yes' or 'I understand'. I've also found it good to write down notes of what other people in my class say while debates are going on. When you do this, make sure you listen first then write down summaries. Don't try to write down every word.

Becca

I tended to become neurotic and obsessive when doing my homework or studying for my exams. In fact, my family found me a nightmare to live with! Nowadays, I try and relax more and not to snap at my family and friends when I feel stressed. In fact, I tend to perform better in exams when I stick to the same routine. This helps me feel relaxed and ready to concentrate fully on the questions.

Hafiz

I didn't much like reading before I started my A-levels, but my sister told me to look at books and articles that were not like textbooks in order to get me interested in the topics I was studying. I started reading novels to do with the British Empire and now I am a big fan of Rudyard Kipling!

George

Your teachers will tell you to read widely and will probably give you reading lists linked with each topic. Don't try to read everything – the lists should be compiled to give you a choice of the types of stuff that you could look at. Also, start with more simple books and internet articles before attempting the more challenging texts.

Mel

I never bothered much with planning my essays, especially in exams. But my teacher kept telling me that my answers were poorly structured and didn't address the question and that I just had to plan or I wouldn't do myself justice. Now I use a spider diagram or chart type plan for all of my written answers and my results have improved massively.

Janko

I got hold of an examiner's report and it went on a lot about analysing questions before answering them, so as to maintain relevance. I found out that this meant unpacking the question to identify the command statement, the topic and key words that might need defining. This was very important in helping me see how to stay on track when writing my responses.

Chinnie

You need to read books from authors from different countries when studying something like the British Empire, otherwise you will get a culturally-biased viewpoint. Things fell apart for my brother when he studied British imperialism because he relied too much on a book that was written by someone who thought the Empire was a good thing.

Emma

Remember that the specification covers a period of just over a hundred years. That means there is a lot of factual information to take on board. It's easy to get bogged down in details. The key purpose of the specification is to get you to develop your ability to analyse and evaluate the different *interpretations* of British imperialism.

Daniel

Case studies are useful for bringing a topic alive and making it seem more relevant. Nevertheless, it's important to realise that they should not be used in isolation. It is helpful to compare case studies but also vital to place them in the appropriate historical context.

Tackling part a questions

Oz

Always identify when the extract was produced, who produced it and any other relevant information that might help you make a judgement about why the historian chose to pursue the particular approach that he or she did.

Kinza

Our teacher says that it is really important to resist the temptation to start writing your answer too soon. You've got plenty of time and you need to read the extract very carefully at least twice. I reckon that you should use about a third of the time that you have been given to analyse the extract, look things up and make a plan.

Sammy

As well as writing about what the extract contains, I always try to think of one or more approaches or methods that the historian could have used but didn't. My teacher told us this will help to achieve a top level answer. There are so many alternative interpretations, approaches and methods, it's never difficult to think of something that has been left out!

Tackling part b questions

Reuben

Part b questions always ask you to consider how a particular approach had contributed to our understanding of imperialism. That means you have to evaluate the approach and talk about its strengths *and* its limitations. Also remember to compare that approach with others. Since I started to do that my marks have improved a lot.

Refresh your memory

Revision checklist

Key areas of knowledge and understanding are:

▷ the concept of change and continuity in regards to the development of the British Empire

▷ the imperialism of free trade

▷ the interpretations of Hobson and Lenin

▷ the Cain and Hopkins thesis of gentlemanly capitalism

▷ European rivalry and the impact of this on the expansion of imperialism

▷ the importance of domestic politics and ideology

▷ the relationship between European elites and the spread of Empire

▷ the extent to which Britain was able to exert informal imperialism

▷ the metropolitan context – policy formation through a focus on security, economic development and trusteeship

▷ the significance of factors on the periphery – direct and indirect rule, 'men on the spot', collaborators and indigenous elites

▷ the use of force to govern – technology and 'native bashing'

▷ constructing hegemony – hegemony and false consciousness (tradition, legitimacy and colonial knowledge), negotiation, the public transcript, contesting colonial rule through hidden transcripts and the weapons of the weak

▷ the representation of the Empire by Europeans – the significance of discourse theory and Orientalism

▷ the experience of the Empire for those living in it – the social, cultural, economic and political change and continuity

▷ the relationship between gender, sexuality and imperialism

▷ the question of how the Empire was perceived in Britain – who was 'for' and 'against' the Empire; what were their motives?

▷ the impact of imperialism on metropolitan politics and the metropolitan economy – infrastructure, agriculture and industry

▷ the Metropolitan, International and Peripheral approaches

▷ the way in which regional studies have contributed to a better understanding of the British Empire.

Common mistakes

▷ Don't forget that historical interpretations are not made by historians working in isolation. Academics working in other disciplines such as social anthropology and political science have done much to enrich our understanding of the past. A multidisciplinary approach to studying history reaps many rewards.

▷ It is easy to get carried away in an exam, quickly putting down your ideas as they come thick and fast. However, your exam answers will be assessed for the quality of your written communication, including clarity of expression, presentation of ideas and the structure of your arguments as well as your grammar, punctuation and spelling. You need to pay attention to this aspect of the specification throughout your preparation by further reading and using a dictionary and thesaurus when practising answering exam questions.

▷ Always read through extracts first before looking at the questions so that you get a general idea of what they are about. Don't try to answer the questions just by looking for the relevant information in the extracts, as this just slows you down and may lead to misconceptions. Highlighting key words and writing mini-summaries in the margin can help you to identify the key aspects of the extract.

▷ Remember that extracts are usually just snippets of a bigger piece of information and can give a false picture of what the author really meant. If possible, it is always best to get hold of the complete book or paper from which the extract originates in order to get an idea of the 'bigger picture'.

▷ Adopt a realistic approach to revision – don't construct very elaborate revision timetables with ambitious targets, as it's likely that you will not keep to them. Divide your revision into manageable amounts and also include plenty of short breaks and 'rewards' for completing part of a timetable.

▷ Once you are in the actual exam, try not to give way to panic – if a question seems tricky then attack it logically and just do what you can. Many students lose points by poor time management in an exam. Taking time to plan your answer is essential, even when you feel you should already be writing! Make sure you know how long you have left and adjust your time plan accordingly.

1. Taking effective notes from written and verbal sources is an art and essential if you are to have a complete record of what you have learned throughout your course. If your record is thin or non-existent you will have nothing to revise from when it comes to the final examinations. At A Level, your teacher will not spoon-feed you with notes. You will need to make your own personalised records from the books and articles you read and the verbal input from teachers, guest speakers and classmates. When constructing notes, use the following guidelines.

   a) A note is a shortened or abbreviated version of what you read or hear. Put the information that you take on board into your own words. Don't try to write down everything you see in print or hear spoken unless you want to directly quote.

   b) Develop your own system of note-taking. Experiment with different colours, headings, sub-headings, underlining, abbreviated words, numbers, letters, pictures, diagrams, charts, paper size (A4, A5, Post-Its, index cards) and writing equipment (pens, pencils, felt pens). Also, try out different approaches such as linear note taking (straight down the page), spider diagrams and mind mapping.

   c) Leave room to add to your notes at a later stage. You can either write on every other line or else write on just one side of a piece of paper leaving the reverse blank for extra notes to be included.

   d) Be prepared to revise and rewrite your notes. This helps you remember and understand information more easily. Some students find it very helpful to rewrite their notes on a computer shortly after each class. This makes editing even simpler.

   e) Keep your notes and handouts in date order in a separate file from your other A-level subjects.

2. Listening to other class members' points of view can be very useful, since it forces you to clarify your own arguments, as well as introducing you to arguments that you may have overlooked.

3. Studying History at A2 requires you to pay even more attention to developing your reading skills than you did on your AS course. Read actively and engage with texts by highlighting key words and phrases and by annotating in the margin. However, don't do this with material you borrow from libraries or friends as this is considered to be very antisocial. When using loaned reading material you will have to make notes. With good writers of history it is easy to spot the key points being made as these are often stated in the first sentence of each paragraph. Also, a good overview of a book is usually obtainable by reading the introduction.

4. Use these guidelines when preparing for and producing an extended piece of writing, whether for homework, as a classroom exercise, or in an examination.

   a) Analyse the question: you need to start by identifying:

   ▷ the topic – pay careful attention to any dates, names, places and events that might be mentioned

   ▷ the key words and/or concepts that might need defining

   ▷ the command stem, that is, what the question setter is asking you to do – for example, 'What can you learn…', 'Explain your answer…'

   b) When reading a question for the first time, try running your first finger over every word in it to ensure that you focus on and log the meaning of each one. Students often skim read questions especially when working under time constraints and misread what the topic is about and what is expected of them.

   c) Plan your answer: use a spider diagram or table; don't use a linear plan as this is likely to represent a list of ideas that you have written down as they entered your head. This will result in an answer that is randomly structured and lacking clear focus.

d) Write your answer in paragraphs using the **PESEL** formula:

  ▷ **P**oint – the first sentence should make the key point or argument that is to be put forward

  ▷ **E**xplain – the next few sentences should develop the key point or argument

  ▷ **S**upport – the point or argument should be supported with evidence based on contextual knowledge and/or the source material that is provided, depending on the nature of the task set

  ▷ **E**valuate – you may need to make some balanced evaluative comment about the evidence you use depending on its nature

  ▷ **L**ink – the last sentence in the paragraph should provide a link to the next one.

e) Remember that one sentence does not constitute a paragraph! Pay careful attention to spelling, punctuation and grammar. Examiners *will* take this into account when assessing your work.

5. When handling extracts and answering questions based on them, you should consider the following general points.

a) Although historians have access to a range of different sources and also have the so-called benefit of hindsight, it is not necessarily correct that they can offer a more balanced and objective account of the past than contemporaries. In the end they interpret information in a way that makes sense to them and it may not be the way in which someone else makes sense of it. This is simply due to the way individuals process information differently.

b) The words 'bias' and 'biased' are not particularly helpful when discussing the merits of an historian. These words simply mean a one-directional or prejudiced view; all historians are likely to project a particular viewpoint even when claiming to be objective. It is far more useful to think about the significance of bias in terms of what this tells us about the views, attitudes, beliefs and ideas of the historian during the time that they were writing. It is also worth thinking about the motives of the historian and their target audience. It is interesting to consider whether historians write to reflect the interests of a particular readership or to shape and influence the views of their readers.

6. When preparing for an exam, it is extremely important to organise your time well.

  ▷ Creating a workable revision timetable is vital if you are to prepare for an exam properly. You should divide all that you have to revise into small chunks. Put aside a particular time or day for revising each chunk. This should help make revision more manageable. Some useful revision tools include mnemonics and ideas maps.

  ▷ Practising past papers is a great way to prepare for an exam, since it allows you to get to know exam-type questions. The more you practice past papers, the better your exam answer will be. Studying past papers also helps you to 'question spot', i.e. identify what type of question is likely to appear on the next exam paper.

Part (a) questions

▷ Make a list of all the interpretations, approaches and methods you can think of and keep it near to you in the exam.

▷ Make sure you understand the distinction between a method and an approach. Refer back to the *Historical Controversies* Student Book to brush up on the theory of history.

▷ Read the extract(s) very carefully to identify the historian's interpretations and the approaches and/or methods used.

▷ Always consider which interpretations, approaches and methods are *not* covered in the extract. A top-grade response will consider alternative interpretations, approaches and methods that are relevant to the extract.

▷ If the opportunity arises, comment on the shortcomings of a particular interpretation, approach or method.

▷ Good answers are tightly structured and show a real understanding of key terms and concepts. Use the Glossary on pages 156–7 as a checklist.

▷ One way of structuring your response is to divide it into three sections – interpretations, approaches, and methods.

▷ Make sure every paragraph you write is clearly focused on the question and the extract.

Part (a) question: example 1

Read the following extract about how the British Empire developed in the nineteenth century, and then answer the following question.

(a) What can you learn from this extract about the interpretations, approaches and methods of the historian? Refer to the extract and your own knowledge to explain your answer.

Extract

After its defeat of Napoleonic France in 1815, Britain became the world's dominant naval and commercial power. Its territorial empire was larger than ever, and technological innovation would combine with capital investment to continue the process of imperial expansion even beyond the imperial borders. This process, known as 'informal empire', drew countries like Siam (Thailand) into Britain's sphere of influence even though they remained technically independent. Britain also took advantage of a series of nationalist wars which terminated Spain's enormous empire in the Americas during the early nineteenth century. British army and navy officers advised the nationalists, and the newly independent Latin American republics often rewarded Britain with trade privileges and the use of strategic ports. Argentina in particular would become the site of intensive British investment.

Sheer lack of competition allowed Britain to sustain this dominant position throughout the early and mid nineteenth century; a period often said to feature a 'Pax Britannica'. There was little that was peaceful about the process of imperial expansion but the Royal Navy's extensive mapping and policing made maritime trade safer than it had ever been before. Although France and Russia also went through expansionist phases, this did not bring about a return to the near-constant European warfare of the eighteenth century. Only during the later nineteenth century would the competition from the other powers challenge Britain's commercial and imperial pre-eminence. Britain was especially worried about the so-called Great Game – Russian encroachment in Afghanistan and other areas near India – and allied with other countries against Russia during the Crimean War of 1854–6. But for the most part, the nineteenth century saw an unprecedented freedom from British military expenditure in Europe.

At home, the Industrial Revolution was transforming Britain into a commercial superpower. No other country would industrialise to the same extent before the 1870s, giving Britain a near monopoly on the production of manufactured goods. But this did not mean that Britain could afford to ignore the outside world. The growing British population required imported food from Europe and the United States; British factories required imported raw materials. Although the expanding empire could meet some of these needs, the empire was not self-sufficient. These developments revived the free trade debate of the late eighteenth century and, this time, the old mercantilist system was almost completely overturned. Free trade suited Britain well for most of the century; only after the 1870s, when other industrialising powers threatened British commercial dominance, did protectionism begin to appeal once again to British statesmen and industrialists.

At the end of the nineteenth century, this new atmosphere of competition prompted a 'new imperialism'. Germany and the United States had consolidated economically and politically, enabling them to industrialise and to challenge Britain's predominance in manufacturing. They wanted to enhance their status and the identity of an international 'Power' in the late nineteenth century depended on the acquisition of an Empire. Various European nations, including Germany, scrambled to divide the unclaimed areas of Africa and the Pacific between them. The United States expanded through informal imperialism in Latin America (where it surpassed Britain in investment and political influence) and by acquiring Cuba, the Philippines, and other territories after the Spanish-American war in 1898. Japan meanwhile was fighting a series of expansionist wars in east Asia and beginning the industrialisation of its economy. Not to be outdone, the British also increased their imperial territory and the British Empire had almost reached its greatest extent by 1914.

The challenges of the late nineteenth century created an intensified imperial rivalry and prompted new interpretations of Britain's imperial identity. At the political level, ideas about protectionism, imperial federation, and joint imperial defence were proposed. At the popular level, the images and literature of Empire found an enthusiastic audience due to increased literacy and the proliferation of inexpensive books and newspapers. Empire-wide societies such as the scouting movement helped to express this renewed popular support for imperialism, and the sense of rivalry with Germany and other nations only served to make British nationalism more aggressive and xenophobic than ever.

Examiner says:

This is a very solid introduction that clearly identifies how the historian interprets Empire and the approaches and methods that they use. Of particular note is the correct use of terminology and concepts to support observations about the work of the historian, e.g. 'synthesised narrative', 'Anglo-centric viewpoint'. The introduction gives a clear indication to the reader what the candidate is intending to discuss and argue in the main part of her response. She is well on the way to achieving a high mark.

Part (a) answer: example 1

(Only the introduction and conclusion from the student's answer are shown below.)

The interpretation of the development of the British Empire by the historian seems to revolve around Britain's response to the rise in status of other nations such as France, Russia, Germany and America throughout the nineteenth century. Maintaining and expanding an empire is seen as a way for Britain to respond to challenges to its economic and political power base across the world. Connected with this is the way in which change is viewed, with reference being made to the concepts of 'informal' and 'formal' Empire. The general approach and methodology is based on a synthesised narrative that is linked to the growth of the British Empire in the late nineteenth century. The narrative is very much from an Anglo-centric viewpoint and offers little insight into how those on the periphery explained imperialism. It also focuses on the interrelationship between the international struggle for political and economic power and only hints at how this affected those who governed the Empire. This kind of historical writing has clear strengths but there are also significant limitations when attempting to use it to explain changes in imperialism.

In conclusion, the author of the extract has provided a very helpful overview of how the British Empire developed during the nineteenth century and gives the reader a clear idea about both change and continuity. However, other historians have questioned the usefulness of labels such as 'informal' and 'formal' Empire and have stressed that expansionism, to a greater or lesser degree, was a constant feature of the foreign policy of British governments throughout the period. Also, the author's comments concerning international rivalry are a bit thin and lacking balance as there is no mention of the Austro-Hungarian Empire. With respect to approach and methodology, the use of a top down narrative has its place, but it provides only one perspective on what is a very contentious aspect of Britain's past.

Part (a) question: example 2

Read the following extract about the methods the East India Company was still using in the 1850s to govern India, and then answer the question below.

(a) What can you learn from this extract about the interpretations, approaches and methods of the historian? Refer to the extract and your own knowledge to explain your answer.

Extract

For Marx, the nature of East India Company rule was best demonstrated by its seldom acknowledged reliance on torture. Writing after the outbreak of the Great Rebellion, he discussed 'the official Blue Books on the subject of East India torture, which were laid before the House of Commons during the sessions of 1856 and 1857'. These reports established the 'universal existence of torture as a financial institution of British India'. It was admitted that revenue officers and the police routinely used torture in the collection of taxes. As he observes, while this was freely admitted, 'the admission is made in such a manner as to shield the British government itself'. The practice of torture 'is entirely the fault of Hindu officials', while British officials were not only not involved but had 'done their best to prevent it'. This claim, as Marx points out, was contradicted by much of the evidence assembled in the reports.

What did this torture involve? It ranged from rough manhandling through to flogging and placing in the stocks and then on to more extreme measures. According to the historian Mukerjee 'extreme measures' involved: 'searing with hot irons… dipping in wells and rivers until the victim is half suffocated… squeezing the testicles… putting pepper and red chillies in the eyes or introducing them into the private parts of men and women… prevention of sleep… nipping the flesh with pincers… suspension from the branches of a tree… imprisonment in a room used for storing lime…'.

What is remarkable is how little the regime of torture has figured in accounts of British rule in India. It is a hidden history that has been unremarked on and almost completely unexplored. Book after book remains silent on the subject. This almost calls into question the whole historiography of the Raj.

Part (a) answer: example 2

(Only the paragraphs discussing approaches from the student's answer are shown below.)

The historian's approach to discussing the governance of India by the East India Company involves drawing heavily on the writings of Karl Marx to support and develop an argument. The thrust of the historian's view is that governance was carried out in a brutal and immoral way through the use of torture and that this was purposefully kept hidden from the records. One problem in using material from another writer in this way is that it is taken out of context and has to be highly edited. It is not clear as to what Marx was focusing on. Was it misrule in just India or are his comments part of a larger critique about the 'evilness' of the British Empire in general? However, Marx was an opponent of imperialism per se and therefore it is safe to assume that the historian has deliberately chosen to use the writings of Marx to support their own left-wing views about the Empire.

It is also noteworthy that the author has concentrated on discussion of torture as a tool of governance although it is possible that they talk about different methods in other parts of their book. The emphasis on torture over-dramatises the more negative aspects of governance that undoubtedly existed. It is not made evident how widespread torture was in India or, indeed, in other parts of the Empire. The use of material from the historian Mukerjee is also questionable as it appears to be used selectively and without any comment concerning validity or reliability. Mukerjee is quite likely to be an Indian historian who has wanted to make a case for the oppressive and obnoxious way in which he thought the East India Company ruled.

Finally, the historian makes a judgement about governance through the use of sweeping statements in the last paragraph. Wide reading of other secondary works on British rule in India reveals much discussion of torture and other equally-distasteful forms of repressive measures of coercion.

Examiner says:

The response so far indicates that the student has fully understood what is meant by 'approaches' and has identified one obvious way in which the historian has gone about analysing the way in which India was governed. There is also some very apt evaluative comment about context and the possible ideological leanings of the author.

Examiner says:

This is sound comment about the importance of torture in the extract and how it is used by the author to develop an argument. The judgement about Mukerjee may well be valid but it is best to be absolutely sure about the provenance of such a source before expressing a view like this.

Examiner says:

A useful point is made here, but although the historian's statement appears to be assertion it is actually factually correct. Most of the key texts on imperial India, such as those by Lawrence James and, more recently, William Dalrymple, do not discuss the use of torture by the East India Company. This partly highlights the fact that the answer is lacking a bit of 'own knowledge' and is based mainly on what is contained in the extract. Answers that lack balance, even if well written, are likely to be given a mark in one of the middling bands.

Get the result!

Part (b) questions

▷ Make sure you have all of your most valuable resources with you in the exam.

▷ Make sure you know where to find particular types of information. Use the contents page and index of your textbook(s).

▷ Use a dictionary to check your spellings.

▷ You must compare the approach you are asked to comment on with other approaches.

▷ Remember to assess the disadvantages or shortcomings of the approach identified.

Part (b) question: example 1

Some historians have focused on particular regions of the British Empire in order to shed light on the nature of imperial rule. What are the advantages and disadvantages of this approach?

Part (b) answer: example 1

Some historians use regional studies when approaching the British Empire; they focus on particular localities or colonies in order to study an issue in greater depth. It is advantageous to study the British Empire in this way for a number of reasons. Firstly, regional studies are manageable; they allow historians the opportunity to look at all the necessary evidence from a particular place, rather than having to skim the surface of evidence taken from a wider area.

Secondly, historians are able to formulate more nuanced pictures of imperialism, rather than painting a universal picture that might not be applicable to every area under British control. Thus, indirect rule in Southern Nigeria had different effects to indirect rule in Northern Nigeria.

Thirdly, studying particular regions allows historians to gather detailed information that might support a more general thesis. For example, Britain exerted political, economic and cultural influence over Argentina, and some historians have used this example to support the thesis of informal Empire. A closely-related point is that regional studies allow other historians to produce synthesised accounts of the British Empire as a whole.

The main disadvantage of using regional studies is that some historians lose sight of the main issue and become bogged down in detail. Also, just because something happened in one colony does not mean it happened in another colony. Therefore, historians have to be careful about how they evaluate the significance of their regional studies.

Examiner says:

A solid introduction, but it would have been useful if the student had explained why some historians choose to study Empire over a wider area in order to make comparisons.

Examiner says:

A valid point, but the student needs to support his example of Nigeria with evidence.

Examiner says:

Again, the point is valid, but thin. The student could have given examples of British influence over Argentina.

The student should have used an example to illustrate an historian becoming 'bogged down in detail'. Overall, he makes some good points, but the answer is generally thin.

Part (b) question: example 2

Some historians have emphasised the importance of discourse theory when analysing the way the Empire was represented by Europeans. What are the advantages and disadvantages of this approach?

Part (b) answer: example 2

Discourse theory relates to the way in which language has been used to depict people within the British Empire. Language has often been utilised to create a certain kind of picture of indigenous peoples which usually revolves around them being inferior and subordinate. The most important proponent of this theory was Edward Said, who developed the concept of 'Orientalism'. For Said, an Orientalist was a person who represented all non-Western peoples in a way that showed them to be a mixture of the exotic, weak and powerless.

The advantages of this approach revolve around the way that it emphasises the need to question the use of language by imperialists who recorded their experiences, since this dictates the way in which the 'truth' was presented. Moreover, discourse theory forces attention to be paid towards the experiences of indigenous peoples, especially those from 'below'. The disadvantages are mainly to do with the fact that other approaches are largely ignored or dismissed out of hand.

Discourse theory is very useful in the way it pushes the reader of colonial literature of various kinds to question whether what is being depicted is a true account. At the heart of the theory is the idea that a huge amount of evidence about imperialism was produced by those who were largely supporters of it and were therefore unlikely to depict it in a bad light. This evidence includes official written reports by politicians, the writings of travellers and explorers such as Mary Kingsley, novels such as Kipling's *Kim* and the work of scientific theorists such as Spencer. Orientalism is not confined to contemporary accounts as even more recent works by historians sympathetic to Empire could be described as 'Orientalist' in approach. All of this evidence has something in common; it supports the idea that Western society and culture was superior to that found in the East and that one of the main aims of imperialists was to civilise what they regarded as undeveloped and medieval-like societies. Thus, discourse theory enables us to critically evaluate sources of information by ensuring the focus is on the way knowledge is presented. Discourse theory is also helpful in the way in which it brings attention to cultural bias in other non-written sources such as paintings and photographs.

Equally important is the way in which discourse theory has given a voice to 'ordinary' people on the periphery, since it has forced attention to be paid to the search for testimonies that have been left by the 'powerless'. In India, for example, reference was commonly made to the importance of Hindu Brahmins while ignoring the experiences of lower-caste Hindus. Discourse theory has led to the development of subaltern history which has given an alternative viewpoint from the perspective of less powerful people in Indian society.

Examiner says:

This is a very solid introduction that defines the key term in the question and outlines the key advantages and disadvantages that are going to be discussed. It gives the reader a very good idea of where the answer is heading.

Examiner says:

An important use of discourse theory is discussed. The student clearly understands the relevance of the theory although the comment about paintings and photographs is 'bolted on' and needs developing. In particular, it requires supporting with some examples.

Despite these strengths, discourse theory and Orientalism has been severely criticised. The most obvious disadvantage is that it largely ignores other theories that could be used to explain social and cultural relations in the Empire, such as hegemony and romantic idealism. Hegemony emphasises the importance of control through the imposition of a particular ideology that occurred mainly through negotiation and that was not forced upon indigenous peoples. The work of James C. Scott has even suggested that the 'oppressed' were very aware of the methods being used by imperialists to impose cultural values and were willing to comply if it meant a peaceful life. However, in many ways, Scott's work is similar to discourse theory since he uses the word 'transcript' in a comparable way.

A further disadvantage of discourse theory is that, according to the historian David Cannadine, it downplays the importance of social class in the development of imperial social and cultural relations. In his book *Ornamentalism*, Cannadine argues that supporters of the British Empire aimed to 'domesticate the exotic' which meant acknowledging and valuing similar social norms and characteristics, especially social hierarchies. Thus, the caste system of India was not seen as inferior but something that was similar to the British class system and therefore to be valued. Cannadine believes that, in general, Said exaggerated the way in which 'otherness' was used as a way of claiming superiority and therefore power over those in the periphery.

Finally, a major fault of Orientalism as a form of discourse theory is that it ignores the way in which it is itself a form of discourse. Any form of communication involves affecting the behaviour of others either with positive or negative intent. It is true that the imperialists seemed to communicate their experiences in a way that was intended to influence the values, beliefs, ideas and behaviours of indigenous peoples. Equally, Said communicated his thesis about Orientalism using language designed to influence the reader and therefore exert a certain kind of power and control over them. Interestingly, what both the imperialists and Said had in common is that they probably all thought that what they were communicating was in the best interests of their respective audiences.

To conclude, discourse theory is invaluable mainly in the way it gets one to analyse and evaluate language that forms the basis of much of the source material available on Empire. However, it is not the only approach available to the historian, especially when looking at the changing nature of imperial social and cultural relations.

Examiner says:

The answer has moved on to consider disadvantages and links the discussion with skilful explanation about the usefulness of another theory.

Examiner says:

This is another good example of an approach that is ignored by discourse theory. Good use is made here of the student's own knowledge to develop the answer further.

Examiner says:

This is an interesting evaluative comment about the Said thesis. Maybe it could have been supported with material taken directly from Said's *Orientalism*.

Acknowledgements

p. 3: Definition of 'State' from 'The Concise Oxford Dictionary of Politics' by Iain McLean and Alistair McMillan © 2009. Published by Oxford University Press. Used with permission; p. 12: Terry Eagleton quote from 'Review of A Critique of Post-Colonial Reason: Toward a History of the Vanishing Present' by Gayatri Chakravorty Spivak. Used by kind permission of Terry Eagleton; p. 12: Extract from Robert Young from 'Postcolonialism: A Very Short Introduction' © 2003 by Robert Young. Used by permission of Oxford University Press; p. 13: Terry Eagleton quote from 'Review of A Critique of Post-Colonial Reason: Toward a History of the Vanishing Present' by Gayatri Chakravorty Spivak. Used by kind permission of Terry Eagleton; p. 14: Extract from 'Africa and the Victorians: The Official Mind of Imperialism' by J. Gallagher & R. Robinson. Used by permission of Palgrave Macmillan; pp. 22, 23: 'The Imperialism of Free Trade' by J. Gallagher and R. Robinson from The Economic History Review, New Series, Vol. 6 No. 1 1953. Used by permission of Wiley-Blackwell; p. 24: Extract from J. Hobson from 'Imperialism: A Study'; p. 26: Extract from 'Empire' by Niall Ferguson (Penguin Books Ltd, 2003) Copyright © Niall Ferguson, 2003. Used by permission of Penguin Press; p. 43: Martin Lynn quote from 'Oxford History of the British Empire: The 19th Century' © 2001. Edited by A. Potter. Used by permission of Oxford University Press; p. 44: Extract from 'The Lion's Share' by Bernard Porter. Used by permission of Longman; p. 46: EHH Green quote from 'Oxford History of the British Empire: The 19th Century' © 2001. Edited by A. Potter. Used by permission of Oxford University Press; p. 47: Sir Author Dawe of the Colonial Office quote from 'Oxford History of the British Empire: The 19th Century' © 2001. Edited by A. Potter. Used by permission of Oxford University Press; p. 48: Kenneth Bradley, a district officer in Northern Rhodesia quote from 'The British Empire' © 2001 Edited by Jane Samson. Used by permission of Oxford University Press; p. 51: Extract from 'The Ruling Caste: Imperial Lives in the Vi Raj' by David Gilmour, published by Pimlico; p. 52: Extract by John Newsinger from 'The Blood Never Dried: A People's History of the British Empire' used by permission of John Newsinger and Bookmarks publications www.bookmarks.uk.com; p. 54: British Officer writing to the Times. Quote from 'The British Empire' © 2001 Edited by Jane Samson. Used by permission of Oxford University Press; p. 57: Extract by John Newsinger from 'The Blood Never Dried: A People's History of the British Empire' used by permission of John Newsinger and Bookmarks publications www.bookmarks.uk.com; p. 57: Hillaire Belloc quote from 'Oxford History of the British Empire: The 19th Century' © 2001. Edited by A. Potter. Used by permission of Oxford University Press; p. 57: Sir Henry Newbolt quote from 'Oxford History of the British Empire: The 19th Century' © 2001. Edited by A. Potter. Used by permission of Oxford University Press; p. 57: Extract by Mike Snook from BBC History Magazine, January 2008. Volume 9 No. 1. Used with permission; p. 60: Edward Robert Bulwer-Lytton Earl of Lytton, Viceroy of India, quoted in 'The Invention of Tradition' © 1983 By Hobsbawm and Ranger. Used by permission of Cambridge University Press; p. 60: Peter Borroughs quote from 'Oxford History of the British Empire: The 19th Century' © 2001. Edited by A. Potter. Used by permission of Oxford University Press; p. 61: Hugh Clifford, Colonial Officer quote from 'Empire Writing: An Anthology of Colonial Literature' © 1998 edited by E. Boehmer. Used by permission of Oxford University Press; p. 62: Extract from 'Domination and the Arts of Resistance' by James C. Scott. Published by Yale University Press. Used by permission; p. 62: 'The Selected Essays, Journalism, And Letters of George Orwell' by George Orwell. Copyright © George Orwell. Reprinted by permission of Bill Hamilton as the Literary Executor of the Estate of the Late Sonia Brownell Orwell and Secker & Warburg Ltd; p. 63: Elspeth Huxley quote from 'The British Empire' © 2001 Edited by Jane Samson. Used by permission of Oxford University Press; p. 63: Lord Roberts quote from 'Oxford History of the British Empire: The 19th Century' © 2001. Edited by A. Potter. Used by permission of Oxford University Press; p. 64: Extract from the Nigerian Eastern Mail from 'Oxford History of the British Empire: The 20th Century' © 2001. Edited by Brown and Louis. Used by permission of Oxford University Press; p. 64: Extract from 'Domination and the Arts of Resistance' by James C. Scott. Published by Yale University Press. Used by permission; p. 65: 'The Selected Essays, Journalism, And Letters of George Orwell' by George Orwell. Copyright © George Orwell. Reprinted by permission of Bill Hamilton as the Literary Executor of the Estate of the Late Sonia Brownell Orwell and Secker & Warburg Ltd; p. 69: Extract from 'Culture and Imperialism' by Edward Said. Published by Chatto and Windus; p. 71: D.A. Washbrook quote from 'Oxford History of the British Empire' © 2001 edited by Robin Winks. Used by permission of Oxford University Press; p. 76: Extract by David Fieldhouse from 'The Cambridge Illustrated History of the British Empire' (1966) © Copyright P. J. Marshall. Published by Cambridge University Press, reproduced with permission; p. 76: Extract by David Fieldhouse from 'The Cambridge Illustrated History of the British Empire' (1966) © Copyright P. J. Marshall. Published by Cambridge University Press, reproduced with permission; p. 76: Kikuyu Chief, Koinage Mbiyu quote from 'The British Empire' © 2001 Edited by Jane Samson. Used by permission of Oxford University Press; p. 78: Diana Wylie, 'Disease, Diet and Gender' quote from 'Oxford History of

Bibliography

Primary resources

Elleke Boehmer (ed.) (1998), *Empire Writing: An Anthology of Colonial Literature*, Oxford: Oxford University Press

Jane Samson (ed.) (2001), *The British Empire*, Oxford: Oxford University Press

Barbara Harlow and Mia Carter (eds.) (2003), *Archives of Empire Volume I*, Durham: Duke University Press

Barbara Harlow and Mia Carter (eds.) (2003), *Archives of Empire Volume II*, Durham: Duke University Press

General

Stephen Howe (2002), *Empire: A Very Short Introduction*, Oxford: Oxford University Press

Bernard Porter (4th edition) (2004), *The Lion's Share*, Longman

P. J. Marshall (ed.) (1996), *The Cambridge Illustrated History of the British Empire*, Cambridge: Cambridge University Press

Alan Palmer (1996), *Dictionary of the British Empire and Commonwealth*, London: John Murray

Andrew Porter (ed.) (1999), *The Oxford History of the British Empire, Volume III: The Nineteenth Century*, Oxford: Oxford University Press

Judith M. Brown and William R. Louis (eds.) (1999), *The Oxford History of the British Empire, Volume IV: The Twentieth Century*, Oxford: Oxford University Press

Robin Winks (ed.) (1999), *The Oxford History of the British Empire, Volume V: Historiography*, Oxford: Oxford University Press

Robert Young (2003) *Postcolonialism: A Very Short Introduction*, Oxford: Oxford University Press

Formal and informal Empire

John Gallagher and Ronald Robinson (1953), 'The Imperialism of Free Trade', *The Economic History Review*, 2nd Series, Vol. 6, No. 1

Economic factors

J. A. Hobson (2005), *Imperialism: A Study*, New York: Cosimo Classics

P. J. Cain and A. G. Hopkins (2001), *British Imperialism, 1688–2000*, Longman

Political factors

C. C. Eldridge (1978), *Victorian Imperialism*, London: Hodder Arnold

Ronald Robinson and John Gallagher with Alice Denny (1965), *Africa and the Victorians: The Official Mind of Imperialism*, London: Macmillan

The nature of colonial rule

David Gilmour (2007) *The Ruling Caste: Imperial Lives in the Victorian Raj*, London: Pimlico

John Newsinger (2006), *The Blood Never Dried: A People's History of the British Empire*, London: Bookmark Publications

J. C. Scott (1990), *Domination and the Arts of Resistance,* New Haven: Yale University Press

Culture

Edward Said (2003), *Orientalism: Western Conceptions of the Orient*, London: Penguin Modern Classics

Edward Said (1993), *Culture and Imperialism,* London: Chatto & Windus

John M. MacKenzie (1984), *Propaganda and Empire: Manipulation of British Public Opinion, 1880–1960*, Manchester: Manchester University Press

John M. MacKenzie (1987), *Imperialism and Popular Culture,* Manchester: Manchester University Press

John M. MacKenzie (1995), *Orientalism: History, Theory and the Arts*, Manchester: Manchester University Press

Ronald Hyam (1990), *Empire and Sexuality: The British Experience*, Manchester: Manchester University Press

Impact of Empire on Britain

Roderick Floud and D. N. McCloskey (eds) (1981), *The Economic History of Britain since 1700: 1860–1939*, Cambridge: Cambridge University Press

Niall Ferguson (2004), *Empire: How Britain Made the Modern World,* London: Penguin Books

D. Judd (2008), 'The Impact of Imperialism', *BBC History Magazine* Vol. 9, No. 1

Decolonisation

Ronald Hyam (2007), *Britain's Declining Empire: The Road to Decolonisation 1918–1968*, Cambridge: Cambridge University Press

Fiction

George MacDonald Fraser, *The Flashman Papers, Vols. I–XI,* Harper Collins (a series of novels about the depraved exploits of Harry Flashman, many of which take place throughout the Empire)

Internet resources

For useful websites, go to www.pearsonhotlinks.co.uk and enter the express code 2480P.

Glossary

It is crucial to have a clear idea of what historians mean when they use particular words such as 'Empire' and 'imperialism'. Definitions of the most important terms are given below. The meaning of each word is not set in stone, however, and historians often prefer to use their own peculiar definitions. Sometimes, altering the meaning of a concept such as 'colonialism' can bring greater clarity to the subject and allows someone to understand the development of the British Empire more fully.

Africanist someone who studies the cultures and/or languages of Africa

atavism the process of returning to an ancestral or 'primitive' state

cathartic the cleansing or purifying of feelings and emotions

clientage the relationship between a patron (master) and a client or servant; dependency

collaborators a common term used by historians of the British Empire when talking about indigenous people who worked with the colonial authorities

colonialism the 'systems of rule by one group over another, where the first claims the right (a 'right' again usually established by conquest) to exercise exclusive sovereignty over the second and to shape its destiny' (Stephen Howe (2002) *Empire, pp. 30–1*)

colonisation the settlement of territory in a foreign land by migrants whose links with a mother country enable them to develop political supremacy

dacoity armed robbery

deindustrialisation the move away from an economy based on manufacturing (secondary level production) to one dependent on services (tertiary level production)

Empire a multi-national political unit, in which a dominant metropole (centre) exercises political power over a subordinate periphery (outskirts)

formal Empire territories officially administered and governed

free trade governments taking away restrictions on trade so that markets would become self-regulating

gin an offensive term for an Australian aboriginal woman

globalisation the process whereby world-wide, international concerns are placed above national or local concerns

imperialism the ideas and actions that contribute to the construction and maintenance of Empire

jingoistic excessively patriotic

Kolonialverein a pressure group made up of industrialists and businessmen, formed in 1882, which aimed to persuade Bismarck to follow an expansionist imperial policy for commercial purposes

legation a diplomatic presence in a foreign country below the level of an embassy

mandarins high-ranking public officials in the Chinese Empire

metropole the name given to the centre of the British Empire, i.e. the United Kingdom. The term has also been extended to refer to London as the metropole of the British

Empire, in that British politicians and businessmen determined the economic, diplomatic, and military character of the rest of the Empire

monocausal refers to a single rather than multicausal explanation of an event

monopoly this occurs when an individual or business has the sole power in selling particular goods and services. Thus, a monopolist usually has total control over what prices to set for goods, how much to produce and the quality of finished articles

Occidentalism a term which generally refers to stereotypical and unflattering views of the West, particularly Europe, the US and Australia; an inversion of the term Orientalism

opium a narcotic drug derived from the sap of the seed pods of the opium poppy

Orientalism a term used originally by Edward Said to describe antagonistic and disapproving views of the East by the West, shaped by the attitudes of imperialism in the eighteenth and nineteenth centuries

paramountcy dominance in world affairs

physiognomy the idea that a person's outer appearance, particularly the face, gives some insight into the individual's character or personality

polemic describes the practice of disputing accepted political, religious or philosophical conclusions. A polemic text on a particular subject is written to dispute or refute a theory that is generally acknowledged and established

policy the guiding principles and courses of action adopted by the authorities to achieve particular objectives

Post-colonialism either the era after colonialism, or the body of academic work concerned with giving colonial and ex-colonial subjects an historical voice

protectionism policies instituted by governments which restrict trade between nations through tariffs, quotas and other regulations in order to protect a country's own industries and economy

retrenchment reduction in expenditure

revisionists a term given to historians whose work challenges traditional, orthodox interpretations

subaltern in the British Army, the term refers to a commissioned officer whose rank is below that of captain. In a political context, the term has been used, mostly since the 1970s, to refer to social groups who (supposedly) lacked the agency to speak for themselves

suzerainty when one country has power or control over the affairs, usually foreign, of another country

syncretism the fusion of two different practices or belief-systems

Index